WITHDRAWN
NDSU

LEARNING TO LEAD

Recent Titles in
Contributions to the Study of Education

The Democratic Tradition and the Evolution of Schooling in Norway
Val D. Rust

Diffusion of Innovations in English Language Teaching: The ELEC Effort in Japan, 1956–1968
Lynn Earl Henrichsen

Improving Educational Quality: A Global Perspective
David W. Chapman and Carol A. Carrier, editors

Rethinking the Curriculum: Toward an Integrated, Interdisciplinary College Education
Mary E. Clark and Sandra A. Wawrytko, editors

Study Abroad: The Experience of American Undergraduates
Jerry S. Carlson, Barbara B. Burn, John Useem, and David Yachimowicz

Between Understanding and Misunderstanding: Problems and Prospects for International Cultural Exchange
Yasushi Sugiyama, editor

Southern Cities, Southern Schools: Public Education in the Urban South
David N. Plank and Rick Ginsberg, editors

Making Schools Work for Underachieving Minority Students: Next Steps for Research, Policy, and Practice
Josie G. Bain and Joan L. Herman, editors

Foreign Teachers in China: Old Problems for a New Generation, 1979–1989
Edgar A. Porter

Effective Interventions: Applying Learning Theory to School Social Work
Evelyn Harris Ginsburg

Cognitive Education and Testing: A Methodological Approach
Eugene J. Meehan

American Presidents and Education
Maurice R. Berube

LEARNING TO LEAD

The Dynamics of the High School Principalship

GORDON A. DONALDSON, JR.

Foreword by Roland Barth

Contributions to the Study of Education, Number 45

GREENWOOD PRESS
NEW YORK · WESTPORT, CONNECTICUT · LONDON

Library of Congress Cataloging-in-Publication Data

Donaldson, Gordon A., Jr.
 Learning to lead : the dynamics of the high school principalship /
Gordon A. Donaldson, Jr. ; foreword by Roland Barth.
  p.   cm. — (Contributions to the study of education, ISSN
0196-707X ; no. 45)
 Includes bibliographical references (p.) and index.
 ISBN 0–313–27743–5 (alk. paper)
 1. High school principals—United States. 2. High schools—United
States—Administration. 3. Leadership. I. Title. II. Series.
LB2831.92.D66   1991
373.12'012'0973—dc20   90-23094

British Library Cataloguing in Publication Data is available.

Copyright © 1991 by Gordon A. Donaldson, Jr.

All rights reserved. No portion of this book may be
reproduced, by any process or technique, without the
express written consent of the publisher.

Library of Congress Catalog Card Number: 90-23094
ISBN: 0–313–27743–5
ISSN: 0196–707X

First published in 1991

Greenwood Press, 88 Post Road West, Westport, CT 06881
An imprint of Greenwood Publishing Group, Inc.

Printed in the United States of America

The paper used in this book complies with the
Permanent Paper Standard issued by the National
Information Standards Organization (Z39.48-1984).

10 9 8 7 6 5 4 3 2 1

To Cynthia, Morgaen, Cary, Nell, and Ben
who wondered what I did all those days
and nights for seven years

Contents

Tables	xi
Foreword by Roland Barth	xiii
Acknowledgments	xvii
Chapter 1 Disjunctions in the Principalship: Role Versus Reality	1

Current Confusion Over the Principal's Role; The Functional Approach; The Functional Approach as a Lens on One Principalship; Postscript: An Introduction to My Principalship.

Part I The Principal's Activities Advance the Purposes of Schooling	**13**
Chapter 2 The Dominant Activity Patterns of My Work	15

Availability to the School's Clientele; Student Supervision; Organizing Central Staff Functions; Teaching and Curriculum Involvement; Availability to Teachers; Responsive Versus Assertive Activity.

Chapter 3 Everything Else: The Less Obvious Activity Patterns	31

Omniscience and Omnipresence; School Representative to the Public and Profession; Structuring School Operations; Running the Office; Satisfying the Hierarchy; Concluding Observation: The Overburdened Principal.

Chapter 4 The View from the Classroom 47

Staff Views of My Activities; Nature of Communication with Me; Staff Perceptions of My Goals; A Mixed Portrait.

Part II Identifying Others to Involve in School Management and Leadership 65

Chapter 5 Who Are the Faculty and Staff? 67

"Welcome, Mr. Donaldson. What Do You Want Me To Do About X?"; Learning in Action; Getting to Know Teachers Professionally; Five Factors That Affect the Principal's Knowledge of Faculty; My Operational Faculty Map.

Chapter 6 Students, Community, and Learning Our Mission 87

Learning About Students; Schools Are for Students . . . Or Are They?; Who Are the Community Members and What Do They Want?; The Principal as Purveyor of Purposes.

Part III Fashioning Productive Relationships 101

Chapter 7 The Development of a Working Relationship: My View 103

Beginnings; The Middle Period; The Final Posture.

Chapter 8 The Principal from the Faculty Perspective 119

My Leadership Style; Was I Effective, Or Was I Not?; My Success at Reaching My Goals; Implications: So, What Was Our Relationship?

Chapter 9 Leadership Within a Shifting Complex of Views 135

In Their Own Words; The Impacts of External Circumstances; Making Some Sense of Our Relationship.

Part IV The Impacts of Principals: How Do They Make a Difference? 153

Chapter 10 Taking Activities, Partners, and Relationships from Intention to Impact 155

The Principal's Activities Must Serve the School's Purposes; The Principal Must Attract and Support Capable People; The Principal Must Develop Constructive Relationships with Staff; A Final Note About the Principal's Intentions.

Chapter 11 Paradoxes of the Principalship 171

The High Expectations Paradox; The Accountability Paradox; The Agenda Paradox; The Authority Paradox; The Success Paradox; Implications for Practice and Training.

Chapter 12 Capacities and Qualities for High School Leadership   185

A Capacity to Understand the Goals of the School; A Capacity to Translate Purposes into the School's Daily Routines; A Capacity to Communicate with and to Direct and Motivate Adults; Three Rootstock Qualities; On the Education of Principals.

Appendix: Principal Leadership Study Survey   205

References and Bibliography   215

Index   221

Tables

1	Common Time Allocations to My Activities	17
2	Staff Contacts with Me	49
3	Staff Communication with Me	52
4	Staff Perceptions of Goal Salience to Me	56
5	Staff Perceptions of My Personal Style: Fiedler's Least Preferred Coworker Scale	121
6	Staff Evaluations of My Personal Effectiveness with Them	126
7	Staff Perceptions of My Goal Attainment	130

Foreword

Gordon Donaldson is a remarkable educator. This lively volume is, above all, his story. It is a story about his search for leadership told uniquely from three vantage points: Donaldson's as principal, his staff's, and Donaldson's as analyst of school leadership. It begins with his appointment as principal of the 800-student public high school in Ellsworth, Maine. From there, we see the inside of his seven-year principalship as he experienced it and as his faculty saw it. "What does the principal *do*?" many ask. Through time studies, journals, and conversations the reader is privy to all of the recurring work of a high school principal from bathroom checks to forging a personal vision. We go where the principal goes, see what he sees, do what he does, and feel what he feels.

Not only are we informed by Donaldson's introspective account, but also we view him through the eyes and with the words of teachers. Thus, we come to know the person and the principalship of Gordon Donaldson well. Most importantly, his staff and faculty teach us about his leadership—and the nature of school leadership—as only they can. It is a revealing portrait, intertwining the perspectives of leader and led with unusual candor, courage, playfulness, analysis, insight, and self-criticism.

But this book is far more than the fine-grained picture of one high school principal. It is a generic depiction of the principalship itself. A principal's office is an extraordinary epicenter from which to view the panorama of public education. From this vantage point all of the hopefulness and difficulty of currently popular school qualities come to life—school culture, shared leadership, teacher empowerment, vision, community involvement, collegiality, and student-centered inquiry. Donaldson presents these qualities not with antiseptic, scholarly clarity but as they occur in the day-to-day realities of school leadership and institutional renewal.

A recurring theme in Donaldson's story is that of paradox—the puzzling, self-contradictory, and unsettling realities of the job. For instance, he repeatedly explores the incredible lack of congruence between the conventional wisdom about the principalship and what he finds at Ellsworth High School. I was a principal for many years. Over 100,000 others are now school principals in the United States. It is refreshing to see the work of the principal portrayed not as it might be, not as outsiders conclude it must be, but as it is—with warts and paradoxes. This is what the author's Functional Approach is all about.

One of the strongest messages here is that of the leader as learner. All too many see the principal as "head leader," one who is learn*ed*. The most important contribution of this book is its illumination of a new conception of the principal as the head *learner* in, and thereby a leader of, the schoolhouse. Through probing analysis, feedback from staff, and thoughtful reflection Donaldson models, articulates, and celebrates the possibility that the leader can be a serious learner and, hence, a powerful influence upon school culture. When one visible adult engages in sustained inquiry, others join in and soon a community of learners develops. And that, above all, is what schools and school leadership should be about.

The knowledge base for improving schools is fed by social science research *and* by the immense craft knowledge of schoolteachers and principals. Those who work daily in schools have much to bring to debates about school reform. But in order to introduce these insights, teachers and principals must transform their discussions about schooling from war stories into craft knowledge. The former is rich in description of practice; the latter is rich in description *and* rich in analysis. Gordon Donaldson in this volume relives his life as school principal through the lens of his current life as university professor, providing abundant description and analysis of practice. We find the craft knowledge of a reflective practitioner made visible for all to see.

Finally, these pages depict a struggle to understand the principal's effects. It is a struggle of a principal trying both to set firm limits on pupils and unlock their capacity to learn; a struggle to form relationships with teachers and forge a disparate faculty into a team; a struggle both to comply with the central office and to educate it; a struggle to "involve parents" without giving way to them; and a struggle of principal Donaldson to discover how the leader of a quite typical U.S. high school can make a difference in the education of students. We also experience the struggle of author Donaldson as he plumbs the depths of the principal's experience and seeks to convert this uneven practice into even prose.

This book will encourage many to become school principals, and it will probably discourage some. All to the good, for we are not all cut out for the job. Better learned now than later. Yet Donaldson's story and his reflections on it will, I am confident, inform and energize the struggles of others in *their* important work—interested teachers, those who want to become principals and those who are, and the many educators who support the growth and professional development of aspiring and practicing principals. In the end, this book is not just about Gordon Donaldson but about the responsibilities we all have for the leadership of our schools.

"What does the principal *do* all day?"
"What difference can the principal *make*?"
Read on!

Roland Barth

Acknowledgments

This book is truly the product of many people whose dedication to public education, to leadership, and to our work together have made my professional life stimulating and fulfilling.

The many teachers, support and professional staff, and students of Ellsworth Junior-Senior High School and of Boggy Brook Vocational School between 1976 and 1983 taught me about leadership. They are responsible for a large part of this book and the insights it contains. As with all teachers, my colleagues in Ellsworth were at times tough, at times gentle, often perplexing, and never dull. I am especially indebted to the fifty-four faculty and staff who responded to the questionnaire about my leadership; their forthrightness and thoughtful comments both instructed and touched me.

Numerous colleagues in the Maine Principals' Academy and the National Network of Principals' Centers contributed greatly, if unwittingly, to my education as a principal and thus to this book. Not only have we learned about school leadership, we have learned together, encouraging and challenging each other to substantiate our beliefs and practices. In the process, we have proven that principals and other school administrators can, given the opportunity, create for themselves a true professional culture. I am especially grateful for the gatherings with other concerned Maine educators at Tenants Harbor in the spring of 1989 and for Alan Snell's coleadership of the Academy's development; they have both prompted my thinking repeatedly.

Several colleagues at the University of Maine made special contributions to my self-study and to the production of the manuscript. Drs. Ted Coladarci and David Fink introduced me to the magic kingdom of SPSS-X and made analysis of the questionnaire possible and bearable. Lori Reynolds, a champion of patience and accuracy, steadfastly and with good humor produced and kept organized the multiple drafts of the manuscript. To the College of Education for its support and to my colleagues and students in our "nondepartment" of educational administration for their stimulation, I am most grateful.

A special acknowledgment is due Roland Barth for his persistent but gentle queries about "that manuscript." His championship of reflective writing made me think that somebody might find my story useful.

David Sanderson provided detailed and good-willed commentary on a draft at a key time and remained on call for consultation as only a friend would. The eagle eyes and restive minds of Morgaen and Cynthia roved the manuscript in search of errors, omissions, and nonsequiturs at a point when I needed them badly. To you two and to Cary, Nell, and Ben: thank you for indulging my absences at the word processor, for understanding my compulsion to finish this during your summer vacations, and for being a loving family.

Chapter 1

Disjunctions in the Principalship: Role Versus Reality

Sunlight burst from a thousand shards of glass, offending my eyes, adding physical discomfort to my mounting anger. The job bore the markings of our students: the small window in the door to the cafeteria was not only smashed carelessly, it was surrounded by spray-painted messages to me and other school staff. The foodstuffs they had upset in the kitchen were not readily edible; their goal had been to make a mess, to aggravate us through more work. They were succeeding.

The glass and kitchen mess were only the tip of the iceberg. I not only had to see to the cleaning and repair, I had to sleuth out what evidence I could about who might have broken in. Should I involve the police? Nothing had been stolen and the damage was slight. How did the kids get into the building during the night? Is the night janitorial staff locking up? Can we clean and repair quickly enough to avoid a public scene? At a more complex level, what was it that provoked these students of ours (if they were) to do this? Caprice? Retribution? Generalized anger against authority? Against me? Who were the culprits and what sort of treatment would be appropriate for them (if we could even find them)?

Another school day had begun with an unexpected event. For me, the principal, this day was similar to most of my 175 "student days" in this respect. The day before, leaving school, I had planned activities and checked tasks for today, only to arrive at school to find the life of the school itself messing up my schedule and my purposes. Most frequently, this disarrangement of plans was not as literal as the case above. But a swarm of small issues can be more disruptive and frustrating even than a major crisis.

The impact of this pattern of events on the school principal is both grave and insidious. At risk is the very essence of the school's mission: Does the school exist simply to respond in knee-jerk fashion to the hourly stimuli it experiences? Or has it a purposeful design that itself structures the life and activities of the environment? The principal, we are learning, has substantial influence over the answer to this question. How we define our goals for and roles in school signals to staff, students, and community the essence of their purposes in school, the degree to which they are reactive and aim to maintain normalcy, the degree to which they are proactive and aim to create and develop. But what if the principal is so buffeted by events that he or she cannot maintain a healthy balance of purposes?

What is insidious about the "unexpected event" phenomenon is its very etiology. By definition, unexpected events are not controlled. They can, however, be minimized and they can be dealt with in such a way that they do not disrupt the movement and temper of the school. If the means to do this are not available to the principal and staff, the inexorable march of unexpected events will become the agenda-setter for each day. The function of the school will become management of those events, its purpose the avoidance of unexpected "accidents." Every school, and every classroom, must effectively orchestrate the cramming together of bodies, minds, egos, and emotions for six hours a day. The ultimate challenge is to see that coping strategies for doing so do not become the only plans or the major purposes for schools.

How do school principals accomplish such a task? We certainly are not formally prepared for it. My training consisted primarily of experience as a classroom teacher. I took only two courses in supervision and administration in order to be certified. Until very recently, that was the extent of most states' certification requirements: experience as a teacher and coursework (generally from two to four graduate education courses). These alone are baldly inadequate. As many others have done, I learned on the job the most practical lessons, those that allowed me to avoid the unexpected and manage the school environment. But neither education, the university's or experience's, gave me goals and strategies for carrying my mission and my school's beyond this level.

Further, our current understanding of the principalship does not provide working and aspiring principals with the intellectual and interpersonal tools both to manage *and* to lead the schools of the United States. While we view current qualification standards for the principalship as inadequate, they are so in large part because we do not understand the job well enough to know how best to prepare people for it and to support them professionally once they are in it. Principals most often fly by the seat of their pants in the early going; as they hit stride in their careers, they tend to reproduce the folkways and folkwisdom of the principals they have worked with and admired. None of us, it seems, can stop school life long enough to understand what it is doing to us or to imagine how we might influence it differently.

It is this dilemma that has led me to this book. As a practicing principal, I found that the descriptions of the principalship in books and courses did not, by and large, fit what I did and what went on daily in school. This may be because most writing about principals has, until recently, been in textbooks on administration. These set forth conceptions of the principalship that reduce the role and work to manageable and predictable units (basically for teaching and writing purposes). Thus we have chapters on "the community," "the law," "the office," "student needs," and so on (Lipham, Rankin, and Hoeh, 1985; Roe and Drake, 1986). But principals do not work according to such neat compartments, nor do we gain from this segmentation a sense of the purposes of our work, the kind of purpose one needs in constructing a path of action in the daily forest of school events.

Some works about the principalship, however, have resonated with my experience. Wolcott's (1973) ethnography of an elementary principal and Blumberg and Greenfield's (1980) biographical sketches informed my conceptual grasp of school leadership with the real experiences of principals. More useful were principals' writings: Roland Barth's *Run School Run* (1979), Lucianne Carmichael's *McDonogh 15* (1981), Marcus Foster's *Making Schools Work* (1971). These captured some of the insides of the job, including the principal's thoughts, beliefs, and feelings as he or she had acted and reacted in the bubbling milieu of the school. These works gave me insights into my own work and into the effects of my work life on my performance.

I discovered that these books—and many recent articles—include one key dimension that many texts do not: they seem to revolve around the principal's interpersonal work life. These books are filled with teachers, students, superintendents, and parents; principals are enmeshed in social networks, trying to get something accomplished *with and through* people. This is no great revelation; we know principals spend most of their time in face-to-face "people" work. What was revealing was that these books began to do justice to this essential dimension of the job. For the first time, writing about the principalship was including a subjective, dynamic, and often inarticulable part of the experience of being a principal. These authors were getting closer to the essence of the principalship than anything else I had read. So I set out to make sense of my own experience, resolving to capture more of the interpersonal baggage of the role.

I soon discovered that I could not understand or evaluate my own leadership in this respect without the aid of those whom I purportedly was leading. In fact, the more I considered my work, the more convinced I became that a principal's function and success might perhaps *only* be understood accurately by consulting the teachers and staff who have experienced firsthand the principals' effects. If the principal is to lead, then the evidence of his or her leadership must be found in the led. The issues raised by this observation are legion. I needed to learn from teachers and staff about myself. I needed not simple quickie evaluations of how well Mr. Donaldson did X, Y, or Z but a level of consultation that addressed fundamental questions, examining the very purpose of having a principal in a school in the first place. That is, if schools are to educate children, and if all personnel are hired for their ostensible value in that effort, how is it that principals are justified? In what respects do principals play any role beyond the clerical/managerial arena? We are told we should be educational leaders, to become involved in the classrooms of our teachers, to inform ourselves of curricular and student phenomena so that we can make the best decisions for the instructional program. But in the broad picture of the school's effect on a student's learning, where do these principal activities stack up? Near the top? Near the bottom?

I have not set out to answer these questions definitively. Indeed, these questions lie at the root of every principal's effectiveness and ought to be asked regularly in every school in the nation by its principal, faculty, and staff. I will contend, in the ensuing pages, that it is the asking of questions like these that has a greater bearing on a principal's impact than do the particular areas of knowledge that are typically imparted to principals during their training and professional development. In short, while the knowledge is important to have, it is no more useful to a principal without feedback on his or her actual functions than a wrench is to a seamstress.

CURRENT CONFUSION OVER THE PRINCIPAL'S ROLE

What makes one principal more effective than the next? In the past ten years, we have heard theory after theory. The effective schools research contended that "strong, forceful leadership" made the difference (e.g., Edmonds and Frederikson, 1978). Rutter et al. (1979) found that the principal who could create an "ethos" of productivity and caring stimulated the school to greater success than those who did not. Typically, we have been exhorted to become instructional leaders, not merely managers, and lists of the characteristics of instructional leaders have been paraded before us (Brandt, 1989). Since 1986, most standard texts on the principalship have been edited to include this new perspective (Lipham et al., 1985; Roe and Drake, 1986; Wood, Nicholson, and Findley, 1985). Works capitalizing on the reform movement of the late 1980s have attempted to draw together lessons from effective schooling literature and the agendas of the school productivity movement to recast school leadership as an executive function (Lane and Walberg, 1987).

More recently, writers have begun to address the inadequacies of these views. Blumberg (1989), for example, points out that the everyday realities of school principals mitigate against fulfilling the logical prescriptions of these scientifically derived expectations; he argues instead that administration is a craft requiring judgment and continuous learning. Dwyer, Barnett, and Lee (1986) suggest that principals, in this renewed effort to create new prescriptions for success, have been scapegoated for their lack of leadership in the instructional arena. Leithwood and his associates (1988) have commenced a seemingly productive line of inquiry examining the decision-making function and culture-building of principals (e.g., Leithwood and Jantzi, 1990). Similarly, Blase (1988) and others have continued the descriptive tradition of Morris et al. (1984), Wolcott, and Barth to examine what it is that principals, good and bad, actually do. Sergiovanni (1987) offers a "reflective practice" approach to understanding the principal's impacts on the climate and culture of schooling that shows promise of integrating personal, professional, and worksite factors for better practice.

These works are supported by a cluster of new studies that help us portray principals at home in their schools. Sarah Lawrence Lightfoot's *The Good High School* (1983), Gerald Grant's *The World We Created at Hamilton High* (1988), the *Horace's Compromise* trilogy of Ted Sizer and his associates (1983), and Alan Peshkin's *Growing Up American* (1978) offer principals and students of the principalship rare opportunities to know and understand how real principals act and interact within their schools. Although they do not focus exclusively on the principal, these works begin to identify the functional life of principals—the manner in which the principal's activities and personality act on teachers, students, and community to create a constellation of effects. Quite unlike the disaggregated view of principals provided by textbooks and effective schooling studies, these allow us to see principals as interactive influences. More importantly for the student of school leadership, they permit us to see the person who is the principal, to experience the doubts, the dilemmas, the joys, and the lessons learned by those people who lead, manage, and survive as principals.

A growing literature about the professional culture of schools deepens our understanding of the context in which principals function. This literature originates partly in the suspicion that principals are dinosaurs. Rosenholtz (1986), Devaney (1987), and others essentially claim that principals *should* be managers and that teachers should be empowered to create and sustain the instructional leadership of their buildings. Lieberman and her associates (1988a) have begun fruitfully to explore the teacher's world and the professional culture of schools in an effort to identify how the value systems, personal relationships, organizational structure, and work of schools affect the teacher's personal and professional motivations and capabilities. These are exciting and extraordinarily valuable for the principal and the prospective principal, for they begin to chart the organizational environment into which principals must productively introduce themselves. Here, we can begin to understand the function of the principal by identifying how he or she can and cannot be influential and how we can predict the direction of those influences.

All these works reflect the unusual attention that the educational and political worlds have lavished on the principal in recent years. Their diversity and richness embody both a valuable opportunity for principals to learn about themselves and their work and a potential for confusion. What view of the principalship should one take? Who should one believe? Is the principal the most important player in the building? How is being forceful and strong different from being authoritarian? How does one lead with vision but in a participative, democratic style? How do principals prove themselves accountable to superintendents and boards while also empowering their teachers?

It is indeed a confusing time to be a principal or to contemplate becoming one. No doubt, the rising expectations for principals and their schools and the expanding literature prescribing roles for principals are convincing some prospective principals to finish their graduate work and certification for the principalship but *not* to seek positions (Kleine, 1990). In this climate, we need to find new ways of understanding what principals do, in the hope that they will help coalesce some of the knowledge and ideological posturing currently flooding us. For this purpose, I propose that we take a new look at the fundamental functions a principal serves in a school.

THE FUNCTIONAL APPROACH

All too often, professionals of all walks find themselves fully immersed in the problems of their work, wondering why they were not prepared in graduate school to handle the issues around them. Certainly, we educators have not been shy in this regard. This common lament, however, is based upon an assumption: that we can learn all important aspects of a role *prior to* assuming it. While fields such as medicine have developed internships to offset the effects of this syndrome, education (and educational administration) has not substantially altered its training and induction practices.

We continue to saddle ourselves not only with too few bridges between the preparation experience and the job but, as I have argued above, with a literature that unrealistically depicts the principalship. Our texts, much of our journal literature, and certainly our prescriptions for reforming the principalship characteristically draw their models of the principalship from three sources: (1) legal/financial role definitions set in a rational bureaucratic organizational framework; (2) instructional leadership role definitions delineated in effective schools and "best practice" literature; and (3) change-agent role definitions depicted in school innovation literature. All of these conceptions of the principalship make the same mistake. They start with a model of what principals ought to be and develop recommendations for preparing or improving principals from there, instead of starting with the common realities of the position and asking how a person can best prepare to handle these *and* adhere to best practice at the same time.

This dilemma has led me to what I call the Functional Approach to the principalship. Instead of beginning with an idealized picture of what principals ought to be and do, I begin by examining what American school site leaders have commonly been expected to be and do. I begin by asking the question, "What functions do principals typically serve in the school and community?" I assume that no principal who is hired into a school and community is likely to succeed (or perhaps even survive) without in some manner seeing that these basic functions are fulfilled. I will argue in later chapters that it is *how* these functions are fulfilled that often determines the successful leadership of a principal.

What do I mean by functions? I mean the essential work done by the principal that affects the ability of faculty and staff to teach and nurture children. This essential work has three basic aspects: activities, partners, and relationships. Hence, the principal's functions can be understood as: (1) committing time, energy, and attention to activities that advance the education of children; (2) identifying the proper people to involve in essential activities and providing for their success; and (3) understanding and developing proper relationships to maximize these people's and the school's success. Clearly, this conception of the principalship is built on an assumption that principals' work is primarily for the purpose of making the work of teachers, counselors, secretaries, coaches, custodians, and other specialists succeed. Hence, principals' functions are defined in terms of other people and the facilitation of their success. Indeed, these are the fundamental roots of the position, both historically and organizationally (despite the fact that practical demands on the principalship often obscure these roots).

The first of the principal's functions is to commit time, energy, and attention to proper *activities*. The principal must be engaged in daily, weekly, and annual behaviors that affect successful student outcomes. What the principal does him- or herself has great consequences for the institution on both practical and symbolic planes (Bennis and Nanus, 1985; Schein, 1985). Whether the principal works in the office or in the halls most of the time, for example, signals both what the principal's immediate function is and what the principal views as important within the school. A functional description of principal activities, then, depicts the professional expertise of the person and the value structure he or she brings to the work.

It is not uncommon to hear teachers wonder aloud, "What does the principal do all day?" At the root of this query is some bafflement about this first function. Similarly, principals when they gather are sometimes hard-pressed to explain exactly what their work is; what they do is not as readily understood as, say, what teachers do. So, too, the skills and knowledge required to do it are oftentimes a mystery even to principals. This focus, then, on what activities principals devote their time and energies to and how well they identify a task, carry it out, and follow it up is of considerable consequence both to principals in understanding their work and to those who seek effective leadership from the principal.

The second function is identifying and equipping *people* so that the purposes of school are properly executed. While the first function can be understood as what the principal does, the second can be understood as who the principal works with. It involves not only having capable personnel but knowing who needs to be engaged in working on what tasks in the school and community. Again, the function has practical and symbolic sides. Practically, the principal needs effective partners to get the essential work of the school accomplished, since the principal alone cannot educate children and run the school. Symbolically, the principal communicates his or her beliefs about the talents of these partners and the priorities of their work in his or her choice of which people will be engaged in what work.

The principal, for example, who engages only a senior core of teachers in important schoolwide decisions communicates to those teachers their importance in supraclassroom efforts. That principal informs all other teachers, conversely, that their work is only for the classroom and that perhaps their talents are not suited to issues beyond the classroom. Such a principal may develop a style in the school that could be labeled "executive" and his or her staff and faculty can easily come to see themselves and their responsibilities in a tiered bureaucratic framework. Functionally, then, the principal's selection of people for certain tasks—and the principal's provision of resources to support those people in that work—has a sizable impact on not only what work gets done, but how well it gets done and how others come to view the principal and his or her society of partners.

The principal's third function is the fashioning of *relationships* with these partners. As with the first two functions, these relationships are a sine qua non of principals' work; they exist, for better or worse, whether by design or by default. The principal, as the assigned leader of the school, has a working relationship with every adult and child who comes to the building and at least a symbolic relationship with many citizens. In the exercise of this function, the principal builds relationships directly with many people and through reputation and public events with many others. While the first function addresses what work the principal does and the second with whom the principal does it, the third function addresses *how* he or she works with these people and the effects this has on the school's outcomes.

Recent literature on the principalship and on leadership has focused on this third function, particularly as efforts have been mounted to share leadership, to empower teachers, and to make faculty cultures more supportive (e.g., Sergiovanni, 1987; Deal, 1990; Peterson, 1990). Indeed, in describing how any particular principal fashions working relationships, we often use indicators of power, of interpersonal sensitivity, and of collaboration. The feelings these terms often stir in teachers, staff, students, and parents are testimony to the significance of this third function to the principal's success. Clearly, a principal's basic function is to understand his or her relationships with these significant actors and to shape them to productive ends.

THE FUNCTIONAL APPROACH AS A LENS ON ONE PRINCIPALSHIP

In this book, I analyze and evaluate my experience as a secondary school principal, using the three functions outlined above. I first examine in Parts I, II, and III, respectively, my activities, partners, and relationships. This examination permits me to describe the essence of my work and to evaluate the extent to which my performance served the purposes of my high school. Then, in Part IV, with the conceptual distance granted by this analysis, I develop observations about the secondary principalship and about school leadership in general.

When I left the principalship to teach graduate courses in educational leadership in 1983, my reflections were haphazard but persistent. In fact, I found that I could not stop thinking about my experience, wondering how in the long run my work had made an impact on the school, pondering what lessons I could bring from my principalship to my new job teaching prospective principals. I began writing about it to try to reconstruct the essence of the job and the role. As I did so, I began a thorough review of my weekly calendars and notes, documents such as schedules, agendas, and policy or curriculum statements. I sought out conversations with co-workers to reconstruct the patterns of my activities and the details of events, people, and relationships. Most importantly, just after my resignation, I surveyed the faculty and staff of my school to gain their insights into my performance. The ensuing chapters draw from these two essential parties in school leadership: the titular leader and those he purportedly led.

How can one principal develop an accurate picture of his own functioning? I cannot promise that I have. Although I have attempted to be objective about my activities, my partners, and my relationships with them, I readily admit that my subjectivity is very much present. If I had had the foresight to seek outside observers during my principalship to provide more objective data, this book would clearly be stronger for some readers. It simply must be read with the usual caution one uses with autobiographical works.

I urge the reader to view this work as a case study of one principal's reflection-on-practice. Although my school's enrollment matched the median for U.S. secondary schools in the mid-1980s (NCES, 1988), I do not intend to generalize my experience to all secondary principals, to secondary principals in mid-size rural towns like mine, much less to all principals. Instead, it is a baedeker to my professional and personal journey through one principalship, detailing the significant sights and impressions of that journey so that others might learn from it. It is something of an epic tale, as well, concluding with new perspectives and advice learned along the way. I ask that readers take from it what they find useful to their own work as principals, to their work preparing and supporting principals, and to their work with principals and their schools.

Events such as the trashing of the school's kitchen disrupt our days. But they also interfere with our conceptions of what we ought to be doing to lead schools effectively. Every day, such events drive principals all over the United States to comment in frustration, "They never said the job would be like this." In the following chapters, one principal's descriptions and analyses of his principalship display not only what one principalship was like, but how his ideas, feelings, and personality made his leadership both effective and ineffective as he dealt with unexpected events and sought to carry out planned activities. From this case, others might see themselves—and their students—more clearly.

POSTSCRIPT: AN INTRODUCTION TO MY PRINCIPALSHIP

In 1976, when I was thirty, I applied for my first full principalship. I had taught since college, largely at the junior high level, in four different schools. Three of these had been in the inner city; the last was a K–12 school serving ninety-six students on an island twelve miles off the Maine coast. Offered two positions, I elected to accept the supervising principalship of Ellsworth Junior-Senior High School in Ellsworth, Maine, a coastal community of approximately 4,500 located about two hours drive from the Canadian border.

A regional school, Ellsworth drew 600 students from nine towns in grades 9 through 12. They represented the full range of the socioeconomic spectrum and educational aspirations, though not of racial and ethnic backgrounds. Sixty percent of the students lived in Ellsworth and the rest faced conditions classic to rural secondary schooling, commuting daily out of their towns to the big high school in the big town. In addition, 200 seventh and eighth grade students from Ellsworth were housed in the same building and, although my assistant principal was assigned to them, I was to oversee their program and activities as well as those of grades 9–12. The school had seen two supervising principals in the previous three years, including one who had been removed from the position. The school board, which had elected me to the position by a three to two vote, reflected the rising professionalism of the area (then shaking off eighty years of economic and population decline to become one of the fastest growing areas of the state). I reported to the superintendent of the district comprising the nine towns whose office was also in Ellsworth.

The position of supervising principal evolved over the seven years I held it. As the lead administrator for the entire operation of a grade 7–12 school of 800 students, I had as open a contract as one could imagine. Few duties were specified; my responsibilities boiled down simply to everything, all the time. I was to supervise all staff, including the junior high principal who handled junior high functions and ninth grade student affairs. This left me alone with grades 10–12, the entire 7–12 curriculum, the 9–12 cocurriculum, and the supervision and leadership of the high school staff of thirty-five. Because the junior high office was located in the seventh and eighth grade classroom wing of the school, I was often viewed—and I often acted—as the high school principal for grades 9–12. The superintendent and board made no clear demands of me; I was to "run a good school" and keep "everyone happy" (defined half-seriously by the superintendent as two goals that could be accomplished by having a winning basketball team and conducting a successful graduation ceremony). My contract was for fifty-two weeks and I was to consider myself on call whenever the school needed me or the superintendent and board demanded.

Sane readers may wonder why anyone would take such a job. Had I known more about the particular interpersonal dynamics of the system, I might very well have steered clear of it. But the job itself offered the kind of flexibility and wide-ranging opportunity to become involved in all aspects of secondary education that I sought. I was naive about the capacity of a high school to consume my time and energy, especially when my role and responsibilities were so broadly formulated. I saw opportunities and challenges, not potential pitfalls.

I worked in this structure for four years, from 1976 through 1980. Halfway through that period, the superintendent and board shifted my role to allow me to work more fully as the leader of both the grades 7–8 faculty and the 9–12 faculty and as supervisor of instruction and program. The junior high principal became the assistant principal/athletic director, defined in typical fashion to include student attendance and discipline, student activities, athletic directorship, and assistance to me in other functions. After doing it all for the high school in my first two years, my direct responsibility for maintaining student life was now significantly reduced, while my time and focus on faculty life and on curricular program increased.

In 1980 my position changed again. The opening of the county vocational school in Ellsworth, under the administrative aegis of the city, presented a supervisory challenge for the school system and an opportunity for me. The junior high grades were moved into a middle school arrangement in another building, and to my responsibilities were added the creation and supervision of vocational programs in a new building two miles up the road from the high school. I became the supervising secondary principal and the assistant principal took on the rather nebulous charge of running daily operations at the 9–12 building. My responsibilities at the high school remained the same, but I was to conduct the business of the voc-ed school part time and to be available for curriculum coordination and some teacher observation for grades 7–12 as well.

For the purposes of this book, I focus on my work at the high school. My responsibilities there were continuous over the seven years and I was consistently charged with the leadership of that enterprise. The challenges of the high school were indisputably adequate by themselves to prod my thinking and stimulate my self-reflection.

PART I

THE PRINCIPAL'S ACTIVITIES ADVANCE THE PURPOSES OF SCHOOLING

> Leadership consists in attempting to close the distance between ideals and behavior by reminding all members of the community of what is at stake in the attainment of ideals and by suggesting practical actions that can be taken to help realize those ideals.
>
> (Grant, 1988, p. 197)

I, like all principals, felt the expectation from all sides to be *the* leader of my school. As I moved to Ellsworth and began work, I felt the eyes of many watching me, anxious to see what kind of leader I would make. As I began, I confess to having little idea how I would bear the weight of these expectations. Having never been in charge of an adult staff, I was running on gut instinct, all but ignorant of the practical essentials of leadership.

I did, of course, have gut-level proclivities. Raised as I was during the late 1950s and early 1960s, my prominent models were John Kennedy and Martin Luther King in the sociopolitical realm, and postwar take-charge types like John Wayne and Vince Lombardi in other realms. These were men-of-action leaders; yes, they were all men. Despite their golden tongues or charismatic looks, these leaders distinguished themselves both by being active and by spurring others to action. They were, as Gerald Grant notes above, people who could meld ideals with live movement; they could cultivate in others the faith that the activities they modeled would lead to the attainment of the ideals they voiced.

The chapters in Part I explore the manner in which this merging of action and ideals is an essential function of the principalship. The experiences and ideas recounted here, however, do not simply assert that leadership results from tying one's actions to one's ideals. I contend that the principal's actions must manifest ideals that are both consistent over time and viewed widely as constructive for students, faculty, and community. Most importantly, productive leadership regularly stimulates action by everyone toward ideals that indisputably serve the psychological, intellectual, and social development of students. Grant argues that the school's "ideals are most often conveyed in less formal ways, by example and by story" (p. 173). It was in the principal's less formal activities that I found the greatest power to communicate to all members of the school community what the school should strive toward. Here, ideals met daily routines, attitudes, and behaviors and could guide and elevate them in small, concrete ways toward better practice. The principal who understands the potency of his or her activity patterns can select them wisely to shape in the behaviors and attitudes of staff and students the best ideals and purposes for the school.

The problem that Part I will make amply clear is that principals do not often feel totally in control of their own activities. Events and people impinge upon their best laid plans. Consequently, leadership of a school is not a matter of setting goals, developing plans to reach them, and single-mindedly pursuing them. Leadership is rather accommodating such goals and plans to the exigencies of the schooling place and, importantly, allocating one's time, energies, and attention to activities that enhance these both directly and, more subtly, by example.

Chapter 2

The Dominant Activity Patterns of My Work

It seems impossible to tell anyone, even another principal, what one does on the job. So many of my activities as principal were determined by happenstance that my attempts to describe what I did often degenerate into lists of unconnected events. This is a persistent difficulty for most every principal. The job is simply too fast-moving and the role too ambiguous to permit neat structuring. We, too, often thrive on the action, choosing to submerge ourselves in student problems and activities despite the fact that we will lose control of our time and perhaps our vision of the school's purposes as we do so. Yet, to understand and improve our work, we must learn to stop this action and to analyze our roles within it.

In Chapters 2 and 3, I describe the patterns of my activities as principal in Ellsworth. I try to resist the temptation to evaluate my work, and especially to revise it post hoc. I do, however, explain my activities as well as describe them, for my *reasons* for allocating my limited time and energies to certain activities demonstrate important elements of my philosophy of leadership. Here, I describe how my ideals as an educator and as a leader coincided—or did not coincide—with my behaviors. I have organized these activities into clusters and arrayed them by the percentage of my workday and workweek they typically required. These clusters reveal not only what I did with my professional time, but how these various activities balanced against one another.

Two properties of this description seem to defy the rules of quantification, and these are noteworthy precisely because they are not logically predictable and they belie our desire for regularity. First, in the life of an active principal, no such thing as a typical week exists. So I have established a range of time percentages for each activity cluster by judging how much time I devoted to it during active weeks and inactive weeks. Typically, the time I spent fell within these ranges. Second, the sums of the percentages of time I devoted to each activity always, even at the low end of the range, surpass 100%. The explanation is simple, although it is commonly forgotten by people outside schools: principals are always doing more than one activity at a time.

Typically, my day began at home with phone calls from sick or otherwise indisposed staff as early as 5:45 a.m., and usually between 6:00 and 6:30. At school by 7:15, I seldom left for home until 4:30 or 5:00 p.m. During most of my seven years, I averaged over three evenings in each seven-day week out at activities that could be construed as tied to my work (including community service and boards of related agencies but not including social activities). Some days were longer, some were shorter, but the pattern held pretty consistently between fifty-five and sixty hours per week, exclusive of on-call time at home. The days and weeks in which I spent over 100% of my time as noted here were weeks when I tended to surpass the fifty-five to sixty hour average and take more time out of home time.

Table 1 provides an overview of the activity clusters that Chapters 2 and 3 describe. It demonstrates the flights of logic and mathematics I have mentioned. More importantly, it displays concisely how my activity patterns may have communicated to others what I valued and did not value. The hierarchy of activities displayed here might be considered a hierarchy of my priorities for the school as well.

AVAILABILITY TO THE SCHOOL'S CLIENTELE: 90–100% DAILY; 80–90% WEEKLY

Availability to students, parents, and the public was very important to me: I considered my activity at nearly all times to be interruptible for a client concern. Thus, I estimate that I was available over 90% of the time, meaning that I could be reached, in the building or out, directly or by phone, and that others would take advantage of this fact. The demand for my attention, however, varied a great deal; students, parents, or the public actually imposed on only 10 to 15% of my time in an average day. Over an average week, only about 10% of my time was devoted to such unplanned solicitations.

Lacking any clear delineation of responsibilities, I felt first and foremost that I should be responsive. Particularly in the first years, I primarily reacted to the requests, demands, suggestions, and comments of the entire school/community body. I defined my work as that of the public servant. I was to see that the school served the students and the community. Serv-

Table 1
Common Time Allocations to My Activities
(by day/week)

Activity Cluster	Common Daily Range % of time*	Common Weekly Range % of time**
Availability to Clientele (students, community)	90%-100%	80%- 90%
Student Supervision	30 - 80	30 - 60
Organizing Central Staff	20 - 40	20 - 40
Teaching and Curriculum Development	0 - 50	10 - 40
Availability to Teachers	5 - 10	5 - 10
Omniscience/Omnipresence (seeing and being seen)	5 - 10	5 - 10
School Representative in Public Professional Circles	1 - 10	0 - 5
Structuring School Operations	0 - 5	10 - 20
Running the Office	0 - 5	0 - 5
Satisfying the Hierarchy	0 - 5	0 - 5

* based on 7:00 a.m. to 5:00 p.m. (10 hrs.)

**based on 5 days as above, plus three evenings 7:30 p.m. to 9:30 p.m. (56 hrs.) including weekends.

ing students in the mid-1970s had a distinctly reactive flavor (education was to be relevant and subject to student interests). I valued very much the open-door philosophy for students, parents, and staff and I sought to engage students and parents in conversation about what students were doing and learning in our classrooms and elsewhere. This in turn led some to sieze on my availability to discuss what was going on.

Most frequently, I heard from students and their parents about personal matters. Many of these dealt with how students were being treated by school staff or, more commonly, by other students: Billy complaining about those big kids in gym class who would pound on him when the teacher's back was turned; Sally who could not walk through the halls without being verbally accosted by the members of a small group of girls; Ted whose mother was irate because Miss Jones had not handed back corrected tests for three weeks; Jeanie stopping by to claim that Mr. Dickens favored the jocks in his classes, never calling on her or her friends and "you know, kiddin' around all the time with those track kids." Each of these comments usually came in the form of a complaint and necessitated a series of responses, increasing the size and complexity of the interruption to my planned activities. Thus, my availability and responsiveness—qualities most communities want in their principals—created serious obstacles to my successfully accomplishing other goals.

My availability also made me a walking information booth. Students, parents, and staff brought a myriad of questions about procedure (e.g., schedule for today), queries about material needs (e.g., free lunch for Marcia, a lost coat, permission to go to the clinic), and about policy issues (e.g., early dismissal, graduation requirements, athletic eligibility). Students, perhaps in response to my own interest in making contact and keeping in touch with them, sometimes acted as if I had *all* the important information and that my word and only my word was good. This situation placed me in a double bind, one very familiar to other principals: I enjoyed being needed but the irregular and spontaneous nature of these demands (and the research I sometimes needed to do to respond) created abuses of my time and energy. Thus, availability led to some level of interpersonal satisfaction for me, but it also created a serious diminution of my powers to attain other goals.

As time went along, I developed with staff more systematic statements of policy and procedure and worked hard to make them evident to everyone so that some of the nickel-and-dime interruptions that I felt were bankrupting my leadership would not occur. I also provided more people—mostly the office staff, guidance, and teachers—with information and gave them the opportunity and obligation to relate it to students. While this freed me of the numerous interruptions I experienced at first, it also removed treasured opportunities for contacts with kids and for gaining the satisfaction of helping someone directly.

This dilemma haunted my contacts with parents as well. Typically, parents did not frequent our school; when they had a pressing enough concern to drive them to express it to us, they called. They most often called *me*: I was near a phone, I was the head man, so they figured I could do something about their concern. Most parents I dealt with in this fashion wanted information about a school affair or about their child, his or her behavior, or academic performance. I attempted to encourage this type of call as much as I could, frequently by following up on the request personally. Other calls sought resolution of situations involving students; I tended to deal with these by first requiring a period of collecting facts about the situation, then explanation of them to the aggrieved party with a description of what action I could take to help. Contrary to the common view, parental complaints were not frequent; many times calls that might have carried a tinge of complaint were satisfactorily handled by providing accurate information about the matter. Parental demands on my available time were not great and seemed to parallel events that caused a stir at the school, such as a large shift in academic policy or a serious disciplinary event. These activities were voluntary, to an extent. They were the result of my choice to be available; the more I encouraged student and parent contact, the more it seemed to happen.

Other aspects of my availability were less optional. Beginning at 5:45 a.m. and running until 9:30 or 10:00 at night, I was eligible for calls (or so it seemed from my vantage point). These were mostly requests or reports of bad news; thus they demanded response, a condition similar to a doctor's being on call. A surprising number of contacts at school, at home, or in the supermarket dealt with the use of the building for community events or private affairs. Some sought my participation in local causes or matters, such as requests to speak to a community group or for the band to perform for a store opening. Still others sought information about events in the schools, some for purposes of public information and some for personal use (such as parents needing a schedule so they could arrange transportation for their children). Whether I liked it or not, my availability was expected in my job and, unless I chose to have an unlisted phone or to develop a hostile response to calls, it extended my job into time that most would define as their own or their families' time.

While not demanding an overwhelming amount of actual time, this function took a considerable toll on my ability to exercise other functions. These activities gave my work a high "distraction quotient." While 10% of my time may have been spent actually responding to initiated client concerns, 90% of my time was eligible for interruption. Most significantly, it required that I be well informed, so it propelled me into extensive activity around the building and in the community. As the leader, I felt a need to know a lot about all aspects of the school, to resolve glitches when they arose, and to respond productively to those with a public vested interest in the institution. The superintendent and board clearly were interested in smooth public relations and, more fundamentally, in seeing that the school served all its populations as successfully as it could.

The inherent paradox arising here between the responsive principalship and the time-efficient, self-directed principalship shadows nearly every principal I know. The paradox is summoned up daily in each principal's time schedule, reflecting in his or her inability to concentrate fully on matters and in his or her need to develop quick means of dealing with complex matters such as complaints. I found this condition stressful. I was fortunate to be able to select and shape my immediate staff and to shift my job description two times in seven years, each time making the paradox a bit less problematic. Many principals, absent these opportunities, devote themselves to availability through making themselves the ever-present principal, the manager of personnel and plant who responds to everything and keeps the machine moving but for whom questions of the machine's direction and destination are abstract luxuries. This is a path I resisted, but with difficulty.

STUDENT SUPERVISION: 30–80% DAILY; 30–60% WEEKLY

I consistently felt compelled to supervise students, even after my job description changed to focus more on supervision and curriculum. Generally, this meant being in corridors, the lunchroom, study halls, the library, at ball games, drama activities, concerts, and other night and weekend events. At all times, it meant being aware of the areas outside the building where students could be unsupervised or en route to a "skip." Although the assistant principal had primary responsibility for most student supervision in the later years, my awareness of the need for such monitoring was ever-present. I felt it was my responsibility to be ready to pick up the slack where teachers and other staff were neither assigned nor expected single-handedly to supervise students. Although I seldom actively controlled students, I was constantly nagged by the thought that, if supervision of students grew slack, the school's good discipline would disappear.

My supervision of students served two major goals: it was to deter major disciplinary crises and to assert a positive influence on the climate of the school. Often my supervision of students came in the form of walking around. My approach was to make my participation in the public realms of the school proactive. That is, while I was in the corridors, in the lunchroom, or at a soccer game, I tried to initiate contacts with students, to chat about how they were doing in shop or with so-and-so or what they were thinking about school or some public issue. My conviction was, and still is, that true deterrence and true positive influence result from the principal's frequent *presence* with students and the principal's *initiation* of interaction from a noncontrolling stance—before a need arises to control or to become punitive.

I also saw student supervision as the prime opportunity to influence the climate. As I saw and talked with students, I could make them feel they mattered and that the principal was interested in them. Playing no small part in this daily practice was the enjoyment I generally derived from talking to kids. Adolescents are fascinating, creative, dramatic, moody, eager for contact with adults, and easy to rib. Talking with students was a challenge, a kind of dance we must do with teen-agers in order to learn about them. I enjoyed this process and enjoyed plumbing for the usual frankness of most kids. But I also discovered that it was essential to my understanding of the school. In running the school, I was a perpetual collector of information and signals from our prime clientele, the students, and I was constantly using this information to shape their understanding of their purposes in the building.

To my way of thinking, the only way the principal can meet the two student supervision goals—asserting a deterrent presence and providing a positive authority—is by committing at least 50% of his or her time to the student realm (or directing other central staff to this end). For me, this meant walking about the building, being in the halls between periods, being in and out of the lunchroom every day, being near entry doors before and after school, drifting through teaching areas like shops and gyms where kids are physically widespread, stopping by practice sessions after school, and attending popular afternoon and evening events. In a high school, this came to mean "purposeful irregularity"—showing up where students were at unpredictable times and from unexpected directions, as well as appearing on duty at expected points such as the lunchroom and at basketball games.

When viewed from the student's angle, however, my goal was to make my presence, and thus my work and role, very continuous and impressive. One bad actor, after a year and a half of getting caught by me once noted with frustration, "I can't get away from you! You're everywhere!" For adults who dealt with me, however, this pattern meant that I appeared and disappeared from discussions or meetings according to student schedules, depending on whether my barometer of visibility was reading "must show" or "all quiet." This type of activity made my work frenetic and discontinuous when viewed from the classroom or office. It drew me away from office activities and from activities requiring blocks of uninterrupted time and attention. Like being available, the student supervision activity cluster fragmented my work. Teachers, staff, and other administrators undoubtedly witnessed this fragmentation and may well have wondered how firm my grasp was on my role and the school's purposes.

Both these major activity clusters made my work exciting and heavily people-oriented. But they also made it very difficult for me to preserve time to develop programs, to work a single project from start to finish without interruption, or to reflect on what I did. They gave my principalship a distinct orientation to action that, while it may have helped me succeed in some realms, created stresses and problems in others.

ORGANIZING CENTRAL STAFF FUNCTIONS: 20–40% DAILY; 20–40% WEEKLY

Next in prominence to these large activity clusters, my time was devoted to working with the assistant principal, athletic coordinator, guidance counselors, and special education personnel. The extensive time I spent with these staff concentrated on several activities.

My work with central staff, and especially with the two counselors and their secretary, focused on the coordination of student schedules, placement, and evaluation. Although considerable time each year went into creating a master schedule of hopefully delicious courses for students to consume, problems with student interest and placement cropped up throughout the year, and especially at the change of each marking period. As students began courses and experienced problems in them (and sought to add and drop them) or as teachers developed assessments of students' progress and motivation, they often sought assistance from the guidance department or the office. I often found myself drawn into conflicts among teachers, guidance personnel, students, and parents. This work led to numerous direct contacts with individuals and gave rise to a need to coordinate and systematize the efforts of central office staff, guidance, special education, and administration. Given the difficulties of reaching and affecting so many students and teachers, I came to see my work with the central staff as an important means of shaping our collective responsiveness to the individual student and of inculcating responsibility in students for their own learning.

My involvement with central staff allowed me to enlist them to my thinking and to enlarge the impact of my own system for running the school. By regular contact with the two guidance staff and the assistant principal in the later years, I developed with them a collaborative approach to structuring the student management and learning systems of the school. This approach permitted each of us to voice opinions and concerns, to share the responsibility for developing and carrying out procedures such as the orientation of new students or the testing of a group, and to align our joint approaches to staff and students. We met regularly and had innumerable short discussions every day. I came to see us as a team for the leadership of the school on all issues where students were concerned. The message emanating from this nuclear group, in my design at least, was that the student is the basic unit of the school's work and that staff must integrate and accommodate to one another in order to have the student come out ahead educationally.

A second major arena of my central staff activity was special education. In my first year, PL94–142, the special education law, arrived in Ellsworth and with it the expectations and regulations to tailor programs to students. Because I believed in such tailoring and for a variety of local administrative reasons, I became a constant part of the effort to establish effective and accountable special needs programs and to develop a system for screening and diagnosing special students. This required weekly afternoon meetings in probably 75% of the weeks I was in Ellsworth and it required an inordinate quantity of my time to organize a system among teachers because the environment was neither supportive of nor adequately staffed for the intent of the law. As we established three different programs, I became increasingly involved in their goals and procedures and came to know the individual students receiving help much better than I knew most students. Although I do not feel I provided adequate support to the teachers in these programs, my involvement with the students and the development of the programs was often as satisfying as it was intrusive on my schedule.

The third and most continuous claim on my time and energy came from activities involving the assistant principal. Because we shared the leadership of the school, it was essential that we knew each other's daily activities as well as each other's style and goals. We were fortunate to be able to work openly with one another. Few holds were barred in our discussions, even when displeased with one another. We spent perhaps too much time talking to one another, serving as foil, as consultant, as encourager, as companions in a frequently lonely job. Particularly in the last three years when I was not present in the building all the time, my impact on the school came increasingly to be felt through the medium of the assistant principal. We spent easily one hour each day (usually four minutes at a time) in discussion.

These central staff activities were some of the most important and time-consuming events of my work as a principal. They were occasions when the leadership of the school functioned best because we multiplied one another's effects. Time spent discussing how we should act was team-building time. Then, what we valued as we dealt with staff, students, parents, and the public gave the school coherence and character. The inner workings of this team had essential value to the school; the time I invested in them established the leadership of the school effort. I was fortunate to have, at least in the later years, an excellent central staff whose efforts and instincts were such that our collective impact was indeed much greater than the sum of each individual's impact.

TEACHING AND CURRICULUM INVOLVEMENT: 0–5% DAILY; 10–40% WEEKLY

I chose to work as a principal because of an interest in teaching and because I believed that teaching can be improved by the principal. As honorable as these intentions are, realizing them is very difficult. Teacher observation, support, and curriculum planning often required blocks of time uninterrupted by the student, public, and administrative concerns previously noted. The competition on my schedule between pedagogical and curricular issues and "everything else" was continuous and draining. I came to see certain days of the week and particularly certain times of the year as more hospitable to the kind of reflective thought and long-range planning necessary to make these activities work. Mondays and Fridays, periods before vacations, and the months of September, May, and June were times of distraction and interruption that made these more thoughtful activities most difficult.

The major activity in this cluster was teacher supervision and evaluation. To provide fair and accurate information to teachers about their teaching required observations, frequently over several days, a period of analysis of the observed data, a conference with the teacher to share and discuss that data, and usually the development of accurate and helpful written feedback. An observation cycle for an evaluation of a teacher's work done in this fashion usually took three to four hours. In addition, I needed to feel relatively unharried to do this well; the activity is so important both to the school and the individual teacher (for whom employment issues are inevitably raised) that I never felt comfortable doing it when more pressing concerns distracted me. Furthermore, I soon learned that well-executed evaluation required three or four observations to establish a reasonable data base. For a faculty of about forty, a concern for pedagogical improvement thus could easily occupy half a principal's time in direct teacher observation and coaching.

Curriculum planning and evaluation activities also required concentrated thought and unfettered time blocks. I sought to assemble teachers, counselors, and sometimes parents and school board members to examine our academic goals and the success of our courses in meeting them. Inevitably, these studies led to revision, requiring further discussion, planning, and writing. To keep these important curricular matters on the front burner demanded that my daily building supervision and general availability be curtailed. Teachers' schedules and energy levels, as well, often made them unable (and sometimes unwilling) to address long-range program issues, leaving me feeling even more responsible for initiating these activities.

This required that I insert myself into the private world of the teacher and his or her students. To do this well took some bravado on my part: I first had to assert that the teacher's classroom was *not* a private world; and then I had to try to make teacher's involvement with me on instructional and curricular matters valuable enough to the teacher that he or she would support it. Such work is delicate, particularly in a school where no significant history of it exists. While I deal with the interpersonal intricacies of this function elsewhere in this book, the human side of teacher supervision tended to devour greater portions of my day than I usually allotted. I found myself thinking frequently about the most profitable way to approach Mr. X about a course or processing an observation conference with Ms. Z, struggling with maintaining the precious threads of a staff network while trying to stretch individual fibers to endure the light of professional inspection.

On a more concrete level, my activities were designed both to monitor and evaluate each teacher's teaching and each course's content. Although we often think of teacher evaluation, staff development, and curriculum development as distinguishable activities, they are not in fact separated in the lives of teachers. Visits to classrooms provide the absolutely best opportunity to observe all three at work; conferences with teachers after such observations are *the* occasion to discuss all three in a context that has immediate relevance to practice. So my teacher supervision and evaluation activities took me across a threshold with teachers into a realm where shared observation, suggestion, redirection, and open questioning could occur about any number of professional issues.

Most commonly these discussions centered on specific patterns of teaching displayed by the teacher and noted by me or the teacher. But they frequently included individual students, the material of the lesson, and issues relating to the appropriateness of the material and method chosen by the teacher for presenting it. From here, issues of student placement and course coordination would arise. In short, the observation/evaluation sequence, for me, was the richest means available to learn about the instructional life of the school and, based on what I learned, to direct my thinking and planning for the school's development.

I used the information I gained in this fashion to give me both an understanding of the student's experience in each teacher's room and a constantly growing data base for rethinking and redirecting teaching and curriculum. Scheduling, program redesign, teacher assignments, and the ramification of these for the budgeting process were all improved through the collection and use of such information. Being knowledgeable about the teaching practices of faculty (and in our high school, that meant I was the only person knowledgeable about them across the board) and having teachers know that I was knowledgeable gave me considerable authority in professional matters. From an informed position, too, I was prepared to respond to the concerns and queries of parents, board, and superintendent; I could speak with firsthand knowledge about all teachers and most courses and actively head off community anxiety or lead efforts toward instructional improvement. So the significant demands of time and interpersonal energy that these activities placed on me were, in the long run, beneficial to my leadership potential. The problem, as always, was allocating the time, and protecting the quality of that time, to carry off these activities well.

AVAILABILITY TO TEACHERS: 5–10% DAILY; 5–10% WEEKLY

My final major activity cluster incorporated the many ways I felt on call for teachers. Clearly, the principal's direct contact with teachers is vital to the overall coordination and direction of the school as well as to the faculty's sense of professional colleagueship and unity. For this reason, I protected to the degree that I could time and interruptibility for teachers. As was true for the first two clusters, much of this activity was not controlled by me; teachers' schedules and agendas shaped my time more than I shaped theirs.

Early in my principalship, I tended to initiate more contacts than did teachers. Believing that I could mold the staff into consensus and teamwork, I devoted workshops and staff meetings to discussion of goals and means to reach them; I asserted professional matters as the major agendas of our talks together. Owing to a variety of forces, however, I soon came to see these formal approaches to coordination as ineffective. Instead, I came increasingly to work one-on-one or in small groups with staff and to be purposefully informal in my efforts to get to know faculty and to shape their efforts to one another and to my vision of the school's purposes. Thus I came to see my availability to teachers as a key to my success at developing a constructive professional climate. Through these contacts I could keep staff coordinated toward our central tasks, offer encouragement, and at times give corrective feedback and guidance.

The concerns that most frequently surfaced through daily or weekly conversation and discussion fell into five broad categories. Most common were student concerns: How should I, the teacher, handle Bill who has missed every quiz this quarter? What should I do with Kelly who refuses to hand in homework? What should be our response to kissing in the halls? Although such issues were innumerable and extremely varied, the way I involved myself in their solution, then jointly developed with teachers a philosophy and procedure for future solutions, gave me a very powerful means of coordinating and shaping the actual work of the school.

A second category of concerns was procedural. What is the order of periods today? When are warning notices due? Why haven't I heard from you on the legitimacy of Fred's Tuesday absence? These questions to me constituted a set of comments from teachers about the routines and structures of the schools. If I heard a lot of questions, I assumed teachers were unusually concerned with a managerial issue and not able to focus on the more salient teaching issues; if I heard few, I assumed things were going as they should. Thus I worked to minimize this kind of comment through trying to streamline and routinize the managerial aspects of the school as much as possible. I am pretty sure that I also communicated an impatience with this type of procedural discussion and sometimes tended to suppress staff concerns in this area. However, I also tried to have office staff and the assistant principal take ownership for many of these procedures and to direct teachers to the appropriate person for a resolution.

A third type of concern dealt with finances. Since I was required to sit at the controls of both curricular and cocurricular expenditures, teachers needed to deal with me for permission and consultation on purchases and expenditures of all kinds. I tried to use this relatively bureaucratic power to focus on the purposes of expenditures. Why were new texts necessary for Civics? What alternatives were available? How can we be sure we select the best of them? Is a community fund-raising scheme worthy of the goal for which the money is intended? At times I am sure that my insistence on having good reasons for all our expenditures and fund-raising drove some teachers nuts. Discussion of the purposes of financial transactions, however, gave me a significant opportunity to shape not only our expenditures to our common goals but also teachers' and other staffs' thinking to those goals. I assumed that *what* we spent and raised money for indicated in a very real way what we valued in the mission of our school. I also assumed that how we explained those financial purposes to others was critical in spreading the message of our school's goals. So, as impatient as both the teacher and I may have become with budget details and requisitions, the discussions we had often gave us a chance to restate goals and recommit to them.

A fourth type of concern, cocurricular issues, generally consumed more time than the preceding activities. This was true because cocurricular activities were seemingly always occurring, because they excited students, faculty, and parents, and because they often seemed to intrude on life-as-usual. Athletics, music, student government, and club activities tended to interrupt schedules and preoccupy students, staff, and office at odd times. We might need to dismiss a team early or arrange a band rehearsal before school. Or we might have to clear the lobby and gym for three days for an Industrial Arts Fair. Or the student council's clean-up day involved organizing and supervising many students doing community service. Rarely a week went by without such an event requiring my attention and time. These activities, too, created a second tier of demands on me. As cocurricular activities impinged on the regular curriculum, teachers, coaches, parents, and even students raised the perpetual debate over the balance between academics and athletics. Although I grew as tired of the debate and the time it took as anyone, I came to appreciate the chance it gave us to reexamine periodically the adequacy of our programs in light of the purposes of our school.

A final category of concern governing my availability to teachers is more interwoven with the other four than isolated. It includes issues of long-range planning and the process of deliberation over various program options available to staff and me. A teacher's query about teaching with computers, about raising our credit requirements for graduation, or about instituting a policy for work-study credits are examples of this category. Although issues of this sort did not surface as frequently in staff conversations as I had hoped, they came in a trickle and in particular from certain staff who were concerned about the performance of the school as a whole. In addition, I sought out long-range concerns from teachers by holding informal coffees and dropping by teachers' rooms to get a feel of how things were going. The information I gleaned from my availability for this level of discussion was among the most useful to me in understanding where the school's staff thought we were heading and how some of them, at least, felt we should shift our focus. Because I attempted to encourage involvement with the longer range issues of the school and because teachers were so immersed in daily short-range work, I suspect that some staff came to see me (and perhaps write me off) as unrealistic, visionary, and even out of touch.

In sum, my availability to teachers required my time and energy in fits and starts. As teachers' procedural, extracurricular, student management, and resource needs surfaced, I tended to be called upon. I intended to remain available to staff for these concerns at practically all times. But, as will become clearer in later sections of this book, teachers' desires to make use of this availability were shaped heavily by my relationship with each individual teacher. As time went along, my regular contacts with faculty took on increasingly stable patterns and my participation with some diminished almost to the level of weekly greetings.

RESPONSIVE VERSUS ASSERTIVE ACTIVITY

This depiction of my primary activities as a secondary principal portrays my work to be largely responsive. Availability to clientele and to teachers on an on-call basis as well as the supervision of students dominated my work activity. Even my involvement with central staff was designed to head off situations that would interrupt the core functions of teachers and students. This activity pattern left me feeling as if I were perpetually stemming a tide of requests, complaints, questions, and issues. Even though this work gave me the chance for daily personal contacts in which I could be helpful, it was frustrating and tiring because the tide never ebbed. Far from my image of the purposeful, energetic young principal leading his school toward success, I often felt overwhelmed by the sheer number of people I dealt with and by the time that each required. Was being responsive the same as being a leader?

McPherson, Crowson, and Pitner (1986) discuss this condition at length in their book *Managing Uncertainty*. Others, taking a largely nonrational view (Weick, 1982; Meyer and Rowan, 1978) would agree with McPherson et al. that the ambiguities of teaching processes and the unpredictability of students make school administration an extraordinarily fuzzy activity. Hence, many principals do what I did: primarily respond to what comes to us, using occasions such as these to keep the building and its occupants on an even keel through the day, the week, the month, and the year. Our work, rather than fitting more traditional profiles of leadership, takes the shape of the people and events around us. Recent treatments of this portrayal of the principalship (Barth, 1979; Blumberg and Greenfield, 1980; Lightfoot, 1983) stress that principal leadership happens through people (not to people), that problem-finding and problem-solving, and negotiation and listening, for example, are the staples of such leadership. Reflecting on my years as principal, I find many of these writers painting the vivid colors of my own work. I did many of these things. But I remained skeptical that a largely responsive activity pattern really provided leadership.

My skepticism was rooted in two ideas, both of which predispose me to think of real leadership as more assertive and controlling. The first is that schools should be purposeful institutions with professional charters and an orderly organization; the principal is the executive whose purpose it is to see that the school fulfills its charter, delivering its products, so to speak, to society on time and well developed. The second is a spin-off of the first and now enjoys currency in the U.S. school reform movement: The best schools have "strong, forceful leaders" (Edmonds and Frederickson, 1978; Lipsitz, 1984; Persell and Cookson, 1982), principals who will assert goals, programs, and a value system for their students, staffs, and often their communities much the way the successful executives do (Bennett, 1989; Peters and Waterman, 1982). Throughout my experience as a principal in Ellsworth, I was attended by a gnawing uncertainty that I was not adequately fulfilling these expectations for a more assertive leadership.

In fact, I was working within several conflicting sets of leadership expectations that are supported by conflicting leadership and organizational theories. Eventually, I discovered that my leadership style and goals were established more by the manner in which I responded to people than by the programs and long-range plans I initiated. My effectiveness as a principal in the eyes of my clientele and staff was determined by my willingness to accept incoming business, learn what alternatives we had for handling it, and orchestrate as beneficial a response to it as I could. To the extent that I could succeed in this manner, I helped make the school an organization that honored individual and human needs. On the other hand, my doing this did not preclude my also holding high expectations for the school, developing an orderly structure, and asserting programs and goals. The two sets of activities, the two styles of leadership, are not incompatible; rather, they are complements to one another that are indispensible to the effective school.

In this regard, the activities described in this chapter show me to be a principal who valued the interpersonal climate and goals of the school over assertive programming and intellectual ends, although substantial time and energy were properly committed to the latter. As will become clear, I learned that leadership develops not through either responding or asserting. Rather it develops through establishing a foundation of productive responses to people and to the uncertainties of schooling and then being assertive and even controlling in a manner and at times appropriate to both the interpersonal and academic goals of the school.

Chapter 3

Everything Else: The Less Obvious Activity Patterns

> It's not the big things that get you, but all the little things that accumulate like a long, quiet snowfall; pretty soon, you're drifted in.
> (a Maine principal)

While historically we have thought that leadership emerges from grand strategies and daring acts, recent attention has focused on the small and less tangible aspects of organizational leadership. Peters and Waterman (1983) found that "management by walking around" played an essential part in providing direction and unity to top U.S. corporations. Bennis and Nanus (1985), Kennedy and Deal (1982), Schein (1985), and Sergiovanni (1989) have expanded our understanding of leadership as a web of small actions and relationships that shape our schools through the medium of their cultures and climates. This chapter profiles the activities that required less of my time than those in Chapter 2 but that were no less important in establishing my character as a principal. These minor activities frequently influenced faculty views of me as much as major activities did; their influence, however, tended to be more symbolic than instrumental.

OMNISCIENCE AND OMNIPRESENCE: 5–10% DAILY; 5% WEEKLY

My work as principal was accompanied by a fear, usually deeply buried, that some event or condition of the school would come to light and I would not know about it. The fear of being taken unaware propelled me into action on a rather random basis, though the purpose of the action was very clear. It was simply to know what was going on around the school and between the school, the community, and other schools. Behind this activity lay the expectation that the principal should be a step ahead of others and should command an efficient communication network in order to resolve problems and provide informed direction to the school community. Though driven in part by the fear of being taken unaware, the know-all-and-be-everywhere activity (what I call here "omniscience and omnipresence") was nurtured by others' needs to believe that the leader was mysteriously in the know. It nudged me into perpetual and somewhat neurotic data-gathering that was, in the end, healthy for me and the school.

I made it my business to move about the building and to inquire about the activities of students and faculty as often as I could. These activities were seldom planned. Instead, they occurred *while* I was doing something planned or focused, such as any one of the activities in the previous chapter. In part, I viewed this activity as simply observational, collecting daily facts and impressions about the school that I could use to assuage the fear of being caught unaware and to undergird my decision-making and planning. And in part, my collecting of information was evaluative: I discovered important information about staff, students, and the school at large that permitted me with some confidence to encourage positive practices or to discourage negative ones.

Like several other categories of my activity in this catalog, this one translated into a peripatetic pattern. Particularly when I found myself sitting somewhere—in the office, in a meeting that was stalled, on the phone, filling out paperwork, or even at home—I felt compelled to ask myself whether there was an activity in the school that was important for me to cover. Up I would jump, if the answer was "yes" or "maybe;" and I would be off to watch and, if needed, become involved in what was happening. While I estimate that I spent between 5 and 10% of my daily time in this type of activity, that time came in small, discontinuous chunks, tending to divide my attention into as many parcels as the phenomena I observed. Of course, where I chose to devote my attention affected what I saw and what kinds of data I collected. In general, these objects of my attention reduced to public events, students and teachers, program, and the building.

Public events demanded a surprising amount of my time, and much of that time was beyond school hours because these events occurred in the afternoons and evenings and frequently away from Ellsworth. Basically, I reasoned that these were the points at which the public had most access to the work and activity of the school, so they were the samples of school life on which the public was most likely to base their comments, criticisms, and praise. I felt a need to have access to the facts and events on which opinions were made, both to permit me to handle appropriately public comments, whether negative or positive, and to understand more fully how the public reasoned. The longer I was a principal, the more I understood that public relations was less a campaign to put our best face forward and more a function of establishing relationships with the public that demonstrated my informed leadership. Community members were fundamentally more concerned that the principal knew about school events important to them than that the principal painted glowing public pictures of the school's performance. When parents found that I not only knew their children but could converse about what they had done last week in intramurals, for example, the impact was almost tangible. Or when a board member heard me discuss in detail events or issues at school, they could not help but conclude that I was on top of things (even if they disagreed with me).

Within the school, observational antennae were often trained on student and faculty attitudes and what Madeline Hunter might call the "feeling tone" of the school. Were students going busily but happily about their business? Were teachers doing likewise? What particular places in the building took on a special character and how did this character translate into a given educational or social purpose for a given group of students? Which specific students did I see doing good deeds or taking advantage of circumstances in ways they should not? Were specific teachers carrying out specific practices that had beneficial or deleterious effects? All of these questions and many more traversed my mind as I walked around and watched. They all led to what I believe was an extensive knowledge of the activities of the people in the school, a knowledge that provided a fairly accurate base from which to respond to specific demands. The importance to me of this knowledge cannot be underestimated. It provided me the confidence through which I could accept or reject complaints and suggestions, allowing me to maintain a steady direction to policies and practices without caving in to the most recent complaint or most vociferous viewpoint.

One small example of this function comes from my third year. In a school board meeting, a father stood up and fulminated against the atmosphere and student supervision at the high school. Before long, his emotional oratory rose to such a peak that board members' attempts to redirect him failed even to interrupt him. Forty-five minutes of monologue followed, detailing a scene of rampant drug use and immorality in the high school and suggesting a need for locked doors and uniformed policemen with dogs in the corridors. The man claimed to have kept the school, and particularly its outdoor smoking area, under surveillance for some time. I finally grew impatient waiting for a board member to put a stop to his ill-founded diatribe. Because my knowledge of students and of all corners of the school building was so extensive, I finally (and confidently) cut in and challenged the man to come to the school and show me and board members his evidence of illicit activity. The discussion grew heated momentarily and eventually ended; the newspaper account detailed much of the monologue but also included my statements; no groundswell of accusations or even questions aimed toward us occurred. I wondered later how sure of myself and the school I would have felt had I been spending most of my time in the office.

A third focus of my data-gathering was the educational program. High schools present precious few opportunities to observe unobtrusively what teachers and students do in the instructional realm. Formal observations of classroom instruction are nearly always stilted and, depending on the supervisor's relationship with the teacher, will or will not yield reliable knowledge of typical curricular and pedagogical activities. Though incomplete, the knowledge I gathered about the types of activities each teacher conducted inside the classroom through means other than formal observation became very valuable. My mobility produced multiple opportunities to talk to teachers and students and to catch glimpses and hear snatches of instruction in nearly all classrooms on a weekly basis. While each individual sample of this activity was extremely unreliable, the patterns of activity I observed over weeks, months, and years eventually produced a picture of a teacher's program and style that I could corroborate during full formal observations.

For example, the teacher whose classes nearly always were working or chatting amongst themselves by the half-hour mark of the period was the teacher whose students came to me and repeatedly claimed they "did nothing" in class. The teacher whose students almost always sat with eyes glued to him or her when I went by was the teacher with very tightly organized lessons day in and day out. The teacher who typically was seated at a table watching as students rather bumptiously carried out lab activities was the one whose students had not completed work at term's end and who grew to dislike those particular course offerings. The active monitoring process I followed, trying to keep up on what went on everywhere each day, generated information that, over time, distilled into accurate facts and impressions about curricular ingredients and teaching performance.

Finally, my erstwhile data-gathering focused on the building—picking up information about its use and condition as I conducted other business around school. The importance of this agenda grew as I gained experience on the job, from a point where I considered the building only a nettlesome burden to where I understood the quality of daily care of the building to have a major effect on the way staff and students treated it and perhaps each other. Although we had a custodial supervisor, his sensibilities about his work did not always jibe with mine; further, he was beset by challenges to his supervisory role that demanded guidance and encouragement from me. Thus, I came to check almost subconsciously for the cleanliness of corners on the stairwells, whether the cracked window had been replaced, how the new heat-regulating system was working, whether we needed to do any painting or major work before the upcoming open house, and the work habits of the night crew.

Although I never liked this part of the job, it played an oddly central part in my role because a surprisingly large number of people, both public and staff, viewed the principal as the person in charge of maintenance. *I got complaints on heat, dirt, plumbing, snowplowing, break-ins; so I found myself monitoring the facility and standing by for emergencies.* Further, I did grow to appreciate the significance of the building's attractiveness and pedagogical suitability; and I increasingly routed data gathered on daily rounds to people who could take action to improve the facility. It was this thinking that eventually led to routine inspections of the building with the assistant principal and the head custodian, to lists of work needing completion by certain deadlines, and to performance appraisals for our janitorial crew based on the building's appearance.

In sum, what began as a fear-driven function evolved into a very significant daily activity with obvious benefits to my leadership of the school. While nearly every principal I know fears getting caught uninformed, how we handle that uncomfortable possibility is crucial. The fear can drive us to bouncing all over the school throughout the day and into the evening, making sure we know everything all the time. I did that more than I like to confess and found it absolutely exhausting and eventually impossible. No single person can be everywhere at all times. Significant agendas are ignored if that becomes the principal's major activity.

The alternative is to understand the need to know a great deal about the school's functioning, but to reach that knowledge through widespread but incidental observation and through gathering it from other people whose primary job it is to be where the action is. I have known principals to disapprove an activity or practice because their personal schedules would not permit them to oversee it and I have known others to relinquish the goal of knowing the daily habits of their schools because they could not conceive of being omnipresent and omniscient. Neither extreme makes sense. A daily practice of random sampling, with purposeful attendance at significant events, is a compromise of the principal's individual limitations and the goal of knowing enough to keep atop the organization. It is one of the more difficult compromises I had to make in the principalship.

SCHOOL REPRESENTATIVE TO THE PUBLIC AND PROFESSION: 0–10% DAILY; 0–5% WEEKLY

Some principals feel that public relations is one of the most crucial of their activities; not so with me. I believed that our work would speak for itself and that time to do our work well was so limited that to spend some of it creating a public image was foolish. Instead, I sought ways to give parents and public access to life inside the school. While I did not often take the initiative with the public, I did my best to use opportunities that arose to represent the school in its best but most accurate light. I spoke to Rotary, Kiwanis, and Lions and I advocated for our band to play at public functions and I sought newspaper coverage of major events (usually requiring *my* time to actually write the news release). Beyond our monthly board meetings, the only high school activities the local media covered were athletic. Consequently, my efforts at representing our school to the public were aimed at bringing the public into the school to give them a feeling for the climate there and a clearer idea of our instructional activity.

This was no easy task. High schools are somehow inhospitable to adults who do not belong in them, as teachers, principals, secretaries, guidance staff, and janitors do. So creating contacts with parents and other members of the public to open the door for them to come in means more than simply inviting them. We never really succeeded at doing this. We established annual curriculum reviews that brought some citizens in to discuss program with teachers; we held the standard open houses as well as a few festivals to show off student talents; we required parents to play a role in course selection and student placement; and we created an elaborate system of publications and parent meetings for incoming freshmen. In the final analysis, the effects of these steps was difficult to gauge and, in retrospect, I do not think they conveyed a lot of information about the educational program successfully to parents. They did, nevertheless, demonstrate our willingness to be visited and consulted regularly; that openness went a great distance toward establishing trust with the public.

Despite these meager planned means of establishing public relations, most of the time I spent at this activity was in meetings and conversations with people at various school and community events. For me, the most potent means of both conveying a welcome to the public and presenting the school to them was through individual contact. Consequently, I felt a nagging obligation to attend parades, public suppers, bake sales by student groups, community efforts to raise scholarships for our students, church affairs, musical events, and meetings of community groups to discuss social issues affecting the school. These sorts of occasions were prime opportunities both to meet an expanding number of interested community members and to signify my interest and support for what they did. The major difficulty I faced was finding the time and the energy to attend them all (and stay long enough to have those important individual conversations with folks).

More of my public time was devoted to membership in community activities or groups. I am more comfortable belonging to groups that have a function than showing up at lots of places and making public presentations or appearances. I joined the volunteer fire department in my town, the Lions Club in Ellsworth, and the board of directors of a residential adolescent treatment center; and I was appointed to the town planning board. These activities gave me a chance to feel useful while being out in the public and they provided some members of the public whom I would not have seen regularly an opportunity to know me and, not inconsequentially, to fashion impressions about the school from that knowledge. Because these groups met often, a good deal of my community time went to them rather than to appearances at lots of events. I believe the relationships I built through these memberships did more to establish me as a credible high school leader in the community's eyes than would have a thousand cameo appearances.

The problem I encountered with all these public activities was two-pronged: these took time, and the time almost always came out of my family or personal time. As a young husband and father, and as one who needs some time alone each week, the constant menu of public events presented me with a constant dilemma: what was the potential value of my presence, on one hand, and what were my responsibilities to my family or myself? I was convinced the high school needed a better image, that members of the public should feel the teachers and administration were more accessible, and that the school really could be integrated with community affairs. Yet the demands on my personal time were substantial. As my children grew older, I would try to bring my family or a child or two to events where it was suitable. More often, though, I took off after supper to a meeting or event alone, usually enjoyed my involvement in it, but returned home wondering if I had done anything more valuable than show folks that the principal cares. In retrospect, I have little hard evidence that any of these investments of my time (and my family's time) paid off. Most of the time I was a principal, I felt very much like the candle burning at both ends.

In contrast to these public obligations stood my professional relationships. In my first three years, my professional contacts were exclusively with the other five high school principals in our county at a monthly meal and meeting. I at first felt guilty leaving the school during school time, even an hour before dismissal, in order to attend these meetings. But I soon discovered that the benefits of the meetings far outweighed any immediate end I served by being around at school from 1:30 until 5:00. The open exchange among us over all sorts of professional and personal concerns provided one of the best opportunities I have experienced for learning and support. We were a slightly unusual group at first, I think, in that none of us seemed bent on competing with the others. Although the composition of the group changed, and with it the group's usefulness, it provided me throughout my principalship the stimulation, humor, and comradeship that made the time, away from both school and family, renewing and strengthening.

Other professional contacts were not so rewarding. I volunteered for committees of our state principal's association and eventually became involved in a variety of state-level activities. These took me from school for an entire day perhaps five days a year (given the distances across Maine, attendance at a two- or three-hour meeting killed a whole day). All too often I returned to school after such a meeting late in the afternoon to the conclusion that I could have made more of a contribution had I not attended the meeting. Ironically, I often benefitted immensely from the thinking I did in the enforced inactivity of my car as I drove the four hours to and from these meetings across our state. This was often my only prolonged reflection time.

One area of my professional activity deserves more comment, for it not only eventually demanded more of my time but it did so in a way that, I believe, ended up contributing more to my practice than it took away. That was my involvement with starting, running, and sustaining the Maine Principals' Academy, an in-service experience designed for practicing Maine principals. The Academy incorporated collegial learning, personal reflection, and an emphasis on the interpersonal dynamics of the principalship (Donaldson, 1985; Donaldson and McCaul, 1986). I eventually committed over three weeks a year, mostly in the summer, to these activities and they proved immeasurably helpful to me.

STRUCTURING SCHOOL OPERATIONS: 0–5% DAILY; 10–20% WEEKLY

On an annual basis, I was expected to generate schedules of classes for teachers and students, of duties for teachers, of activities for students and the community, and of professional events for staff. Further, I was expected to articulate policies and procedures for staff and students and it was my responsibility to oversee these and to organize improvements when necessary. With regard to the superintendent and school board, I was to help design program and budgetary elements of the school and to take part in policy and evaluation discussions that would affect future practices. Finally, I had purportedly free rein over curricular design and the opportunity to engage community and staff as I wished in examining and redesigning program, subject to the superintendent and board's final approval.

These opportunities to structure school programs and life presented themselves to me every year. I tended to use them as fully as time and past practice would permit (which varied considerably with the activity). For example, I devoted a great deal of time to evaluating and reorganizing our system of course offerings and student registration. I attempted to weave together each winter and spring a community review of our curriculum, board review of our staffing and curriculum, staff discussion (both group and individual), and annual course registration. By doing this each year, I hoped to convey the message that we needed to be constantly evaluating ourselves and opening our practice to at least limited outside scrutiny. During the period when this occurred, usually February through April, I spent easily 25% of my week on matters relating to review and scheduling activities. The results of all this activity did not always appear to merit such an effort on my part, however. Ultimately, early recommendations to change course offerings or revamp a department's structure ran afoul of teachers' established routines, superintendent's priorities, or the Ellsworth board's penny wisdom. What nearly always began with inspired discussions late on a winter afternoon eventually ended up with a well-hammered recommendation for a policy change or a course revision that looked small in comparison to its image at infancy and to the time we had devoted to it.

Particularly as I came to feel my opportunities for asserting major new directions for the school slipping away with my years in the job, I developed new regard for the potential impact of small changes in the work of teachers and the experiences of children. We looked, for example, very hard at our spring freshman orientation procedures for eighth grade students. Through a series of meetings over two years involving grammar school principals, ninth grade teachers, and parents, we built enough of an understanding of the student's transitional experience from small school life to our large high school to be able to restructure the entire sequence of course selection, registration, and orientation. My time, as well as that of the assistant principal and guidance staff, was well spent on this process in part because our planning paid off directly in improved student placement and transition. I am convinced as well that it paid off in increased recognition among eighth and ninth grade teachers that their curriculum selection and student placement decisions were valued by us.

My structuring of school operations occurred in a miasma of short-term planning sessions. These included considering and designing plans for assemblies, course-related programs and trips, staff in-service days, and meetings of nearly every description. A fair number of these opportunities surfaced because teachers, other staff, or sometimes parents or outside agencies suggested a program or new practice. Typically, I weighed the merits of such an opportunity and chose whether to introduce it to wider consideration or not. For example, a visiting mime troupe could present a program on nineteenth-century American dramatists. Did the schedule permit another "disruption" just now? How would the presentation apply to course material? Did it have merits of its own, aside from our curricular considerations? Who should attend? When? These were often suprisingly difficult questions to answer, depending on the time of year and the current frame of mind of staff, students, and community. Making decisions about these opportunities indeed consumed large amounts of time and energy as they inevitably led to frequent and sometimes repetitious discussions with staff, superintendent, and always the author of the proposal.

Some staff disliked my sponsorship of new ideas and activities; others simply objected to the disruptions they caused. But to me, the consideration of new practices—a new text, a different schedule of periods, an assembly, or a workshop topic—performed two vital functions. It brought possibly useful ideas and practices to everybody's attention, and it was a means for establishing an ethos of open-mindedness and participatory responsibility. Each opportunity to examine new or different practices was an opportunity to examine ourselves, to focus our purposes, and hopefully to confirm ourselves as we either reendorsed current practice or chose to plan and execute a new practice. Time devoted by the principal to thinking broadly about the school's work and to involving staff in planning thus generated a vitality in the school's organizational world. It cultivated an ethos of professional challenge essential to the improvement of professional performance and the cultivation of professional pride.

Structuring school operations, for me, was not the calmly reasoned, farsighted activity that we picture occurring in paneled board rooms. It often meant seizing opportunities created by unanticipated events. Clearly, one of my goals as principal was to run a smooth ship, to make daily and weekly activities as predictable as possible so that everyone could focus as completely as needed on instructional and programmatic activities. I learned that when the inevitable crisis occurred, it was often healthier for me not to manage it into submission so the routine could reestablish itself. Rather, once the immediate crisis was contained, I often found that legitimate student, public, or staff needs lay at the root of the crisis; it was most productive then to devote my time and staff time to learn and to consider changing the way we did things. In this manner, I tried to take advantage of schoolwide problems for the purposes of planning and restructuring. The longer I served as a principal, the more I chose to use these opportunities for planning and the less I introduced prepared strategies for change.

An example of problem-centered planning dealt with the course registration scheme we used, which provided students considerable choice and individual liberty in selecting a course of study. Criticism of the scheme, known as "arena scheduling," mounted among some parents who felt their students were out of control, among some board members who agreed with those parents, and among some of the staff of the system who felt student-built schedules made in some instances very poor pedagogical sense. Rather than ride through the storm on past practice, I chose to keep riding for the interim but to engage in an informal, then later a formal, program of fact-finding. To the scheme's critics, I said we were taking a hard look at it. Among the staff, we devoted parts of four or five staff meetings and innumerable corridor discussions to the relative merits, both pro and con, of the arena process. The eventual consensus, engineered in part by my evolving commitment to a more directive approach to student programming, was to change our practice. The fact that the change displeased some teachers meant that the matter of student scheduling did not die with the change. In fact, though it moved to a less prominent agenda position, we continued to discuss scheduling for a number of years, made further adjustments in our procedures in order to increase teacher involvement with students in the selection of courses, and ended up with an excellent process. Once again, our ability to sustain a period of self-assessment and discussion, to make changes we could justify, and to continue examining outcomes of the change was a significant strength.

Although I did not spend a large amount of my work time planning and structuring school operations, the time I did spend was extremely valuable both to me and to the school. Insofar as it forced us all to remember and to reevaluate the long-term purposes of our daily work, this time kept us pulling toward a common end. For me and most others, it maintained our optimism and vitality and thwarted the ever-present tendency toward tedium and routine. So much of my business as a principal, and so much of teachers' daily business, was focused on the immediate and concrete—attendance, assignments, student management, preparing worksheets, correcting quizzes—that this kind of time is indeed precious and hard to come by. I wish I could have protected more of it.

RUNNING THE OFFICE: 0–5% DAILY; 0–5% WEEKLY

Many of us remember our principals primarily in and around the office. I had not considered very carefully my office responsibilities before I took the job of principal. In fact, I had never had a secretary before and did not conceive of myself as an executive. I was mildly shocked at the expectation that I should oversee and direct a myriad of office activities. I soon discovered that I needed to do these things fast and well if I was to devote more time and energy to what I considered the more important functions beyond the office.

The key executive activity of the office is record-keeping. Many records relate to attendance: who is present and who is not and endless investigations into why. Needless to say, the principal need not do most of this work, but that is possible only if a sufficiently well-groomed system exists to handle the many details involved. In a high school, the attendance activities occur throughout the day, particularly if the school has a history of class-skipping. My work in the early years involved periodic monitoring of attendance records throughout the day and every day, an activity that took a great deal of time and included checking on teachers' record-keeping habits as well as the recording system in the office. Some days, I did little else.

The office was also the communications center of the school. It was the place students, teachers, janitors, and the public came to conduct any business outside the routine (and including some routine as well). The student needing to call home or delivering a note, the teacher stopping in to ask about next period's activity, the janitor reporting a leaking sink, and the parent delivering a forgotten lunch sought the office to execute their tasks.

Of course, the list of possible uses is endless and it seemed we saw some of the strangest (most of these dealt with injuries to students or with public requests for services, such as using the school for a dog show). Given this variety and the unexpected nature of the office's function, the principal and office staff needed to be prepared for an assortment of contingencies.

I found I could not create policies for all occasions. Rather, I came to depend on the judgment and good nature of office staff to handle a great deal of what walked through the door and to know when to involve me and when not to. Of course, much was routine, such as the referral of students for discipline, requests for supplies or information, or the delivery of sneakers or a lunch for a child. I found that, in my normal comings and goings through the office, I could quickly check on current activities. If secretaries or student helpers directly or indirectly caught my attention (a raised eyebrow toward a student, for example, or a general air of exasperation), I knew the office needed a few moments of my time. Beyond that, I at times attempted monthly meetings with office staff to adjust procedures and to hear how things were going. Though we worked closely with one another, the pace of my day and of secretaries' days frequently allowed us little chance to talk about anything save immediate concerns. Needless to say, relationships with office staff are among the most important to the principal.

One persisting activity for the office was finances. During my seven years at Ellsworth, the amount of cash annually flowing through our office jumped from $12,000 to over $20,000; the net worth of our activity accounts was easily in the $40,000 range. I frankly was surprised at the amount of time and supervision required to keep tabs on this substantial responsibility. Again, the key to the principal's role is the presence of a good bookkeeping system and a good bookkeeper. But the principal also needs to keep a constant eye on financial procedures and is, at least in my experience, responsible for the major decisions regarding activities that cost or raise money. Because school activities relied on fund-raising, I became the arbiter of conflicting plans to blanket the community with raffle tickets or to run magazine drives. Similarly, I insisted on approving major plans for the expenditure of funds (after I encountered community disapproval of the way one school group spent the money it raised from the community). Finally, I was obligated to ensure security. We used a strict accounting system that required a paper trail for all funds raised and expended; to stay alert to security issues required periodic investigation of these paper trails as well as the account totals themselves. These all took time and were functions I felt only I could exercise. While a conscientious, careful, and communicative secretary-bookkeeper is essential in most schools our size, the principal must remain involved.

The office, too, has character-setting powers for the entire school. How the office staff and the office environment make people feel is, in my estimation, a potent force in the school's climate. For a parent calling on the phone, a student upset about treatment, a lunchroom employee collecting the cashbox, or a teacher stopping in for mail, the office conveys messages to people about how welcome they are and how important the concern is that brought them to the office. Having worked with a variety of office staff, I was able to observe the differences in spirit and affect we as a unit transmitted. Thus, I came to appreciate how my role could affect the character of human interaction in the office. It became increasingly important to me to monitor myself, the office staff, and student help and to open up to discussion with this group the issue of how well we were doing meeting the public and making the office user friendly without turning it into a lounge. The office secretarial function, given its public visibility and potential for establishing the tone of the school, does indeed require extraordinary skills and personal attributes.

I have had long conversations with principals about the office. The concerns of many seem the concerns I had. Underlying many of these was the problem of feeling anchored to the office while feeling pulled out into the school. In part, this dilemma is a result of changing expectations for the principal; the old office-bound manager who conducted business by the public address system, by memo, and by faculty meeting is being replaced by a highly visible instructional leader who monitors and shares in the performance of teaching. In part, too, the dilemma results from a need to see that the management of the school occurs smoothly *before* one can confidently devote more time to the loftier enterprises out in the school. As the dilemma magnifies, as it did for me at the outset, it becomes increasingly important for the principal to find ways of delegating responsibility to others for either the office function or the instructional supervision function. I struggled with finding ways to unburden myself of the office routines, after spending upwards of 50% of my time on those routines in some of my first months on the job. The fact that I eventually pared my involvement down to around 5% reflects my success in finding excellent secretarial help and devising a relatively smooth office system—and the fact that my job changes moved me away from this area. But I left the principalship marveling at how, had I not had the conviction to work on this aspect of the school, it would have been very easy to allow the office to dominate my time and energy.

SATISFYING THE HIERARCHY: 0–5% DAILY; 0–5% WEEKLY

One of the paradoxes of the principalship as I experienced it was that while many school people believed that my work was aimed at satisfying "the system," I felt almost no demands from above in the hierarchy. Certainly, I was expected to fulfill certain obligations, but in Ellsworth these were seldom time-consuming and seldom fit the stereotype of bureaucratic paperwork. Although I now hear that school reform mandates have grown state report forms like mushrooms, I averaged during my prereform principalship no more than twenty minutes daily and two hours weekly on state or district paperwork or system meetings.

What kinds of activities were these? The most prominent were meetings. Aside from the monthly public board meeting, I averaged close to one meeting or extended phone call with the superintendent and/or another principal each week. We tended to discuss events in the school if I called, or specific system needs such as budget figures or enrollment data if the superintendent called. I often spent a few minutes with the superintendent on Friday afternoons, a time when he was always in the office, few others were around, and I dropped off a weekly report on the school's activities. Opportunities to discuss staff and student concerns with the superintendent were important to me; the press of demands and agendas within the school frequently blurred my perspective and the chance to listen to a distanced observer comment was frequently helpful.

I placed more demands on those above me than they did on me. Not only did I use the superintendent as a sounding board, but I also viewed my role with the board as informative and consultative. At monthly board meetings, in committee work, or informally, I typically reported information, volunteered opinions, or made requests. These centered on major events of the recent past or future, proposals for new activities or a large purchase, comments on a specific student or a specific program in which the board was interested. In these interchanges, I normally decided what I was going to present and how; in contrast to the popular view, the board did not often demand specific documents or forms from me. In many of my dealings with the board, especially in my later years, I took advantage of this fact to seek support and ideas for change from them.

Certain times of year demanded more office work for the organization than others. The first three weeks of the school year generally required extended periods of record review as we tried to produce an accurate account of who our students were (a significant factor, since many of ours paid public tuition to attend). Budgeting, in late fall and early winter also demanded examination of current programs and expenditure levels and the difficult task of having busy teachers look long-range to produce a reasonable budget for next year. Following school's June closing, we did a lot of record keeping, both of students and of finances; attendance, grades, test scores, special education individual education plans, as well as student activity and athletic accounts required closing.

My single most time-consuming office activity was writing reports documenting my observation of teachers' performance. Again, this was more self-imposed than system-imposed (though it should have been the latter). Such documentation had not been assiduously carried out before me nor was it being done elsewhere in the system when I arrived. For each forty-five-minute observation I made, I normally spent fifteen minutes analyzing notes, thirty to forty minutes in conference with the teacher, and an hour writing the report. This activity, because it established the teacher's personnel record, required care, precision, sensitivity; hence it was time-consuming. Further, it necessitated continuous, highly focused time; because I could not find such time in my office, I usually wrote these reports at home on Sunday mornings or evenings.

In concluding, I devoted little time to the hierarchy. This was in no small part a result of the superintendent's attitude about paperwork and pointless meetings. Quite simply, he did not value forms or discussion if they had no obvious bearing on accounting for student progress, attendance, or finances or on the immediate operations of the school. Although the board, parents, and occasionally staff sought more written policies and reports on various aspects of the schools, the superintendent steadfastly held to the view that policies and reports tended largely to cloud our assessment of situations and limit our good judgment. I credit his attitude with freeing me to look after the real life of the schools I supervised. Other principals, particularly in larger school systems, do not have this luxury or the benefits of the trust in the principal that it implies.

CONCLUDING OBSERVATION: THE OVERBURDENED PRINCIPAL

The breakdown of my activities reported in Chapters 2 and 3 represents my insider's view of the principal's position and work. This profile is important in part because it depicts the constant pressure I felt to cram more activities than could comfortably fit into the time and energy I had. As Roland Barth (1979) has pointed out, the broad scope of my activities (from dust in corners to evaluating a marginal teacher to crowd control) often left me feeling that I had "more than enough responsibility and less than enough authority" to succeed.

So, I often went to work feeling overburdened. I often returned from work exhilarated by the activities of the day, but not certain of the long-term effects of what I had accomplished. I was a juggler of goals, of tasks, of people, and of schedules. This meant that I was a juggler of my attention, my time, my energies, and thus of those of the immediate staff around me and of my family. I lived and worked with ambiguity and, I suppose inevitably, I communicated ambiguity to those around me.

The reader has been introduced to my inside view of my activities and their rationale. To what extent was I able to establish a steadiness of direction that gave staff, students, and parents a sense of purpose and, ultimately, of accomplishment? To what extent did staff see me in the same light as I saw myself? What impact might any discrepancies between our views have on my ability to develop strong working relationships with staff? In the next chapter, I describe the staff's views of my activity patterns and priorities and begin to examine how differences in perspective shape our conceptions of leader behavior.

Chapter 4

The View from the Classroom

> The function of leadership is to engage followers, not merely to activate them, to commingle needs and aspirations and goals in a common enterprise.
>
> (Burns, 1978, p. 461)

The principal can factually describe his or her activities, but it is the staff's understanding of those activities that establishes his or her effectiveness as a leader. My success as principal of Ellsworth High School was certainly shaped by what I chose to do, but ultimately it hinged on whether faculty and staff believed I was doing the right thing to lead them. Leadership exists within the individual and shared perceptions of the members of the school community of which I, as principal, was but one member.

Did the staff perceive my patterns of work as I did? What did they think were the goals that motivated me as I went about my business? In this chapter, I explore staff views of my activities and my goals and synthesize their collective view of my work patterns and motives. This profile will provide a basis later for examining staff and faculty ratings and beliefs about my leadership as well as the match between these and my own conceptions of my work.

STAFF VIEWS OF MY ACTIVITIES

In the year following my resignation from the Ellsworth principalship, I developed a questionnaire and sent it to every staff member with whom I had worked for at least two years. This group included junior high, high school, and vocational school teachers, other administrators and guidance staff, and secretarial and instructional support staff. Altogether, I surveyed 67 staff members and heard back from 54 (81% return). The questionnaire and a description of return rates are included in the Appendix.

The survey had two parts. In the first, staff were asked to report "what Gordon did as principal"; and in the second, they were asked to evaluate "how Gordon did as a principal." This chapter is based on data from the first or descriptive part. It began by asking staff to describe their contacts with me in two respects: where did they recall seeing and hearing me and what types of interaction occurred? Answers to these two questions permitted me to see how staff remembered my activity patterns and what they understood the nature of those activities to be. Although I emphasized in my principalship being out and around with students, did this communicate to teachers? Did the staff's collective view of my activity patterns bear any resemblance to my own?

The survey results for the entire respondent group indicated that the most frequent contacts staff remembered with me were in the corridors and in the main office (see Table 2). Ninety percent of the staff noted that they "saw, heard, or spoke with" me at least twice weekly in one of these two contexts, with 61% indicating this was a *daily* contact in the corridors, and 47% indicating a *daily* contact in the main office. Close behind these two settings were contacts at school events, through the public address system, and in my office. In these three areas, roughly 60% of the staff reported contact at least twice weekly; contacts in my office were rated somewhat less frequently than the first two. The profile of my activities that emerges from these data has two dominant aspects: staff saw me most often on the fly and they encountered me most often in public situations.

With the exception of "in my office," none of the settings in which they had contact with me is conducive to much more than cursory interaction. The kind of contact most typical of the corridors, the main office, the PA system, and school events is social (e.g., a daily greeting) or a business interchange of a purely instrumental nature (e.g., clarifying policy or procedure). These are also stereotypically principal-like contact patterns: they suggest an active person, but a peripatetic one as well. The dominant activity pattern that staff report is one in which thoughtful and relaxed discussion with me was unlikely to happen.

This image is changed somewhat by consideration of the remainder of Table 2. Contacts that occurred "seldom" (between monthly and weekly) with a majority of staff were "in small, specific-purpose meetings," "in faculty meetings," "through memos," or "through personal notes." These settings, unlike the most frequently reported ones, are generally more task-oriented: they imply associations with the principal in which some official

Table 2
Staff Contacts with Me
(percent of staff by frequency of contact type; N=54)

How frequently did you come in contact with Gordon and in what types of situation?

Situation	Often (once a day or more)	Sometimes (2 - 4 times a week)	Seldom (once a week to once a month)	Almost Never (once a semester or less)
in corridors	61.5%	28.8%	5.8%	5.8%
in my classroom	4.3	21.7	45.7	28.3
in main office	47.2	43.4	9.4	0.0
in his office	13.2	47.2	34.0	5.7
in teacher's room	2.0	24.5	46.9	26.5
at school events	30.0	32.0	34.0	4.0
through P.A. system	26.0	40.0	26.0	8.0
through memos	7.7	32.7	55.8	3.8
through personal notes	3.8	26.9	53.8	15.4
in faculty meetings	14.9	6.4	68.1	10.6
in small, specific-purpose meetings	5.8	7.7	69.2	17.3

agenda of mine or of the staff member was the focus of the contact. Similarly, they imply more interaction than the most frequent contact pattern: meetings, and particularly small ones, permit interchange; personal notes likewise suggest ongoing interchange on an individual basis. I maintained interchanges of this sort with a majority of staff, but only about monthly. Approximately one-fifth of the staff recall these interchanges occurring less frequently and some saw them happening weekly (and these were central staff or vocational faculty). Clearly, the opportunities for staff to discuss and develop ideas and programs with me were substantially rarer than were opportunities for staff to see or hear me on a directive or fly-by basis.

At the "almost never" extreme, we see that between 15 and 30% of the group report rare contact with me in several of the more personal arenas: "in my classroom," "in the teachers' room," and "in small, specific-purpose meetings," and "through personal notes." That some teachers hardly recalled contacting me in these settings suggests that my relationship to some staff was indeed established and carried out at a distance. With these staff, I did not have an ongoing relationship over instructional or similar business issues of a nature that would bring us together in classrooms or small meetings.

This overview of contact patterns not only begins to describe my access to staff, but also suggests how that access existed differentially across the staff group. My most frequent contacts with the average staffer were on the run; the chance to sit down with that average staffer came only monthly. While I managed frequent close contacts with about one-fourth of the group, a roughly equal portion reported that such contacts practically never occurred.

Results of two items illustrate this distribution. My contacts with teachers in their classrooms and in the Teachers' Room were patterned similarly and were different from the pattern in all other contexts (see Table 2). These two settings are the most personal for the average teacher; territorially, they are where the principal is most on teacher turf. The fact that one-quarter of the group recalled contacts with me more frequently than weekly suggests that, as principal, I was close to and comfortable with a group roughly of this size. Similarly, a group of about one-quarter of the respondents almost never saw me in these contexts. To them, relationships with me were likely more formal, discontinuous, and distanced than to the first group. The remaining half of the group recalled my presence in these contexts, but with a frequency that suggests slight impacts.

An examination of responses from only the high school professional staff (teachers and guidance) shows practically no deviation from the patterns above. In fact, the tendencies are slightly strengthened, as the proportion of this group that recalled contacts with me at the extremes increases by a few percentage points. Thus, my image as a corridor presence was a vivid one in the minds of high school staff in particular and, conversely, my presence in teachers' classrooms and the teachers' room is recalled less often.

This brief visit to the staff's recollection of contacts with me held two major revelations for me. First, it confirmed the passing nature of my relationships with my staff. On one hand, this was heartening as it demonstrated my ability to keep in touch with about 75% of these 54 staff and faculty. On the other hand, the brevity and social tone of these interchanges suggest that, most weeks, I was merely keeping in touch. Where and when was I conducting the serious business of professional educational leadership?

Second, these staff reports showed me that I worked differentially with the staff. Some staff had a lot of contact with me, others had very little. By "a lot of contact" I mean daily contact with as high as 60% of the staff (and the reader might wonder, as I do, if this is sufficient for successful leadership). At the other extreme were roughly one-fifth of the staff: these folks almost never sat down with me and a goodly number do not recall seeing or hearing me on even a weekly basis. Frankly, these figures disturb me. They do not at all match my vision of the successful leader who has a working relationship with all staff that he or she sustains through frequent professional interchange. In my case, contact and communication patterns were neither uniform nor always vibrant. As we shall see in later chapters, these patterns reflect a polarization of the faculty, its relationship to me, and evaluation of my leadership.

NATURE OF COMMUNICATION WITH ME

What did faculty and staff recall the form and substance of these contacts to be? Given that staff had less contact with me than I hoped and that the contact pattern was not uniform, how did staff learn what I was about? The questionnaire's second question was designed to probe perceptions of what we talked about when we had contacts and how often we communicated. I asked staff to indicate how often they remembered communicating with me in twelve different modes (see Table 3). Overall, the results of this item are remarkable for their distinctive tilt toward the "infrequent" end of the continuum. Staff more often reported communicating with me "seldom" or "almost never" than "often" or "sometimes" in eleven of the twelve modes. In the twelfth, 57% indicated that "we engaged in casual talk" frequently. In general, then, staff communications with me, in nearly all forms, occurred less than daily and often less than weekly.

For someone who projected himself as an active principal, this feedback was startling. Although most staff reported daily to weekly contacts with me, most of these apparently did *not* involve direct communication with me. That is, they tended to be occasions when staff saw me or perhaps heard me dealing with others rather than occasions when the staff member and I actually transpired some business. Thus, I was a principal who, first and foremost, was remembered for my presence rather than for any specific type of communication or message. These broad observations have given me pause: if I did not communicate often verbally, through what medium was I leading the school (if in fact I could be described as doing so)?

What typified my communication beyond its infrequency? The twelve communication modes were assigned to three clusters: (1) "receiving" a variety of information or directives from me, (2) "engaging" with me in various topical discussions, and (3) "seeking" from me assorted information or ends. Of these three types of communication, the most frequently reported was "engaging." That is, nearly one-half the respondents recalled engaging with me in discussions (either professional or casual) two to four times per week, while no type of "received" communication or "sought

Table 3
Staff Communication with Me
(percent of staff by frequency of communication type; N=54)

Indicate how frequently you <u>usually</u> had an interchange with Gordon of each type or on each topic.

Situation	Often (once a day or more)	Sometimes (2 - 4 times a week)	Seldom (once a week to once a month)	Almost Never (once a semester or less)
I received information from him (e.g., about a student or program	7.7%	30.8%	55.8%	5.8%
I received general instructions from him (e.g., about scheduling or an assembly)	0.0	28.3	54.7	17.0
I received personal instructions from him (e.g., what my responsibility was)	1.9	20.8	49.1	28.3
I received suggestions from him (e.g., what to do with a student or problem)	0.0	25.5	60.8	13.7
I received requests from him (e.g., Would you cover a class; help a group of students)	1.9	15.1	58.5	24.5
I received orders from him (e.g., what I must do/not do)	0.0	7.8	25.5	66.7

out" communication was reported with such frequency by such a high proportion of the staff. More staff recalled the content of these discussions as "casual talk" than recalled it being "mostly professional issues." Although the discrepancy is not great, it is somewhat surprising to me that nonprofessional topics stood in staff's mind before professional topics (in fact, no respondent reported *daily* professional discussion with me, while

Table 3 (Continued)

Indicate how frequently you <u>usually</u> had an interchange with Gordon of each type or on each topic.

Situation	Often (once a day or more)	Sometimes (2 - 4 times a week)	Seldom (once a week to once a month)	Almost Never (once a semester or less)
We engaged in discussion of mostly professional issues	0.0	48.1	44.2	7.7
We engaged in casual talk (e.g., gardening, ballgames, family)	9.4	47.2	43.4	0.0
I sought him out for advice (e.g., how to handle a situation)	3.8	20.8	52.8	22.6
I sought him out to inform him of something I thought he should know (e.g., about a student/ program issue)	3.8	34.6	46.2	15.4
I sought him out to tell him what to do (e.g., to handle problem; change a procedure)	3.8	9.6	17.3	73.1

9% reported daily casual discussion). I was a principal who, for the most part, communicated directly with staff to maintain personal contact, not necessarily to transact business. Communication with me was more collegial than hierarchical, more conversational than instrumental.

Next in frequency to "engaging" modes of communication were two that dealt with acquiring from me specific information. Between 39 and 45% of the staff indicated that they either received from me or sought me out for specific information (the examples given dealt with professional topics). While these modes of communication do not exclude "engaging" with me in discussion (i.e., one can seek out information during a discussion), it is significant that so many staff remembered me as an information source. One of my functions in our communications was to provide information about school, students, and procedures. This impression is strengthened by the nearly equal frequency for "sought him out to inform him of something." That roughly 40% of the staff recall such "informational" interchanges with me more frequently than weekly (though less than daily) suggests a central component of my activity and indeed role involved the transmission of knowledge up *and* down the hierarchy and back *and* forth within the school. This function was, in fact, a part of my "management by walking around" strategy.

The results of other items reinforce staff views of me as an information giver and receiver. Staff consistently reported interacting with me in modes using the word "information" more frequently than those using "instructions," "suggestions," and "advice." These in turn scored consistently higher than subitems in which the object of the communication was described as "requests" from me, "orders" from me, or my "telling" the respondent what to do. I tended not to approach staff often with a coercive or directive purpose; rather, I tended to engage them in conversation or, less frequently, professional discussion or to exchange information with them that, presumably, we both needed.

While the distinctions grow increasingly fine between clusters of findings, two more deserve mention. Next to those communications involving "information," the most frequently reported were "receiving general instructions" and "receiving suggestions." Both modes place staff in the position of passive recipient. "General instructions" may be viewed as relatively benign and necessary for the organization; one might even expect principals to deliver instructions more often than "sometimes." The fact that staff remembered "receiving suggestions" from me more often than "orders," "personal instructions," or even "requests" reinforces my role as one who engaged in discussion rather than operated directively with staff.

I did not often function, it seems, in stereotypically bureaucratic administrative modes with most staff, although I seem to have done so weekly with between 10 and 20%. It comes as no surprise, then, that the staff rarely remembered "receiving orders" from me or, reciprocally, "telling me what to do." Roughly 70% of the group reported these as "almost never" occurring, while roughly another 23% recall them occurring between weekly and monthly.

A final word must be appended to address the last statement on this scale: "I sought him out for advice." This item received a wider spread of responses than nearly any other: one-quarter of the respondents sought me out for advice more than weekly, one-quarter almost never did, and the remaining half did so between weekly and monthly. I am intrigued by these results, as they may well indicate the extent to which staff valued my judgment and knowledge; those seeking me out for advice might be understood to be those who trusted and supported my leadership enough to make this effort and, contrarily, those who did not seek me out perhaps did not respect my judgment as much. The distribution of staff on this item echoes the distribution of staff contacts in teachers' classrooms and the Teachers' Room. Although I had "daily" interchange with only a few people, my active relationships distributed in a 1:2:1 ratio into "weekly," "monthly," and "less than monthly" contacts.

In conclusion, staff contacts with me were fleeting and communication between us was, foremost, "casual talk" and "discussion." These observations lead inexorably to the conclusion that, to most of my staff, I was normally somewhere else, doing something else than what they were doing. The lack of direct contact and opportunity for substantive interchange between leader and staff in this picture is startling to me. Against my rather compulsive self-description, this staff view suggests that my role as leader was more symbolic than direct. Staff, because they had infrequent personal contacts and communication with me, must have formed impressions and ongoing judgments of me substantially on the basis of indirect evidence. Despite this discovery, the predominant staff view of my communication style squares generally with my own. I strived for an active role as principal, rooted in having and sharing accurate information about our students, our performance, and our problems. I eschewed the formal trappings of the directive leader in a bureaucratic role, preferring to meet staff on their territory and on an equal and objective footing. In large part, the staff's survey responses sustained these images.

STAFF PERCEPTIONS OF MY GOALS

I have explored the extent to which staff recollections of my activity and communication patterns appear to have agreed with my own. A third means of examining the congruence of my perceptions and staff's perceptions is to investigate their understandings of my goals and purposes. Many students of organizational life have stressed the importance of visionary leadership. Did I manage to establish a coherent, purposeful direction as a leader—a direction that staff understood, whether they agreed with it or not? Did they understand my goals as I did?

The questionnaire asked staff to rate a list of twenty-three personal and professional goals typical of those principals might hold. Staff were asked to rate the importance of each goal to me. Choices ranged across a four-point scale, from "of no importance to him" to "of utmost importance to him" (see Table 4). I have labeled these the salience scores for each goal. The items provide a lens on staff perceptions of my motives as principal. When compared to my own independent rating of the list, salience scores also make possible a discrepancy analysis that will illuminate the commu-

Table 4
Staff Perceptions of Goal Salience to Me
(frequency distributions, rank ordered by mean; N=54)

Indicate how important <u>you believe</u> each goal was to Gordon.

	% Staff Assigning:				Mean Importance Rating
	1	2	3	4*	
to raise student performance	0%	6%	18%	76%	3.70
to make the school its best	0	4	30	66	3.63
to inspire students to achieve and behave	0	9	26	65	3.56
to involve students actively in school	0	7	32	61	3.54
to make fair decisions, treat everyone fairly	2	9	32	57	3.44
to make teachers accountable for teaching	2	6	43	49	3.40
to create public support for school	0	13	41	46	3.33
to create cooperative faculty team	4	15	31	50	3.28
to make school comfortable for staff and students	2	19	35	44	3.22
to encourage staff creativity	2	15	44	39	3.20
to make school run smoothly and quietly	2	13	50	35	3.19
to put his own ideas to work	2	15	56	28	3.09

nication "fit" of this principal and his faculty. Throughout this discussion, it will be important to remember that respondents were not asked to disagree or agree with any of these goals themselves; their responses only provided indications of what they felt I was trying to do in my job.

Over 60% of responding staff rated the following goals "of utmost importance" to me: "to raise student performance," "to make the school its best," "to inspire students to achieve and behave," "to involve students actively in school." These are ambitious professional aspirations, implying high expectations for students and for the school's improvement. Staff generally agreed that my primary motivation was to cultivate academic and

Table 4 (Continued)

Indicate how important you believe each goal was to Gordon.

	% Staff Assigning:				Mean Importance Rating
	1	2	3	4*	
to implement management's desires	0	15	62	33	3.07
to lead the district out of the Dark Ages	13	26	35	26	2.74
to befriend students	6	26	59	9	2.72
to befriend staff	6	35	50	9	2.63
to use staff for his purposes	18	29	35	18	2.53
to exercise his authority	9	50	33	7	2.39
to work his way up the job	17	42	28	13	2.38
to earn a good income	18	40	32	10	2.34
to force students to behave	26	46	26	2	2.04
to force some teachers out	53	34	11	2	1.62
to keep everyone on the defensive	66	28	4	2	1.42

*4 = of utmost importance to him (mean scores 3.25-4.0)
 3 = quite important to him   (mean scores 2.50-3.25)
 2 = slightly important to him (mean scores 1.75-2.50)
 1 = no importance to him   (mean scores 1.0-1.75)

social progress in our students. They believed that, whatever the particular issue or project I worked on, I was driven by a desire to make the school "its best." The fact that over 90% of respondents saw these four goals as either "quite important" or "of utmost importance" to me suggests that I successfully communicated these central purposes and provided a coherent set of professional aspirations for the group.

Did similar proportions of staff agree about what I did *not* value? A majority of staff rated only two goals so low as to suggest they dissociated them from me and my work. The following goals received "of no importance to him" ratings from over 50% of the respondents: "to keep everyone on the defensive," "to force some teachers out." These results, taken with the top four, indicate that I appeared motivated more by generally altruistic purposes consistent with the traditional goals of school (academic, behavioral, and participatory learning) and less by purely managerial control or enforcement goals. The two sets of results suggest procedural distinctions, as well. Ranked high were the lofty academic purposes, to be attained by inspiration and involvement. Ranked low were short-term administrative objectives, to be executed by force and a campaign to generate paranoia. It is interesting to note that staff agreed less on what I did not value than on what I did value (an observation quite consistent with my own sense that I often had too many irons in the fire).

To identify other goals that staff rated important to me, I combined "quite important" and "of utmost importance" scores of the remaining seventeen goals. Nine goals were assigned to one of the two "important" categories by at least 80% of the respondents. Here we see the blending of goals like the top four achievement goals with another variety of more managerial goal. Ranked with nearly as much unanimity as "making the school its best" and "raising student performance" were "implementing management's desires" and "making teachers accountable." Importantly, staff saw me as driven by concerns for "fairness" despite these managerial ambitions. Staff also believed that I sought to run a "smooth" and "quiet" school and "to put my own ideas to work" while, contrarily perhaps, I encouraged faculty creativity and faculty teamwork.

Taken together, these results suggest a variety of perceptions of my purposes and, in fact, a mixture of some conflicting goals and motives. I was seen, for example, as encouraging and participatory but also as assertive and demanding. I strived for accountability but also for comfort. While some of this variety might be explained by conflicting opinions, once again the staff seem to reinforce the image of Gordon Donaldson, the principal who tries to do everything and wants the school to do everything. They have left me wondering if I in fact did establish a clear vision for the school that helped staff, students, and community know what their top priorities were.

Turning to my low priority goals, only two were rated as unimportant to me by over 80% of the respondents (the same two receiving high "of no importance" scores). The goals that a simple majority rated as either "slightly important" or "of no importance" to me were: "to keep everyone on the defensive," "to force some teachers out," "to force students to behave," "to exercise his authority," "to work his way up the job ladder," and "to earn a good income." The first four of these goals share the common themes of force employed for compliance or to maintain power through its direct exercise or through the undermining of others' power. These form a natural cluster around authoritarian traits, suggesting that I avoided self-promotion and did not endorse coercive goals and tactics. A slight maj" ity of staff agreed that I was not primarily driven by professional or economic mobility.

As interesting as these majority views are, they are not strong enough to obscure the importance of their obverse minorities. For example, 13% of the respondents felt it was important to me to "force some teachers out"; 40% believed that "exercising my authority" was important to me; 41% saw "working my way up the job ladder" as important. This slightly fainter mirror image to the majority view—a view that is substantially in line with my own set of priorities—has important ramifications. Clearly, members of the staff saw different Gordon Donaldsons: some believed that I was capable of manipulating staff, while others did not; some thought me ready to wield my power to get my own way, while others did not; and many found me motivated by personal gain while others did not.

Table 4 also presents mean scores of staff ratings for the twenty-three goals by quartiles (top = "of utmost importance," bottom = "of no importance"). This method of analysis permits another look at the extent to which I communicated a distinct vision for myself and for the school. As a group, which goals did staff believe were "of utmost importance" to me? To what extent did they clearly understand me to support a plank of purposes? Table 4 suggests that staff rates my goals in three discernible clusters.

The staff ranked four goals in a cluster between 3.5 and 4.0 ("utmost importance") and nine goals between 3.0 and 3.5 (what I will call the "quite important" range). This fact, by itself, may be noteworthy, for it suggests that I conveyed the image of "someone knowing where he wants to go," of a goal-driven individual, of an individual who in a leadership or authority position is exerting direction of some kind. The staff strongly agreed that I valued most the four altruistic goals discussed above: "raising student performance," "making the school its best," "inspiring students to achieve and behave," and "involving students actively in school." (Median and modes for all four were 4.0.)

Four more goals clustered a bit below this top group; interestingly, these include two goals that were procedural and relational rather than framed in student terms: "to make fair decisions, treat everyone fairly" and "to make teachers accountable for teaching." These are goals that demonstrate my method and my values as an administrator. High staff agreement about them suggests that my style with them, as well as the rationale I presented for that style, was consistently demanding but not unfairly so. These provide important clues to staff perceptions of my motives toward them, as does a third procedural goal just below these, "to create a cooperative faculty team." These three may be viewed as incompatible aims, in that making teachers accountable is frequently viewed as divisive and not conducive either to staff cooperation or to a view of the principal as just.

The remaining five goals in the second cluster give my profile a managerial overtone, but with a twist: I sought "to make school comfortable for staff and students" and "to make school run smoothly and quietly," but also "to encourage staff creativity." The possible disjunctions between "smooth and quiet" and "creative" and between "comfortable for students" and "smooth and quiet" are interesting to ponder, as is that between "comfortable for staff" and the higher-ranked "make teachers accountable." While many staff viewed my motives as productive, the potential existed for many as well to see these as mixed and unclearly prioritized management objectives. It is important to note, at this juncture, that some staff may have viewed my leadership as neither monolithic and unidimensional nor as the type of leadership that is simple to follow, model, or feel comfortable with.

The last two goals of the "quite important" group suggest that personal ambition and management needs played a part in my motives. That I was viewed as valuing "putting my own ideas to work" suggests that staff found me self-assured enough to seek personal impact on the school, to push my own philosophy and theory into action through the staff and school as a whole. Similarly, a good portion of the staff saw "implementation of management's desires" as a driving force for me. These two goals are more self-centered than the top nine goals and do not slide comfortably into the picture created by them. Staff ratings of both goals came as a surprise to me. As one who viewed himself as a consensus leader and not as a strong management man, I did not think I projected such a directive side.

The eight goals that fall into the "of slight importance" range distribute into three groups. At the top are four goals that staff were really divided about—significant numbers saw these as important to me, and significant numbers felt otherwise. Two of these—"to befriend students" and "to befriend staff"—are interesting. Staff beliefs about my desire to establish comfortable personal relationships were very mixed, perhaps reflecting my relationships with them. Similarly, they were almost evenly divided over my willingness "to use staff for his purposes," suggesting that some may have felt my relationships with them were based more on my ambitions than on concern for them. That roughly 80% of the group felt I was motivated by a desire "to lead the district out of the Dark Ages" reinforces the observation that I was a principal with a sense of mission—or even missionary zeal. These data betray some obviously mixed opinions about the genuineness of my approach to people and the extent to which I would honor personal feelings over professional or personal ambitions. Whereas most staff believed that I was motivated most strongly by professional ambitions, some felt my drive for self-promotion tended to overshadow my concern for them as individuals. Indeed, the remaining goals in the "slight importance" category indicate that from 30 to 40% of staff believed that "exercising my authority," "working my way up the job ladder," and "earning a good income" were driving forces in my work.

Finally, staff strongly agreed about three goals at or near the "of no importance" range. The uppermost of these, "to force students to behave," was clearly not viewed by many as a compelling ambition of mine, yet one-quarter of the staff did feel it was important to me. As noted in the discussion above, very few felt that "to force some teachers out" and "to keep everyone on the defensive" were important to me at all.

In sum, most staff saw me as a principal who was clearly motivated by goals for students' academic, personal, and social growth but also by goals that would satisfy my own personal philosophical contentions and my boss's desires. They viewed me as a principal who wanted to make them accountable while also making them a cooperative team and creative and comfortable in their work. It was more important to me, they believed, that I treat everyone fairly than that I befriend students or staff. On the other hand, a portion of the staff believed that I was motivated by self-aggrandizement and a desire to exercise my authority. More than half the staff felt that I would "use staff for my purposes," suggesting that I did not always hold the staff in as high regard as, perhaps, I held students.

A MIXED PORTRAIT

Reading and analyzing the staff's surveys was an exciting and valuable experience for me; and it raised my anxiety a little. As the reader can see, my understanding of myself and my work as a principal did not coincide neatly with what the staff saw me doing, how they remembered me communicating with them, and what they felt motivated me. I now can see that I portrayed not one portrait, or two portraits, but a mixture of portraits. The question for me is not, "which one was accurate?" but "what was it I did as a principal that created both the points of agreement and disagreement about my activities and goals?" Much of the remainder of this book will address this question. For the time being, however, I will briefly identify several of the points of agreement and disagreement simply to summarize the discussion.

I am struck by two basic conjunctions in my self-portrait and the staff's portraits. We agree that philosophically I was driven by an interest in students and by a belief that the school could, and probably should, improve continuously. These certainly were constant themes as I did my work as a principal. I tried not only to live by them but to project them on others as they raised problems and joined together to resolve them. Second, my style of work was fairly peripatetic: I found myself always juggling more than one thing at once and the staff's recollection of seeing and hearing me (rather than talking with me) in the hallways and main office seems to reinforce this image. I was compelled to work as a hands-on principal by both my philosophy and the job and, in fact, the staff tended to see me in this light.

In the collective portrait, I am trying to do everything and probably spreading myself so thinly over the activities of the school that I may not have developed the relationships I should. A majority of the staff saw seventeen of the twenty-three goals as important to me; I, too, felt pulled constantly in a thousand directions. Some of the goals that staff strongly associated with me may conflict with one another (e.g., "making teachers accountable" and "creating a cooperative faculty team"); in fact, I felt these incongruities and struggled against behaving differently in different situations and with different people. Both my self-portrait and the staff's portrait display these incompatible hues: I was a principal working in many places at once, with many people at once; in that kind of work it was difficult to project a logically coherent attitude, philosophy, and behavior pattern. In part, I suspect, this resulted from my desire to do too much, to support many activities, and to have contact with many people. Once I found myself pursuing responsive *and* initiating roles, it became increasingly difficult to feel, think, and apparently act consistently.

An important contrast in the two portraits deals with our recollections of contacts and personal communication. I strived to be available and to initiate professional discussion with teachers whenever I could. Yet the staff recall only infrequent contacts with me and, when these occurred, they most often were casual talk. In retrospect, I see how my activities supported their description; but I did not at the time believe that these were the predominant sorts of contacts I had with teachers. As the educational leader, I thought of myself driving the instructional and student affairs programs of the schools, not simply passing time in the corridors or office. My recollections are flooded with meetings and conversations about business, but staff reported these occurring only monthly—and some more rarely than that. These reports do not depict a principal who is in touch enough to maintain relationships with staff and to enhance the goals of the school. Short on time and long on ambition, I may have been able only to maintain relationships.

A second contrast in our portraits lies in the absence of a darker side in my description of myself, and the presence of such a side in the staff's description. My self-portrait naturally casts my activities in well-intentioned hues; I was not an authoritarian principal with insidious designs on students or staff; I placed kids above myself; I strived to lead collaboratively. The staff generally agreed with this; but a significant subgroup disagreed on several strokes of the brush. About twenty staffers saw me as more closely tied to the hierarchy and its wishes than did I; a similar number believed that my own personal ambitions drove my activity; some remember me as a giver of orders and instructions, not as a seeker of advice.

The abundance of contacts with me in the main office and over the public address system reported by some faculty support this shadow portrait.

I have always believed that effective leadership requires a substantial degree of consensus between leader and staff regarding the leader's purposes and values. Certainly, authorities on organizational effectiveness over the past century have reinforced this belief (Argyris and Schon, 1974; Barnard, 1938; Peters and Waterman, 1982; Weber, 1912). One reason I sought a principalship in Maine was that it had schools small enough for the principal to establish consensus and unity of direction among staff. My exploration into my principalship has so far demonstrated how difficult it was for me to achieve this unity.

PART II

IDENTIFYING OTHERS TO INVOLVE IN SCHOOL MANAGEMENT AND LEADERSHIP

No principal can do it all, and certainly no principal can provide effective leadership alone. Leadership is an elusive concept. We have, at various points in our past, believed that successful leaders possessed certain traits, or that they carefully deployed certain behaviors, or that they executed certain situation-specific analytic, behavioral, and emotional procedures. Through all of this, nobody has disputed the fact that leadership requires an alliance of, if not a bonding between, the leader and the led.

Hence, the principal, to paraphrase a military expression, is only as good as his or her faculty and staff. The principal is hired to run the school and, in the eyes of superintendent, board, and community, this frequently means organizing, managing, supervising, and leading the adults under his or her jurisdiction. Clearly, a central function of the principal is to learn who these people are, to understand how to deploy them properly, and to find ways to support their successful work (or, if necessary, seek their dismissal).

I have found that this function, though easy to describe, is very difficult to execute. Textbooks on school administration discuss and describe personnel practices, supervision, evaluation, and human resource development. In many instances, these activities are portrayed as if the principal would have considerable discretion in selecting staff, in getting to know their personalities and professional capabilities, and in providing staff development (Castetter, 1986; Lipham, Rankin, and Hoeh, 1985). Yet the press for action described in Part I requires that these activities occur while a whole lot of other things are going on. Moreover, most principals do not hire a staff, they inherit one. And these staff members come with contractual defenses and well-patterned routines and relationships that make it hard for the new principal to assess who they are, much less assign or reassign them at all.

The first chapter in Part II explores the intricate process of learning who staff and faculty are. In Chapter 6 I examine how the principal learns continuously about students and community and uses that knowledge to shape the purposes and programs of the school. Both chapters echo the theme that the principal's knowledge of and attentiveness to these clients not only permit the principal to enlist them as partners in leadership but to establish his or her credibility as leader as well. The partnership that results is the essence of a professionally responsible and continually renewing school.

Chapter 5

Who Are the Faculty and Staff?

> To be interpersonally competent as a school administrator, one needs certain skills as well as a great deal of knowledge about teachers, the teaching task, and teachers' views of themselves, their students, and their work.
>
> (Greenfield, in Griffiths et al., 1988, p. 224)

The principal's choice of daily work patterns is, to a large degree, dependent on his or her understanding of faculty competencies, attitudes, needs, and desires. The principal who has little accurate knowledge of faculty is unable either to know where to deploy his or her own energies or to organize productive working relationships and conditions for faculty. The interaction of the principal's goals, knowledge of faculty and staff, and choice of activities is constant; maintaining a healthy flow of information among these spheres is essential to the principal's effectiveness.

A principal's perceptions of staff obviously do not just happen. They evolve, starting with preconceptions and rumored reputations to probably polite and distanced initial relationships and on into more mature, if not always pleasant or accurate, understandings. In the beginning of my Ellsworth principalship, I attempted to establish an accurate picture of the staff; I relied on certain sources of information to maintain an understanding of staff attitudes and performance; and from these I developed my working profile of the faculty. As I describe this evolution in this chapter, I examine how these means of learning about faculty and staff *and the understanding of them that resulted* disposed me to act toward faculty and staff in certain ways.

"WELCOME, MR. DONALDSON. WHAT DO YOU WANT ME TO DO ABOUT X?"

In the best of all worlds, educators would move into principalships the way textbooks describe "implementing personnel practices": we would read all staff files, interview all faculty, ascertain what staffing weaknesses there were and hire accordingly; then the school year would commence. But I know of few principals who have had this luxury (and those who have were opening new schools). Principals come into their positions either cold, in which case they know few if any faculty or staff, or from inside, in which case they have the colleague's view or, if they were assistant principals, the incumbent's view of faculty and staff. In either case, the principal steps into an environment flowing with activity, relationships, emotions, and many bits of business-in-progress.

The consequence of this ineluctable fact is that principals are asked to act before they know which other actors will be involved or, most importantly, who those other actors are and whether they can play their parts. This certainly was the case for me in Ellsworth. I arrived in town two weeks before school began and, from the outset, began fielding questions from staff about a variety of issues that had gone unattended since the departure of my predecessor. I found myself making decisions not only on issues I knew little about but that affected people whose skills and capabilities were unknown to me. Clearly, one of the first tasks confronting me was establishing a working profile of the faculty and staff. It was a task I was to accomplish slowly and in bits and pieces.

How did I approach the faculty and staff in the late summer and early fall of my first year? As a newcomer to Ellsworth and its region, I had practically no information about the faculty and staff. Through the selection process, I had met only the assistant principal. From him and from the superintendent—and between the lines from board members—I had gathered that there were some tough cookies on the faculty. Of the thirty-five faculty in the high school grades, I met only three before school began and I had no direct contact with any of the eight junior high faculty. Most of my information about staff came from the secretary, a woman with seven years' experience, and from the guidance director. Both came by compliments sparingly and, by the initial faculty meeting, I had a small inkling that these two had their favorites, and their enemies.

I attempted to approach staff, despite these early indications about them, as openly as possible. In retrospect, though, I think I was more conscious of *how I would come across to them* than of learning who they were. I hoped to make the best impression, to appear businesslike but friendly, to instill confidence, to stimulate excitement in our work. Rather than introducing myself and fashioning some process for staff to introduce themselves to me, I found myself planning approaches to assert my leadership and my managerial competence. In the absence of accurate information about faculty and staff, I made assumptions about who they were and how they would approach me. I now see how this uninformed strategy led to a rather defensive approach to meeting my staff and faculty.

Three major assumptions about how staff might view me played a large part in my initial approaches to them. The first stemmed from my Harvard education. I assumed that the Harvard mystique already surrounded me in staff's eyes and perhaps tainted community expectations of me; they likely expected a principal with a doctorate from Harvard to come on like gangbusters. As a result, I decided to downplay my special knowledge and to neutralize the reputed power and authority of the Harvard image. In my initial approaches to staff and to running the school, I avoided highly developed agendas of tasks and policies and especially any that would change practice appreciably.

A second major paradigm that I assumed would influence my initial reception by staff was the in-state/out-of-state dichotomy. In coastal Maine, the out-of-stater is frequently viewed as out of touch, as perhaps naive, as apt to be more full of book knowledge than of useful knowledge. The in-state/out-of-state distinction overlays other polar sets: rural/urban, stolid country/slick city, plain and sensible/fancy and ridiculous. I distinctly wished to avoid seeming like another out-of-stater peddling foreign ideas. Again, the watchwords for my approach were "wait" and "listen."

I made a third assumption about the faculty and staff: they would be older and probably more conservative than I was. I was thirty years old. I was entering a position in which I was to be the overall supervisor for fifty professional and support staff, most of whom I assumed were older than I. I expected, and in fact felt from some quarters, some skepticism about my abilities to run, much less successfully lead, a school of the size and complexity of the junior-senior high. I guessed some senior, and perhaps influential, staff would think, "Who is this young whipper-snapper with the fancy education and out-of-state credentials that he thinks he can make us work?" Thus my age generated two possible approaches to staff. A low-key approach with some older, wiser teachers would, I hoped, lend their knowledge and experience to my activities and avoid radical discontinuities and errors. Others, though, would probably want some clear evidence that I knew what I was doing, a goal requiring some high-profile early steps. So there was a mixed message with regard to what one seasoned teacher called my rookie status: there was a risk I would come on too strong with my green and foolhardy ideas; on the other hand, there was a risk that if I did not come on assertively, staff would not feel that "this new principal" knew enough or was giving them enough control and direction from the office.

So I tried to do both. I began by attempting to be clear and at least verbally assertive in areas in which I felt more confident (primarily relating to the program and mission of the school). Inversely, I approached tentatively those areas in which I had less clear ideas of procedure or in which I felt past practice was at least temporarily best. These tended to be the procedural and structural aspects of school life: regulations, attendance, routines, duty rosters, who was a department head and what his or her tasks entailed. I established an informal collaborative stance in response to a common early question, "Mr. Donaldson, what do you want me to do about X?" My response was, "What have you done before?", which led to my developing with the interrogator a sense of what the problem was, what the standard procedures were for handling it, whether there was any weakness in those procedures, and finally what we would do with the current problem. I worked that protocol down to sometimes a twenty- or thirty-second interchange. When the same problems began surfacing from many teachers, I knew it was time to sit down as an entire faculty and clarify the system or work out a new one.

In summary, I began my work as principal conservatively. I believed that reactions to press accounts of who I was and to informal word around town was already centering around my youth, my education, and my background. My reaction was to "go in listening." I began by informally interviewing people in the high school, on the school board, and in town about their knowledge of the school and their kids and about their expectations of the school. I wanted to make it clear, in so doing, that I did not come to Ellsworth with a loaded agenda. I was most concerned that I not immediately offend these important constituents, either by acting as they might have stereotyped me or by asserting an ill-fitting plan for the school. The problem, of course, was that I did want to assert some personal and institutional goals and standards for the school. In the ensuing years, I have learned that this is a common dilemma for principals: how do you demonstrate sincere concern for staff and faculty views and characteristics while, at the same time, giving active, visionary direction to the school's energies?

LEARNING IN ACTION

Against this backdrop of assumptions and strategies, the school year began. As the pace of business quickened, I found no time to learn who faculty were and what they valued; we learned about each other by meeting each other in the fray. While finding faculty inaccessible in their classrooms, I had quite the opposite experience with students. I got to know them by being out in the building a lot and by fielding the flood of early-year problems myself.

This meant that I established an early image throughout the school from my dealings with students who were not where they belonged or who were sent to me for some infraction. These were the guinea pigs of the new principal's experience, coughed up by the school to test the principal's mettle. I tried hard to discover the favorite hangouts and hideouts early and to establish my ownership of those territories (the smoking area, the bathrooms, the stairwells). I spent most of my time on the move, in corridors, study halls, bathrooms, and lunchroom, accosting some kids and gently questioning others. While my objective at the time was "taking care of discipline," in retrospect I was learning an incredible amount about students, about the culture of the school, and, through them, about the faculty.

My early pattern of activity, then, led to frequent, brief contacts with most teachers, and it was through these contacts that we came to know each other. We learned how each other thought and we developed working relationships (or nonworking relationships) over specific student problems. The result for me was an uneven early knowledge of faculty: I became most familiar with those teachers who had difficult students or difficulties with students and with those who initiated contact with the office or with me. The most active teachers (for example, those who coached or led student groups) were the central part of this latter group. In what became a pattern of my career at Ellsworth, those teachers who kept quiet and who were not involved with students outside their classrooms were the ones I dealt with least and knew least well.

While I most often dealt with faculty individually and in a problem-solving mode, I did attempt to establish more formal means of including their views in the resolution of important issues. I called a monthly faculty meeting, intermittent department head meetings, and met faculty in other gatherings such as Pupil Evaluation Team meetings and student-teacher conferences. In the meetings I conducted with faculty and department heads, my goal was to open issues for discussion rather than to assert procedures or espouse programs. I raised concerns I and others had about life in school and asked for staff involvement in consideration of steps we could all take to deal with those concerns. I operated on what I now regard as a naive faith in open interchange in such forums; I tried to stimulate honest discussion of the pros and cons of questions regarding grading, alternative programming, discipline, and curriculum coordination. Although I frequently met with little response from most of the staff, I clung to the conviction that the entire staff should be involved in deciding matters for which they were responsible. In retrospect, these meetings told me little about individual faculty members' views (except for those of the perennial soapboxers). However, they said a great deal about the culture of the faculty and the willingness of the group to make an effort at open exchange and collective decision-making. The high school I inherited as a principal was not a place that I found ripe for positive faculty participation (although this proved not to be true for the junior high school faculty).

For me, these intermittent formal gatherings did not teach me nearly as much about teachers as did my direct daily contacts with them. Several critical incidents in the early months introduced me dramatically to individual staff and began displaying to me their relationships to one another. The first student days were devoted to arena scheduling, a process through which students registered themselves for classes by signing up directly with teachers seated at tables in the gym. One experienced member of the faculty simply did not come to work the first day, leaving sign-up lists to be filled out by colleagues. With the hubbub of scheduling and an unknown teaching staff of about forty, the new principal was not likely to miss one teacher. I not only missed the teacher, I felt little could justify the unannounced absence. After discussing the issue with the superintendent, I approached the teacher the next day and discovered that the day had been used for one more day's summer wages. We consequently docked the teacher a day's pay, an unusual step in schoolwork but one the teacher did not protest.

The significance of the incident is difficult to gauge. While it was not a public event even within the staff, I am sure everyone knew about it. Its conclusion established that the new principal was observant and willing to take disciplinary action with teachers. On the other hand, I had been forced to handle someone I preferred to think of as a professional simply as an employee. Had I given the teacher adequate opportunity to explain? Should I factor in personal considerations the teacher might have? How much should I listen and how much should I simply decide these things according to policy? I learned to be mistrustful of teacher motives from this first-day experience and it took me a long time to believe that my professional standards were shared by many faculty. I felt thrust into a management role. From the opening gun, I wondered if I would be able to carve out a professional relationship with this faculty.

I somewhat naively precipitated another early critical incident that both taught me about many teachers and influenced their images of me. I intended to make teaching, learning, and curriculum the heart of my work as principal and I made this point early on to the faculty. I found, however, rare opportunity in the first two or three months to become involved with the teaching process of the school. This fact increasingly frustrated me: my initial emphasis on management, on meeting and directing students, and on simply learning about the school left little time for my top priority.

Around Thanksgiving, I decided that I needed to establish my interest in classroom activities, for the patterns of my work were solidifying and, I felt, as time went on they would become increasingly difficult to break. With the help of the junior high administrator, I developed a feedback sheet on a variety of general teacher behaviors and attitudes. We then filled out a sheet for each teacher, rating them and adding comments where appropriate that were based on hit-or-miss observation and impression. In early December we delivered these to the teachers, noting that they were initial readings of their performance designed to open frank discussion between them and us so that we might embark on improving their accuracy and eventually our ability to promote teachers' professional development. We invited individual responses.

As one can easily imagine, this unsolicited and unexpected feedback prompted considerable anxiety, anger, and consternation. A number of teachers felt we were firing from the hip (we were). Many were unsure if these were evaluations for their personnel files or not. We were told we were insensitive to do something of this sort just before Christmas. A few teachers came in to discuss how we had arrived at our judgments. These conversations fulfilled my expectations as we improved our understanding of these teachers' goals, perspectives on their work, and important discrepancies between these and our own outside views. We did not, however, make progress of this sort with many teachers. Rather it seemed that our practices had invoked the specter of repressive and capricious administration. The episode was clearly a setback in the relationship I hoped to build.

In retrospect, it seems our handling of the aftershock was more important than the actual feedback. We attempted to reassure all staff that these initial observations would not be entered into files and that they were intended as the beginning of an open and helpful dialogue about the staff's professional work. Here was the opportunity to convince teachers that our intentions were honorable *and* that we were serious about insisting on an interchange about their work. Many teachers acknowledged our right to do this and, over time, came to expect us in their classrooms. Although my approach had been brash, judgmental, and intrusive, I learned which teachers were comfortable enough receiving feedback and concerned enough about performance to discuss our early estimates of it. Conversely, I learned which teachers were likely to curl into a ball, which would seek protection from the Teachers' Association, and which would do nothing. Thankfully, over the next six and a half years I learned enough about myself and faculty relations to eventually convince most teachers that I was not out on a holiday hunting spree for their heads.

In sum, my first months as principal were characterized by a dilemma: I needed to take action and be decisive but I often had inadequate information about the school and insufficient insight into staff to take action confidently. I had hoped to buy time to learn about staff, faculty, and students and to develop relationships before committing myself to specific actions and goals. Reality prevented such a logical strategy; I had to learn as I acted. The pace I set for myself, the necessity of making many decisions immediately, and my need to feel at the helm ran against my philosophical preference. I came to know faculty views, values, and competencies by brushing up against them. My learning was often reactive: I saw or heard from teachers as they responded to a decision I made or an action I took with a student or policy. Hence, *I* was a factor in the incident—and my learning who staff and faculty were was always confounded by my own participation and relationship with them. Learning about faculty in action meant learning about myself in action as well.

GETTING TO KNOW TEACHERS PROFESSIONALLY

The December feedback incident in my first year proved to be a benchmark for my principalship because it asserted my involvement in the instructional work of the junior-senior high. Although it set back some of my relationships with teachers, it put me and the assistant principal in their classrooms. By midyear I had learned basically who the faculty were in a bureaucratic sense; that is, I knew who were the tough disciplinarians and who were the soft, who returned their attendance slips promptly and accurately, who spoke up in meetings, and who seemed more compliant and who less so. Idealist that I was, however, I needed to figure ways to learn each teacher's strengths, weaknesses, style, and curriculum in their classrooms. This goal was central to my belief that I could (and should) have an impact on what and how our students learned.

The problem of learning about faculty in this instructional realm was twofold. First, logistical demands keep secondary principals preoccupied with noninstructional matters. Second, differences in assumptions and beliefs about the principal's professional role in instruction create barriers between teachers and principals that are more psychological and philosophical than physical. In this latter respect, many teachers make principals believe that teaching and learning processes in the high school are none of their business. Not only did I not believe this, but my training as a teacher in a setting in which my lesson structure, lesson execution, and student management were under constant scrutiny from administrators and colleagues had demonstrated the potency of open professional criticism. My socialization into this professional model of teaching indelibly marked my expectations for myself as a teacher and for others as a principal. Certain premises underlay this model. Teaching was a process that, first, could never be perfected; kids changed, materials evolved, you changed, the conditions of teaching and of the culture shifted; the challenge never ended. Second, I assumed that the most effective and rewarding way for the teacher to approach the challenges of teaching was in a collegial, self-critical vein. Quite simply, teaching was a calling that demanded the brains, creativity, commitment, and colleagueship of the very best professional caliber.

My belief in this model of professional work was tested repeatedly. To create a professional teaching milieu where little organized interchange about pedagogy had existed before was a task matched only by my naive ambition. From the start, I could not find a convenient entree to the classroom. After the first five weeks, I found myself feeling peculiarly shut out from the real business of the school—teaching and learning. To my surprise, I discovered that hitting stride as an institution meant that all the teachers' doors were closed and that I was in the halls rounding up errant students, checking bathrooms, insisting on hall passes, watching closely the new study hall monitors. From the vantage point of the evolving pattern of each day's activity, it looked more and more as if the halls and the office were my territory and the classrooms were teacher territory. To step into a classroom was going to mean *disrupting* the school, creating havoc in the organization I had worked so hard to run smoothly. I felt a victim of my own good intentions.

In the years following my awkward December intrusion into the world of teacher evaluation, I discovered that how the principal learns about teacher performance is a complex and sensitive process, one that is rarely written about or discussed in pre-service or in-service activities. Despite the merits of the clinical supervision cycle, it is exceedingly time consuming and, consequently, hard to sustain. Ironically, I learned more about teachers secondhand, simply by being an active principal, than I did through clinical supervision and formal evaluation. I could not avoid hearing and seeing teachers in a piecemeal fashion, mostly from students, parents, office staff, and other administrators. These *are* influential data sources for all principals, partly because they surround the principal and partly because they convey data about students' direct experiences with teachers. Such data are circumstantial, tangential to the more reliable data one can gather through direct observation and discussion, yet have substantial cumulative authority. The problem principals face is sorting through the data from these unavoidable multiple sources to identify what is accurate, fair, and above all useful in their decisions about students, curriculum, and program.

What were my sources of information about teachers and how reliable were they? For me, students were a major, active source. From students I heard direct reports: "Oh, he's so nice. . . . He makes the work really interesting, the way he tells stories about it." I heard, more frequently, indirect reports, comments about teaching dropped in the transmission of other information: "Well, you know, I never would have been fooling around with Tammy if we'd had something to do in that class!" I gauged a teacher's relationship with students by my daily observation of students with that teacher: Do they speak to him in the halls? How do they speak to him? Are they in her classroom after the bell? After school? I developed judgments of student respect for teachers by students' selection of teachers for their purposes and by their offhand references to teachers in school-wide contexts: Whom do students choose for formal advice, both personally and for extracurricular events? In organizing activities, how are the students' comments revealing their evaluations of teachers as models and leaders? Which teachers' names appear on the bathroom walls and in what contexts? The list goes on and on, for the school is constantly generating information about how we, the adults, are conducting our work.

Direct student complaints about teachers formed a special category of student information. Unlike names scribbled on desktops and bathroom walls, students' reports to the principal describing shortcomings of teachers demand serious consideration. These were always enervating events to me because they brought into play several latent dilemmas in school work. First, should I give the student the same credibility I give a teacher or other adult? Second, if I do, what is the basis of his or her expertise about teaching upon which I can rest a case for addressing a teacher's performance? Third, even if I have resolved the first two dilemmas in favor of the plaintive student, will the teacher place any credence in such information and argument (and will the Teachers' Association)? If I do not act on the complaint, will I merely prolong poor practice? Will we face parental anger? Legal action? Student complaints always engaged these questions, raising for me the issue of what to do with the *information* about the teacher contained in the complaint. Such information played a significant part in my assessments of teacher performance, whether passed on to the teacher or not. I am sure it affected how I dealt with teachers and the varying relationships I developed with them.

I experienced less conflict, if not less anxiety, over information about teachers passed on to me by adults. Parents, neighbors, guidance counselors, special education teachers, other classroom teachers, the superintendent, school board members—the list of sources is endless. As principal, I was viewed as the school's ear for this kind of information. Moreover, when I was told "what that teacher did," the speaker usually expected me to do something with the information. Although issues of validity and credibility similar to those raised by student reports accompanied such adult information, I tended to act more frequently on this kind of information than I did on student complaints. Adults more directly expected me to use the information about a teacher in my role as supervisor of the teacher. Here, *my* job performance was manifestly involved. I did not want to run into that parent again and have him or her raise the tender subject of "that teacher" without being ready to report that I had acted on his or her report. I wanted to be responsive to the public, to show that we take to heart feedback from parents to upgrade our school.

A special place must be reserved in this discussion for information from "inside" adults. While reports on teachers that travel through the community before returning to my ears were subject to obvious interference and bias, those from within the school, from professional staff particularly, created a different pool of data. Teachers, counselors, specialists, and even secretaries have the access and frequently the professional training to fashion credible evaluations of fellow staff. Comments dropped in meetings or conversation, as well as forthright reports on peers, carry a significance not easily dismissed by the principal. In my experience, these kinds of data were the most difficult to use constructively. To make this information an explicit part of a supervisory conference violates collegial norms, brings into doubt the teacher's trust, and assaults the collective morale. Once again, however, such data stuck in my cerebral file, perhaps more permanently than any other data save my own direct observations.

A third information source is more direct than these first two. From the first day on the job, I was involved in direct observation of teachers *outside* the classroom far more often than inside. What was I to do with this information? It did not explicitly relate to classroom instruction and did not fall into the neat categories of the clinical supervision observation formats. In fact, much of the directly observed behavior I noted was more clearly related to teachers' interpersonal skills and teachers' attitudes, values, and beliefs than to pedagogy. I saw, heard, and worked with teachers in staff meetings, committee meetings, the teachers' room, the hallways, the office, at extracurricular events, and in the community. Whether I was even conscious of it, data about teachers' interpersonal styles, philosophical stances, and psychological maturity came to fashion my perspectives on their suitability to their work. I am convinced that these data were very powerful in setting the stage for my approach to teachers in the supervisory relationship. Deep down, I judged people more on how they functioned in small ways than I did on how they performed formal procedures under the examination light.

Beyond these omnipresent data-gathering moments my direct interactions with teachers shaped my knowledge of them in a rather perverse way. Like most principals, I began my work with teachers within a typically bureaucratic relationship, one that placed teachers in a compliant, responsive posture. The relationship is part of our culture: administrators give directions, make demands, expect work, keep order; teachers take directions, carry out demands, produce good work, comply with restraints. So, like most principals, I learned about teachers as they participated in my bureaucracy: Did they respond quickly to office directives? Did they get attendance in promptly, count lunch money accurately, get grades done on time, follow correct procedures in referring disciplinary cases, call home when I expected them to? I developed rank orderings of our teachers by their responses to these tasks (and joined other principals in complaining to one another about how poorly they did it). My perceptions of my teachers, then, were subject to a natural bias, one that automatically rated their work on criteria of compliance, managerial efficiency, and dependability.

If so many sources of information daily present themselves to the principal, where does the reputedly scientific, objective data of the classroom observation fit in? As I have noted, I desperately injected myself into classrooms in my first year on the assumption that the teaching I would see displayed there would be the most valuable source of data for my evaluations. Based on that data, I could move to improve and facilitate learning. From that point on, as I described in Chapter 2, I committed varying amounts of time to classroom observation and conferences. At no point, however, did I feel that the data I gathered in this manner was as representative of a teacher's real performance as was the compilation of less formally collected evidence. I reached this conclusion because of the sheer impossibility of seeing enough normal teaching through observation. With a faculty of about forty, I simply could not get to all teachers enough to gain a fair and accurate picture; I probably averaged two visitations per year in the classrooms of each teacher (I was in some teachers' rooms ten times and in others' not at all). While I valued the observations and particularly the postobservation conferences, in the end these may have been more important as forums for sharing my expectations than for gathering valid evidence of teaching.

In summary, my learning about staff was more heavily influenced by the information that naturally crept my way than by discrete, purposeful observation and evaluation. Though I tried to assess fairly the source and the completeness of what I heard and saw, I found that a gestalt, created by living with staff in a busy environment, grew on its own for each staff member. My views of staff and thus my approaches to them as a group and individually were the product of an unconscious mixing of my personality and perceptivity and those of many other people. After a year of trying to control these data and stay above the informal gossip, I gave in and strived mainly to balance everything I heard and to avoid jumping to hasty or blind conclusions. In a world where the administrator's evaluations and decisions about staff are protected by most contracts from being arbitrary and capricious, the evolution of my working knowledge of teachers may seem to fit both terms. I learned, however, that principals can neither censor their perceptions nor information that abounds in busy schools. They can, though, be very discriminating sorters and analysts of the information they receive about staff. They must learn how to weigh what they learn and to apply it justly as they make decisions about students, curriculum, and, most of all, personnel.

FIVE FACTORS THAT AFFECT THE PRINCIPAL'S KNOWLEDGE OF FACULTY

I assume that most principals (and leaders of all kinds) take actions, whether by design or not, within the context of two major forces: their paradigms for what should happen and their accumulated data on what is happening. At the start of a new job, the ideal dominates our thinking. As we come to know more about the realities of our organizations, we increasingly fuse our ideals with our growing map of the actual terrain we must cross to reach the goals. The staff are the single most prominent feature on this landscape for the school leader, for without an accurate idea of their abilities, the leader and the school cannot optimize their contributions to the learning of children. In my case, I found this map developing into discernible shape toward the end of my first year and taking on permanent features in my second and third years.

My map of who the staff were and of how I should approach them was never static over the seven years I served as principal. In my early months and years, I assumed naively that teachers would give their best. From there, as a result of my experiences with teachers who persisted in not fulfilling some basic obligations, I moved through a period of questioning every teacher's contribution and every teacher's motives for working in the school. Through much of the first three or four years, I tended to lump the staff together in my characterizations, the result of my desire to treat them all the same and of my attempts to develop a sense of unity and joint effort among them all. In the last three years, in part because my job changed and in part because I decided to work with staff individually and in small groups, I came increasingly to see and to work with teachers as subgroups requiring different supervisory approaches and different working conditions.

In Chapter 7, I will explore more fully the map of my own faculty. Here, I describe five major factors that, I discovered, deeply affected that map and significantly shaped my approach to sharing trust and leadership. First, the faculty was extraordinarily difficult to unify around a professional mission. I held the conviction that the school can do its best only if the staff works together from a shared conviction in the school's goals, policies, and practices. At Ellsworth High School (EHS), I learned that high schools do not work that way without exceptional effort and good fortune. Instead of responding enthusiastically to my overtures for harder work through team play (which would of course reward us with better education for our students), the faculty was generally silent. My invitation to join forces and to generate greater internal commitment to our joint work appeared to meet with indifference from most. When my appeals to professional responsibility generated positive action from some, it always seemed punctuated by skepticism, grumbling, or pleasant noncompliance from others. I learned that the principal does not move a school toward better performance solely by appealing to the staff's higher principles. The task is incredibly more complex and grimy than this rather righteous conception implies; high school teachers, it seems, need to be individually convinced by the principal's appeals for professional commitment and work. My rather simplistic belief that we would move forward together because we were all professionals gave birth to a growing cynicism on my part about the professional quality of the staff I worked with.

A second discovery preyed on this budding cynicism: the culture of school administration is laced with a watchdog mentality with regard to teachers. The superintendent, other principals, and even the school board made it amply clear that all teachers were not to be trusted to do their work conscientiously. While this belief was not necessarily to be applied to every teacher ("Oh, he's terrific at what he does"), it threaded through conversations and even policies to the extent that it was clearly a prevailing attitude among administrators. The prevalence of this ideology made it doubly difficult to know faculty accurately and, more importantly, maintain optimism about their work. Surrounded by a culture that viewed teachers with a jaundiced eye, questioned their motives, and sought evidence of noncompliance, it took extra effort to get to know teachers on their own merits. When I encountered teachers who did not uphold their fundamental responsibilities, starting with my first day on the job, the prevailing motif of the untrustworthy faculty took on new life. As I came to know and have confidence in each teacher at EHS, I had to overcome the persistent strains of this motif, one teacher at a time.

I learned a third lesson about the high school staff through the management arena of my work. School administration requires some fairly mundane operations on everybody's part, such as daily attendance, the supervision of students, and the communication of and adherence to school policies and procedures. Having little patience for these kinds of activities myself, I tried to minimize demands on teachers' and students' time for such menial work. That such demands *practically never* met with 100% compliance or accuracy, however, shook my belief that the entire staff could ever work as a unit on more important and more complex endeavors. If teachers cannot carry out simple tasks together, how will we succeed jointly to move our schools ahead? My experience with teachers consistently failing to pull together on simple procedures did not, I remind myself, mean that they were not pulling together on more fundamental issues. Nevertheless, daily instances of sloppy management by teachers sustained nettlesome doubts about the commitment (and the attention span) of some teachers. Over time, my doubts about staff teamwork drove me toward rewarding compliance and punishing noncompliance in teachers; these two aspects of leadership are neither classically professional nor healthy for the self-motivation of the faculty group.

A fourth factor that played a part in my evolving conception of the staff was the pervasiveness of a union/management mentality. Although I was seldom directly asked to take a traditional, hard-line management stance toward a teacher or on an issue, the district had a recent and continuing history of adversarial incidents. Postures of the school board and superintendent were characteristically recalcitrant, fueled by the relative conservatism and financial tight-fistedness of the electorate. Beyond that, the superintendent's rather brusque personal style and outspokenness cultivated considerable suspicion among teachers concerning the actions and motives of administration. In this climate, I found it difficult to build an ethos of optimism and hard work among the staff. Teachers would, in diverse ways, let me know that they might share my goals but they would be darned if they would (or could) put in more time and effort at the current pay rate and under currently unsatisfactory working conditions. The persistence of this theme in my dealings with some staff took a toll on my own optimism and patience. Again, I found that seeing teachers for what they were was an uphill battle; individual strengths and idiosyncracies were often obscured by the corrosive presence of the "I'll be damned if I'll put out for them" attitude.

A final factor influencing my view of the faculty stemmed from my belief that I was to be in charge—the director and coordinator of the entire school operation. This belief grew in part from my own inbred definition of what the principal does, in part from my conviction that someone needs to pull the strings to keep any organization working smoothly, and in part from the school board and public's desire to have a principal who was in control of the school. This belief structure proved unexpectedly hazardous for me. Schools, and particularly high schools, are notoriously difficult environments to control. Students are testing their wings in all sorts of spheres and against all sorts of authorities. Physical movement around the building and access to the building after hours have expanded from lower grades, presenting infinite options for behavior that the administration does not sanction. High school teachers, a group already resistant to control by virtue of their professional status, tend to be diverse and to lay legitimate claims to academic freedom.

I found Ellsworth High to fit these descriptors; it was, indeed, loosely coupled (Weick, 1982). As principal, I could not keep tabs on everything, so I nursed a dread that this dynamic collection of independent people was not measuring up. This gnawing sense of vulnerability, in turn, tempted me constantly to increase monitoring and enforce uniformity. Given the impossibility of knowing all teachers' strengths and weaknesses and my unwillingness to impose policies and practices uniformly, however, I had but one choice. I needed to have faith in each teacher's motives and judgment and to trust that their performance was beneficial to students. I was expected to be in control, but ultimately I controlled very few things that affected the quality of education directly.

These five aspects of the principalship—staff diffusion, administrative cynicism, failures in managerial compliance, the union/management rift, and the expectation to control—are familiar to many school administrators. Their significance in this discussion lies in their effects on my approach to my own staff. Without doubt, each of these factors had a depressing influence on my ambitions to develop a cohesive, energetic, professional staff. As I learned that most teachers were not going to accept my leadership on face value, their reserve and even open cynicism tested my objectivity and optimism about them. In some respects, these discoveries might be seen as evidence of my coming of age as an administrator, the erosion of my naivete, and my joining the mainstream of seasoned high school principals.

Thankfully, I was able to overcome many of the negative overtones. With time and teachers' help, I came to see teachers for who they were and to identify a significant majority of faculty who did match my aspirations for them. With each month I put in as principal, I learned to appreciate better the need to support and sustain these faculty members and—for my own good, for their good, and for the good of our students—to fight the tendency to conclude that these five disheartening discoveries meant that the entire staff were unprofessional, untrustworthy, union-mongering resisters to leadership.

MY OPERATIONAL FACULTY MAP

The high school faculty varied in size over my seven years from thirty-two to thirty-five. All the departments of a comprehensive high school were represented (some, like media or music, had single members). As I have noted above, the faculty was seldom cohesive, speaking with one voice. My evolving relationship with them was less a uniform experience than it was an increasingly fractured one in which my single contacts with individual teachers led to accurate knowledge about one another. This knowledge, in turn, generated bonds of various kinds that, interacting in staff associations, gave birth in my view to several major clusters of staff. In the following pages, I describe my summary assessment of these major clusters and how those assessments shaped my ability to deploy those staff well.

The largest single group within the faculty were committed teachers whose first responsibilities were to their subjects and students. They constituted perhaps 40% of the faculty. Their days centered around their classes and their relaxed and friendly associations with one another and with students. They were distinguished by their rather indifferent view toward administration: the office was necessary but best when kept to a minimum. I frequently felt that I was an intrusion for these teachers, a person who was probably liked and even supported for his idealism but who basically was tolerated. This group, in my view, did good yeoman's work in the classroom and generally presented a positive and warm face to students and public, giving the school a professionally competent central core. From my standpoint, they made Ellsworth High School an average high school; the absence of fervor to constantly improve made me view them as something of an inert mass. At times I was extraordinarily thankful for this average core. But I pretty consistently tried to ignite spirit and action in them through teacher observation, curricular discussion, and personal motivation.

The next largest group of faculty, numbering around 30%, were those who had some of the fire I sought in the rest. These were teachers who would come to school prepared to put in time before and after classes planning, thinking, discussing, and enjoying themselves with students. They understood their work to be unending and they accepted an obligation to continually seek ways to do it better. They drew sustenance and vitality from students as well as from each other. These were teachers who would initiate with me discussions about their own and our collective professional tasks. They responded to optional opportunities to become involved in the planning or evaluation of our school's work, giving time and energy on top of their teaching (and often coaching or supervising student activities as well). These staff stimulated my thinking and rewarded me most, and they were the ones I worried least about monitoring. They were also the teachers with whom I found it easiest to share professional criticism and with whom discussions of performance seemed the most fruitful. This group was weighted more heavily with teachers I had hired and grown up with than other groups.

A third group varied in size over my years at EHS from perhaps 30% early on to 20% later. I characterize them as mediocre classroom teachers whose approach to work was covering the bases. They were predominantly interested in things *other* than students and formal curriculum. They varied widely in what they taught, as did the other groups, but consistently showed up as the staff members who used most of their sick days, found most reason to miss meetings, and had the least time for schoolwide issues or activities unless they had a personal stake in them. I came increasingly to see these teachers as evasive and sheltered by the negotiated contract. They were the object of my classroom evaluations each year and, it almost goes without saying, theirs were the motives I least trusted and whose practices came under the most scrutiny.

This group also syphoned much of my attention in my initial years, first as enigmas to my naive expectations about professionalism and then as nuts I could not crack. Eventually, I grew to resent them and to feel their presence as one accepts the pain of a chronic ailment. By and large, their activity in the school was benign, but to my way of thinking that constituted a negative force for students and the rest of the staff. The outcroppings of sarcasm, defeatism, and noncompliance that they occasionally exposed took a considerable toll on me and, to some extent, on other teachers. My patience with this group decreased steadily over the years and I came increasingly to confront them over their behavior and attitudes.

A fourth group deserves mention, although it is not exclusive of the three already described. Its salient feature is its obvious dislike for me, or perhaps for central administration under any guise. Importantly, the roughly 15%–20% of the faculty who fell into this group was not uniformly poorly performing in the classroom. They did tend to take an approach similar to that of the third group, but some whom I count among this group were clearly effective in the classroom and with students. These contumacious teachers seemed heartily opposed to any organization beyond the bare minimum. Whether this organization was represented by me asking for a review of curriculum or a colleague raising a concern about disciplinary consistency among teachers, these few persisted in actively resisting involvement of any meaningful or positive kind. All too often, their cynicism or outspoken critiques muffled the idealism of others, shutting off potential for open debate and sharing. Much of the latent or manifest hostility from such individuals landed at the feet of the administration, playing into the themes I have described above and leading in my case to a sense of futility. My experiences with these teachers convinced me, over time, of the limits of interpersonal communication and trust. While we generally worked together civilly, I grew confirmed in my inability to change their attitudes and performance and became, myself, the object of their defamatory rhetoric.

In the end, my map of the staff at Ellsworth High School was shaped not only by what teachers' competencies were but by my faith in their motives as well. We had a critical mass of good solid folks, most of whom were not going to chart new pedagogical waters but who were committed to our quite normal student body and curriculum. To one side were a considerable group who came to work breathing a little fire, feeling a little passion for their work with students, for their material, and for melding the two. On the other side were the remaining groups, generally less predictable in terms of their pedagogical contribution and uniformly less wholesome in terms of their attitudinal and affective effects. I viewed the first two groups as partners and the second two as obstacles. I looked to the solid core and the fire breathers to lead others and for advice. My faith in these teachers' motives and competence allowed them to operate more autonomously than other staff in my school. Unfortunately, I could not feel as confident about others and this severely hampered not only the formation of a broad partnership but each of these teachers' sense of professional worth.

The work required to cultivate and maintain faith in teachers never ended for me. The principal constantly gathers information, sorts perspectives, and duels negative forces in the faculty-administration culture in order to see faculty accurately. Some faculty will not survive this discrimination process because they lack competence; some will not because the principal has poor information or skills. Thankfully, most will prove able and willing to justify the principal's faith. It is this important process that permits the principal to formulate assignments and plans with teachers so that tasks and talents are matched and the chances of success are maximized. I was fortunate to lead a faculty who by and large proved dependable and perspicacious; and unfortunate to have a minority that gave me continuing reason to doubt.

Chapter 6

Students, Community, and Learning Our Mission

> Successful leaders . . . are great askers [who] do pay attention.
> (Bennis and Nanus, 1985, p. 96)

The task of building knowledge of the faculty never really ends. As the principal faces decisions about class assignments, student placements, committee appointments, and a raft of curriculum issues, his or her assessments of teachers—and the trust that is or is not thereby established—comes into play. As the faculty grows and as student and community demands shift, the principal must adapt staffing and structures to match these evolving realities. To succeed, he or she needs constantly to learn who those students are and what their parents and community dreams for them.

In most U.S. high schools, the principal is positioned at a critical crossroad: information about the purposes of the school, the needs of students, the preferences of community is presumed to be linked *through the principal* to decisions about teacher assignments, curriculum, and the arrangement of the learning environment. Decisions about the length and number of periods, the nature and substance of curriculum, and the composition of student groupings are orchestrated if not made by administration. While many secondary school principals eschew this busy and sometimes dangerous crossroad, leaving the work to guidance staff and department heads, pressures for principals to act as instructional leaders in recent years have made this increasingly difficult. I came to Ellsworth intent on directing traffic at this crossroad between student and community needs and the organization, assignment, and supervision of faculty. From my first days on the job, I was heavily involved in student placement, scheduling, articulating curriculum within departments and by student need, initiating an alternative program, creating a vocational training capacity. They offered the opportunity to shape what students took from their years at Ellsworth High School.

Each new curricular or pedagogical agenda demanded that I know a great deal about our students and their educational needs. What were their abilities? What were their interests? To what kinds of futures did they aspire? What should be the school's contribution to them? These questions could not be answered without considering their parents' and in fact the entire community's goals and mission for the school. What did they believe the school should do for their children? How did they expect the school to treat kids? What were they willing to pay in taxes to see that we succeeded? As the liaison for the school in public circles, I was expected to develop answers to these questions and to be capable of fitting the school's work to match what students needed and the community valued.

LEARNING ABOUT STUDENTS

I prided myself on my energetic contacts with students. As I have pointed out elsewhere, these contacts had a dual nature. From students' and staff perspectives, they were intended to be proactive, to assert both control and a positive climate. From my perspective, however, these contacts were most important data-gathering opportunities. Regardless of how informal or how task-oriented, my observations and conversations with students gave me names, faces, personalities, and personal agendas to store away, to be used at some future planning point. This activity might seem obvious and even inconsequential to some. What good educator, after all, does not continually record this kind of personal and interpersonal data about his or her students? Very few. But how many of us use this data consciously to build a student reality base into our thinking, our decisions, and our planning? Frequent student contacts showed that I cared about students individually; and it provided me with a constant flow of new data to shape my sense—and others' sense—of our mission.

This task came easily to me because I enjoy kids. I am naturally inclined to chat with them, tease them, and want to make them feel significant if I can. That activity is what made teaching a stimulating and enjoyable profession for me and it is an aspect of our work that I did not want to give up as an administrator. To be accurate, it was not so much that I did not want to give it up as it was that I just kept on operating with kids as I always had. I would approach them gently if I could, in something of a cracker-barrel-conversation tone, attempting to plug into their interests, ideas, and concerns. While this was often difficult for the principal to do—

I usually had a specific objective as I approached a student or the student approached me—I enjoyed most the tangential discussions I often had with students. Although I cannot be sure, I believe that my success as a principal was shaped heavily by my interest in and enjoyment of kids.

Driven by these motive forces, I daily learned a lot about the 800 students in my school. I could not always keep names, faces, and issues straight. Clearly, some students entered my mental directory faster than others and, for the sake of discussion, I have categorized them into three sets: kids with problems, kids involved in activities, and kids I saw outside school. Altogether, I estimate that I knew names and faces of about 75% of the students after two years, a data base that then kept refreshing itself as each new class entered.

Most principals will acknowledge that they get to know the problem kids best, and I was no exception. Some of these students only experienced academic difficulties, but more frequently classroom weaknesses were paired with behavior problems, class skipping, truancy, tardiness, and other infractions. These were perhaps 10% of the students in our school. They were kids I saw repeatedly and for whom I built the most extensive mental background files. I learned what their families were like, where they spent the night, how tough it was to get up in the morning, what their work hours were, who their enemies were, what they thought of teachers, and occasionally "where you can put this god-damned school." I often did not go looking for this information; it found me as I followed referrals, spoke to kids in the hallways, consulted with teachers and counselors, and attended Pupil Evaluation Team meetings. It became vital data for my decisions about these kids and, in the grander scheme, in my thinking and faculty discussions about curriculum and programming for this kind of kid. Given the countless hours we spent with these students and how well we came to know them, we succeeded haltingly at improving their education. Mostly, the personal relationships I and other staff developed with them merely made them feel better about us and about being in school.

I learned about a much larger group of students through their participation in school activities. At Ellsworth, between 40 and 60% of our students took part in sports, student government, math team, chess team, American Field Service, peer tutoring, office aides, and the like. Although I did not get to know these students as thoroughly as I did those in the first group, by attending activities or being involved in them myself I met many of them. More importantly, I came to know them in a nonpunitive manner and, quite unlike my acquaintance with the first group, in situations where I cheered them on, encouraged their planning of activities, or participated in decisions with them. It was from these interchanges and activities that I fashioned my normative picture of EHS. These were the kids I pictured when I thought of the average student and what we were doing, or should be doing, for him or her. That "normal" student was happy to be at school, eager to participate in its social life, and not terribly inspired intellectually. These were good kids, responsive to me and to their teachers, coaches, and advisors for the most part.

These kids formed a compliant core majority among the student body. For the principal, their presence was a blessing, as they made my managerial life easier. I saw them as a solid majority whom we needed to keep feeling positively about EHS, a task requiring diversification of student activities and the maintenance of our own optimism. Because they appeared to adjust well and thrive at school, we seldom had reason to question our academic practices with them. Despite my regular attempts to wonder aloud if we were challenging them enough, the fact remained that, as one teacher put it, "the good kids always do well."

The third group were students whom I met and often saw outside the school. They were neighbors, children of friends, residents of the small town I lived in, employees at stores I frequented. As a rural principal, this means of learning about students was of considerable consequence. I estimate that I had contact with roughly 20% of the students through this nonschool network. These contacts were of course tinged by our school relationship (I never quite felt that "Mr. Donaldson, the principal" was displaced by "Gordon, my neighbor"). Nevertheless, I saw students while they were not being students, and they saw me while I was not being principal. I met parents and younger siblings, saw kids at work and in community activities like theatre and church, and developed an appreciation for the place school played in some of their lives. This information instructed me in the life-styles of these students. I learned, for example, that work played a large role in the daily lives of many and tended to undercut the plans of some for further education. My associations with students outside school provided me a basis for understanding what they valued, how they spent their time, and how their families (or lack thereof) appeared to affect their self-esteem, their future goals, and their current life-styles.

No principal's portrait of the school's students is complete without reference to the invisible students. I knew perhaps 25% of our students well: their interests, personalities, and backgrounds were part of my working knowledge, accessible to me when I needed it. I was well enough acquainted with another 50% to greet them by name in the hallway and place them in a grade, an academic track, a hometown, and often a family relationship with former students. The remaining 25% of our students were relative unknowns. For the most part, they behaved, did well enough in classes to escape our safety nets, and participated in few if any school activities. Many of these students were nameless to me until they became juniors or seniors. They were, as is common in the U.S. high school, the middle of our student body. They probably felt rather neutral about the school and they were undoubtedly not challenged enough by our academic program. These were the students with whom I simply could not establish personal contact, given the size of our student body and the nature of my job. I thought of them more in programmatic terms than in personal terms. These were also a set of students that, I learned over my first few years, I did not need to worry about; they would come to school each day, go dutifully about their rounds, leave on the afternoon buses, and seldom if ever cause a disturbance in this routine. Many days I was thankful for them.

SCHOOLS ARE FOR STUDENTS . . . OR ARE THEY?

How did I use these varying levels of knowledge about students to fashion my purposes and those of the school? Ideally, schools exist to educate children. Our purposes as educators are tempered to meet the needs of our specific students, calling upon us to monitor our students regularly and adjust practice accordingly. I found at Ellsworth that the matter of understanding student needs is a complex one for the high school principal. This was true in part because I could not know all the kids; and in part because the mission of our school was so thoroughly structured by the traditions of U.S. secondary education (see, for example, Goodlad, 1983; Hampel, 1986).

Plainly, I was not at first in a position to judge how the school should respond to our students and their needs. I had to rely on others' interpretations, on others' old baggage with previous administrations. I have described in earlier chapters how some of these interpretations grated on my values, but here I wish to emphasize the relative powerlessness I felt early in my career to act on my intuitions. Teachers, counselors, the superintendent, and parents simply knew their kids and the school better than I did. The best I could do as a new principal was religiously to observe the practice of inquiring of others about students, existing practices, and the rationale that might (or might not) link the two. So I found that the only true teacher was time, time spent actively moving about the building, sticking my nose into everyone's business, and meeting as many students as I could.

The problem was that I had little time. As with faculty, I had to act on student issues immediately, with inadequate knowledge. Everyone expected me to contain the kids and to promote an orderly start to the school year. Such a start-up strategy communicates a dangerous value system. Rather than sending the message to students, parents, and staff that students are to be encouraged and stimulated at EHS, containment communicates doubt, caution, and mistrust of student motives. In the mid-1970s, with bomb scares, sit-ins and walk-outs, and drug use commonplace in U.S. schools, I like most principals had additional reason to be cautious. In the very important first months of my relationship with students, staff, and community, my central message was that students would be controlled in my school—suggesting of course that they needed to be.

The problem for me—and for most new principals—is how to break out of this mold, to push one's purposes, activities, and role beyond the minimum of management. I contend that the only way this can be done is through developing a purpose founded clearly on the educational needs of the students in the building. For me, this meant learning enough about our students to be able to construct a rationale for improved work with them and to sell it to faculty, superintendent, and board. Ellsworth, as is often true of schools, provided me the honeymoon period to learn enough to establish control and even to make mistakes doing it. I had to push beyond that minimum myself if I were to do more than just manage.

Here is where my knowledge of students became so vital. The first beachhead was with the hard-to-educate. Because I dealt most often with kids referred for behavior and academic problems, they were naturally the first group about whom I generated questions regarding the adequacy of our work. Referrals of individuals led to firsthand knowledge for me about the kids and about the classes and teachers they had. It is surprising how rapidly the knowledge base grew; first one student from one class or teacher, then from other teachers, then more students floated to the top of my daily lists. By November or December of my first year, I had grounds for asking more fundamental questions about our course structure, our grading practices, and the competence of some teachers.

These led to my first changes: a new grade reporting system; an early warning procedure for seniors unlikely to graduate; the creation of an alternative night school; the removal of a teacher. Understandably, these dealt mostly with the 10% of the population I was coming to know the best. As the years went by, they remained a central focus of mine, leading to rethinking the lower level courses and the way we taught them and eventually placing me in a leadership position over the new vocational school. I still do not know how much my philosophical preferences and teaching experiences disposed me toward this subpopulation, or whether it was the fact that I knew these students first and the best that put their needs in the forefront for me.

Over the first three or four years, I gradually became more involved in examining our curriculum and teaching for all students. As I have noted, teacher supervision and evaluation were a central goal for me; and, as I examined how we taught, I inevitably engaged with teachers and department heads in discussion about what we taught and its relevance to our students. This became one of the most rewarding and interesting facets of my job, albeit one that I spent less time and energy on than I had hoped. Here, my growing knowledge of students could be augmented by the often more extensive contacts and perceptions of teachers and counselors. Limited as I was by meeting kids in my office, in the halls, on the playing fields, or in social activities, I needed the insights teachers and counselors could give me in order to fashion valid notions about where the school should be headed. I came to rely heavily on secondhand knowledge of kids' academic lives and, as I attempted to engage the staff in rethinking and changing how we worked, to see that my success in moving the school was inextricably tied to my relationship with staff.

Outside the academic arena, my relationship with students had a more direct role in fashioning my purposes. I was expected to sit atop the school's student activity function from the very outset of my principalship. Although I started out cautiously—my first response to requests was "wait and I'll get back to you"—I more rapidly found a direction than was possible in the academic arena. This was in part because I felt immediately comfortable fielding student requests to do fund raisers, organize the sale of class rings, and set up a new club. These requests gave me something positive over which to engage with students. Within a few months, I had granted permission for the first school dance in two years and had set up a financial management system that placed the responsibility for activity accounting partly on student leaders' shoulders. As I look back, it seems that I was eager to establish working relationships with student leaders over these matters and that the social curriculum of the school was much more accessible to me than was the academic curriculum. I suspect that my willingness to become involved in these affairs determined student attitudes toward me and my leadership from the very outset.

I do not think that my principalship was distinct from most other high school principalships in its emphasis on the "problem" kids and on student activity functions. Most of my time in the early years was devoted to these two agendas and I knew best the problem kids and those in activities. As time went on, however, my work focused increasingly on the academic program. I spent more time in classrooms and in conversation with staff about curriculum and teaching, attempting to link what we knew about kids and what we wanted for kids to what we did with kids. In turn, I initiated more discussions with teachers about the relevance of their textbooks, materials, and teaching methods and with departments about their curricula and course selections. Importantly, my direct knowledge of students and of teaching activities provided the examples and the concreteness to make me credible. Board members and parents became involved in curriculum reviews, as well, making it possible to engage directly the custodians of student needs and community interests in decisions about academics. Although much of my learning about students was piecemeal, most of it was extraordinarily useful to me and to schoolwide curricular decisions simply because I possessed it.

In conclusion, my experience in the principalship suggests that linking what we know about our students to clear purposes, programs, and practices in the high school is an extraordinarily imprecise matter. First, the principal him- or herself must rely heavily upon the perceptions of others to understand who the student body is and what they require. Second, the press of the principalship forces those who occupy the role toward involvement with special populations (in my case, the problem kids and the school leaders). If most principals are propelled by desires to be directly involved with students as I was, their purposes will likely be dominated by these subgroups. The invisible middle is likely to be left to its silent progression through schooling. The principal who brings to the job an interest in the academic performance of all kids will be constantly submerged in student life and in classrooms—and constantly fighting to scatter his or her contacts to *all* students and *all* classrooms. The academic life of the school is relatively inaccessible to everyone when compared to student activities, discipline, and management issues; to represent it accurately and to advocate changes in it, the principal must be widely informed.

Information-gathering and informed decision-making, ultimately, are cooperative ventures. The principal simply cannot do much alone. Most of the information I needed to make decisions at Ellsworth High School originated with a student or staff member. More critically, most of the actions that followed upon a decision needed to be executed by staff and ultimately by students. Especially at the high school, people and functions were scattered physically and philosophically and few staff were even capable of being widely informed. So it fell to me, as it falls to most secondary principals, to build, share, and use an information network about students. My own effectiveness finally depended on the quality of my relationship with teachers, students, and parents to enliven such a network.

WHO ARE THE COMMUNITY MEMBERS AND WHAT DO THEY WANT?

U.S. public education has the longest tradition of democratic control of any education system in the world. Nowhere is this tradition longer or exercised with more conviction than in New England. Local school committees are directly elected in most towns and cities and they serve (in theory at least) the will of the people. For principals like me, the school board and its agent, the superintendent, were constant reminders of parental concern, citizen interest or disinterest, and the need to offer an educational experience that served the purposes of the immediate community.

What did the greater Ellsworth area want from its high school? I must start this discussion with a confession: I am an educator's educator; I do not believe that laypeople should make most of the decisions in running a school. On the other hand, they have a proper role articulating the purposes of their schools. They should identify what schools should be doing for their children and they have a vital role in helping schoolpeople see whether they are fulfilling these expectations. In Maine, the board's legal powers extend to budgets, buildings, and policies and practices dealing with personnel, students, and curriculum. Nevertheless, I jealously guarded my and the staff's prerogative to make pedagogical decisions, student management decisions, and most administrative policy decisions for the junior-senior high.

The perennial school-community relation question for me, as for most principals, had two parts: who are the community members and how can we involve them enough in school so that they trust that we are doing well by their children? The question is perennial because I never felt I had a clear and permanent answer to either part of it. Learning who the community is, after all, can be a full-time job, particularly if one sees, as do most theorists and practitioners, *many* communities of interest in each school community. I had little time and even less idea how to identify the multiple client interests of parents, town officials, nonparent taxpayers, and business leaders in nine towns. Tending to student and faculty matters was job enough without having to traipse around these communities sorting out Rotarians, city councillors, band mothers, athletic boosters, and concerned parents. Even if I could have learned who these communities were, ascertaining their various goals, attitudes and assessments regarding EHS seemed impossible indeed. So, despite the well-argued rhetoric of textbooks and educational politicians, I never managed to launch any systematic campaign to learn what my communities wanted from EHS and to relate this to our program.

As with other tasks, however, I chipped away at my ignorance mainly by keeping my ear to the ground. My initial contacts with the community were with the Ellsworth school board, first in the employment process and, after I was hired, through interviews with each member that I requested. Through my first months and years, the most consistent contact I had over professional matters with any community member was with these five board members. Not only did I see them at monthly board meetings but I involved them at the school in curriculum reviews and other matters. Although these contacts were not numerous, they gave me some inkling of what the community wanted the school to be. To say that their message was garbled in this respect would be to understate the matter. True to the democratic canon, the five members could always articulate differing perspectives on a request, an issue, or a policy matter. Through my tenure as principal, we saw fiscal conservatives sitting beside reform-minded moderates, student advocates sitting beside defenders of strict authority, athletic promoters sitting beside stalwarts of academe. I needed, of course, to tend attentively to the views of these five (despite the fact that they changed over time) because they felt directly responsible for my school and they controlled my future employment. But I learned early that they did not truly speak for the wider set of communities that Ellsworth Junior-Senior High served.

This wider community, oddly enough, was easier for me to read than was the school board. They were the parents of our students, spread over the nine towns. They did not come to the school often, nor did I come to know many of them well unless they lived in my own town or in Ellsworth. This community was easier for me to understand precisely because of this more limited contact. I basically heard from people in three situations: (1) when they had a complaint or a concern for their child; (2) at student activities or other public events, such as an open house; and (3) when I encountered someone on the street (i.e., in stores, at the gas pumps, at church, at my children's school events, at a movie). By and large, these contacts were pleasant; parents approached me with the tentativeness of people who, as high school students, had held their principals in awe. They were respectful, not terribly specific about their concerns unless they were angry, and seemed more anxious to make personal contact with the principal than to initiate action.

Of course, we had our share of disgruntled citizens. Some were neighbors of the school who complained about loud music at dances or kids walking across their lawns. Some were parents of kids whom we could not handle and who we constantly called for assistance. Some were adults who themselves had had poor experiences at Ellsworth High School and who believed we were still mistreating students. And some saw us as too loose, too student oriented, overlooking pot smokers and pill pushers in our very midst. Over my years as principal, my responsiveness to these complaints changed markedly. I was, at the beginning, very concerned about them and spent inordinate amounts of time attempting to remedy the problems that underlay them. As time went on, however, I came to see some of these as the grousing of disaffected citizens, others as calls for assistance from very frustrated parents, and others as important commentaries on how well we did our job. This separating of "problems we can affect" from "problems we can't affect" marked an important maturation in my leadership in that it permitted me to feel better about not healing all wounds that presented themselves. It also was testimony to the fact that I had learned that the school can in fact fail with some students (and probably must fail with some because of the nature of their needs), but it can still be successful as an institution and be viewed as such by its constituents.

I sought to make the school receptive to parents, and particularly to their complaints, even if we could not do much to remedy them. I found that by politely listening to their concerns we often could, at a minimum, make parents feel as if the school cared about their kids and about them. By involving teachers and counselors in conversations either directly or secondhand, we were able to pass along parental worries and perspectives and, in ways I cannot document, even change the way the school dealt with their children. Of course, practices like Pupil Evaluation Teams helped to institutionalize meetings of teachers, counselors, administrators, parents, and kids around a concern about the student. More and more administrator time was devoted to such meetings as the years of my principalship went by. In the long run, this investment of my time and that of the assistant principal paid off not so much because we were able to solve the problems that kids and parents faced as because we demonstrated to parents again and again that we were willing to sit down, talk hard together about their concerns, and try to ameliorate their situations. Investments of this kind impress parents and, especially in a rural area like ours, that impression is rapidly passed on to others and becomes a dominant factor in public perceptions of the school.

The school, too, benefits from the flow of parental contacts that it can encourage. As well as putting information about students immediately to use with the students, the school picks up a constant stream of information about parental preferences. These, writ large, are statements of value; when a parent complains or commends the school for its work with his or her child, implicit in the comment is a statement about how the school ought to work. Many of our parent-initiated contacts dealt with the treatment of students by other students and, less frequently, by staff. A decidedly smaller number involved academic matters—usually student performance but sometimes faculty performance as well. The most telling of these were communications that formed a pattern suggesting that the school was operating in such a way as to produce a systematic effect. For example, we launched a program review of the freshman year experience because of a pattern of parental and student concerns.

Our reading of public preferences, in the final analysis, contained an irony. The entire staff lived in a rural area where the community was small and very personal, yet we all worked in a vacuum of reliable information. In its place, we operated on our intuitions about what our neighbors valued and, more often than not, interpreted the infrequency of complaints as a demonstration of general public support. Whether this perception was accurate we will never know, for the fact remains that we seldom if ever heard from the vast majority of parents or citizens. Crowds of 1,200 might show up at a basketball game and were always guaranteed for graduation, but these fleeting contacts certainly did not give us much feedback or much direction on what we should be doing differently. Although I was somewhat active as an ambassador, the contacts I made at Lions Club or speaking to a parent group did not, except in indirect conversation, help me or the school to know more clearly what to do with the kids. In this regard, even our intensely locally controlled school did not mirror the conscious values or address the articulated goals the community held for it. Contrary to democratic principle and extant theory, we did pretty much what we believed was right and gave those members of the public who wanted contact the opportunity to initiate it. I think we were a typical high school in this regard.

THE PRINCIPAL AS PURVEYOR OF PURPOSES

I always felt that I, as the principal, stood alone at a unique intersection in the school's life. I could see life within the school from many angles (with the major exception of life inside the classroom). And I was a part of most of the school's interchanges with the community and the world beyond it. While counselors, the assistant principal, the athletic director, coaches, and others dealt with the public, none did so from as broad a perspective of both school and community as did I.

The consequence of this was that I felt most responsible for creating a link between the community's educational ambitions and the school's performance. As I have described it above, this task was so complex that it cried for oversimplification; the fact that the community neither spoke with one voice nor spoke loudly about the life or goals of the high school permitted me this oversimplification. In the final analysis, too, we did little to encourage members of the public to feel that their voice had a legitimate and valued part in the development of the school's mission. Yes, we formed curriculum review committees, involved the public in accreditation self-studies, invited parents to open houses and meetings on special topics. But we relied much more on bringing them into school to see what students were producing: sports, music, art, drama, industrial arts, and home economics. Ours was an unconscious strategy born of decades of tradition to give parents and the public a show to watch at their high school, not to play an integral part in shaping the education their children received there.

I take responsibility for this posture. Looking back, I think I was motivated by a mixture of naive faith and convenience. I believed that the staff, many of whom had lived in the area for a long time, knew the community well and in fact adapted their teaching to the kids and to the values of their neighbors. Further, we all had enough to do without creating the added burden of parents and other citizens running around the school correcting what we did. It was simply easier on all of us to put up some prophylactic barriers that would permit us to work with the kids as we saw fit. Both motives made some sense. The faculty were well-versed in local culture; a number had graduated from Ellsworth High School; they knew families well and had evidence of the role the school had played in previous students' lives. And we had enough to do to smooth out our curriculum, our student management procedures, and our internal differences without inviting even more perspectives and preferences.

The longer I served as principal, however, the less I felt that these rationales held water. It is important to recognize the maturational effects of the principalship in this regard. Coming into a high school from outside, it is natural both to assume that staff are responsive to local values and to avoid complicating an already complex job with a lot of community opinions. As a principal learns about the community, about students, and especially about staff, he or she gathers information that may be dissonant with observed practice. And, if he or she is so inclined, resolution of the dissonances can become a major focus of energies. It did for me. I began to see, for example, that some faculty and staff bought into local social stratification formulae. They simply believed that certain students would (or should) do well in school because of who they were or that they would not succeed in school because an older brother or sister had not. Here, my values entered the picture and I began challenging, and in some cases confronting, some staff practices that were in a sense too compatible with local community values. The longer I served as principal, the more I found myself challenging staff to make their practices fit a more egalitarian and more cosmopolitan educational ideal.

What interests me about this, in retrospect, is that it meant that I increasingly imposed my purposes on the school. While these purposes were shared by many other staff (and I suspect by many community members), they clearly ran against the better judgment of some staff and some community members. I sought to give all students repeated chances to prove that they could perform as students and as decent citizens. I sought to make all our classes stretch students beyond their current knowledge and academic capabilities. I sought to develop a supportive climate among students that, at the same time, clearly put work at the top of everyone's personal agenda. And I sought to make the school a jumping-off-place for students, a place from which students could seek their own future paths without feeling we had predestined them for any single path.

Few educators and few parents would disagree with these purposes in the abstract. In fact, it was only when one of them materialized in a specific problem that I found people arguing against them: The student who had skipped class ten times should *not* get another chance, he should flunk the course, even if it was only October 10; the student who, one teacher contended, was "nothing but a dub, just like his father" and should not be permitted to take the teacher's course; the parents who argued vehemently that their daughter should not apply to college because "she can get a good job right here"; the student groups that persecuted individual students to a point where they refused to come to school. The experience of dealing with these sorts of opinions gradually pushed me into a fairly consistent posture that opposed local standards and practices in some cases.

My position as principal gave me a platform from which to take these sorts of stands. Because I had access to all faculty and staff and because I rubbed elbows with a variety of community members, I usually knew that I had some support for the stands I took. That is, I was usually sure that others would agree with my purposes and values in the abstract, even if they disagreed with the impact that a decision had on their student, on their son or daughter, on their friend or enemy, or even on themselves. Importantly, I seldom knew whether stands I took would play well politically in Ellsworth—or lead to reductions in my support (or my pay or employment status) with board members. I worried about this dimension of my work a fair amount in the beginning of my tenure because I had so little indication of the board's purposes and expectations. As time went by and I realized the diversity of opinion on the staff, on the board, and in the community, I increasingly believed that I could garner some support for nearly any position I felt I could reasonably argue. More to the point, I came to realize that, if I waited until I knew I had support for a decision, I was likely to spend so much time trying to locate and tally my support that I would never make the decision at all.

This, then, explains my operating principle: assess each issue on its own merits by considering how it will affect the student(s) involved and make the decision that will enhance them as people, as students, and as future citizens. This posture places local community values in second place in some instances (although it is not on its face in conflict with local values). This principle meant that, as a political actor, my positions were not always predicated on *who* was involved in a decision; my positions hinged on the arguments that were mounted concerning the various possible impacts of alternative choices. It meant that I might side with a student against his or her parents or that I might side with parents against a teacher or that I might side with a special education teacher against four mainstream teachers. Interestingly, some teachers and some parents found me inconsistent as they saw me sometimes siding with one faction, sometimes with another. Try as I might, I always found it extremely difficult to communicate the reasoning for my decisions—and particularly for my unpopular ones—to people who saw the school and its world as a function of contending factions not of a common mission.

In the final analysis, I made limited use of my knowledge about the community, its preferences, and its goals for the school mainly because these were not uniform and because, on occasion, they ran against my own understanding of what was good for our students. I learned that I could not rely on some unwritten canon of opinions and values mysteriously labeled "community goals." My work with teachers and students and my work with the faculty as the group responsible for curriculum and student management required a value system that was much more internally coherent than any expression of community preferences could ever be, even in a conservative rural area. I found that it was I who had to assert this internally coherent value system through my actions and my words. Most importantly, it was our willingness and ability to stay attuned to our students and the values of their parents that assured that our practices, for the most part, served our students.

PART III

FASHIONING PRODUCTIVE RELATIONSHIPS

> . . .'tis a common proof,
> That lowliness is young ambition's ladder,
> Whereto the climber-upward turns his face;
> But when he once attains the upmost round,
> He then unto the ladder turns his back,
> Looks in the clouds, scorning the base degrees
> By which he did ascend. . . .
>
> (Shakespeare, *Julius Caesar*, Act II Scene 1)

We often think of teachers moving into the office as Shakespeare's climber-upward: our former colleague has ascended the ladder and has turned his or her back on us, forgetting if not scorning common origins in the teacherhood. This perception is, I am sure, accurate in some cases. But much more often it simply signals a reality of school organization: the *relationship* between principal and teacher strains and sometimes dislodges the collegial relationship. For the principal, surviving this relational dislocation and coming to understand the positive potential of principal-faculty relationships determines his or her success as a leader.

I approach this complex matter with three premises in mind. First, I mean by relationship the way two or more people think of, feel toward, and interact with each other. In this sense, relationships can be of many varieties—good, bad, *and* indifferent. Two or more people who work together have a relationship that can be somewhat objectively described at any given time. That relationship affects their attitudes toward work and their performance in the workplace. Second, I assume that the functioning of a school is intimately affected by both the individual and collective relationships of principal to faculty. In the 1980s we saw growing attention to this dimension of school performance (Lieberman, 1988a; Levine, 1989). Teachers' and students' faith in their school and its policies and their willingness to care for it and for one another, for example, are likely to be influenced by the level of respect and communication between principal and most teachers (Sergiovanni, 1989). Third, studying principal-faculty relationships is very difficult. We might think we understand a principal's relationship with faculty when suddenly events conspire to change it (the way nasty contract negotiations might turn the interpersonal tone sour in a building). Moreover, when we think we have a handle on a principal's relationship to the faculty, we suddenly become aware of the exceptional individual relationships between the principal and a specific one or two teachers. We are just beginning to learn how to describe these relationships and to understand how they shape both teacher and principal thought, emotion, performance, and job satisfaction.

These caveats notwithstanding, the question, "What were the relationships of Gordon Donaldson with his faculty and were they productive for the school?" is the basic question of my principalship. Principals, if we expect them to be leaders of their schools and not simply technocratic functionaries, must be capable of relating with faculty and staff in manners that make faculty and staff maximally effective. This assignment is fluid; it involves ample two-way communication and sensitivity; ultimately, the principal must be capable of accommodating numerous different personalities and styles while not losing his or her own sense of direction and personal integrity.

In the following chapters, I discuss my relationship with faculty from both my own perspective and the faculty's. Although I cannot fully represent faculty viewpoints, the questionnaire I circulated to faculty when I resigned my position generated considerable information about me and my work. As will become clear, teachers, counselors, and others freely evaluated me and my activity as principal, providing the analysis of my relationship and my success as principal with a modest data base. Most importantly, this mixture of perspectives allowed me to understand more deeply how the principal-faculty relationship operates and affects the work life of teachers.

Chapter 7

The Development of a Working Relationship: My View

> The problem of how to change things from "I" to "we", of how to bring a good measure of collegiality and relatedness to adults who work in schools, is one that belongs on the national agenda of school improvement—at the top.
>
> (Barth, 1990, p. 32)

How does a principal assess his or her relationship with faculty? The task resembles that of catching the water from a disintegrating jug: you cannot catch it all, so you grab for handfuls here and there; and with each handful you grab, you become painfully aware of the others that are getting away. The task here requires my stepping back from the particular incidents and personalities and grabbing an overview of myself as I dealt with faculty in a more or less consistent pattern. In this chapter, I attempt a description of my relationship as it developed over the seven-year course of my principalship, focusing on the patterns of my early years, the middle years, and the final relationship.

BEGINNINGS

I recall my initial relationships with faculty as starchy. I was stiff with unease, uncertain how to get to know these important people who were the teachers while getting the school off the ground at the same time. The two activities did not mix well for me. Establishing a rapport and some understanding of one another required time and perhaps a social setting. Organizing schedules, student handbooks, assemblies, and duty rosters required talking *to* the faculty, directing them to do things I was unfamiliar with, and making a million assumptions about them and their attitudes. My concern with getting school started and my ignorance of staff combined to make my approaches to teachers more task-oriented and formal than easy-going. In early meetings, I wanted to assert a businesslike tone, to ensure both that school started well and that I appeared competent. Interpersonally, my early ventures with faculty were stabs in the dark, structured by my stereotypes of high school faculties and bits of secondhand information from office staff (for a superb alternative strategy, see Cheever, in Jentz, 1982).

I relied heavily upon guidance, secretarial, and administrative staff to inform me about faculty. This central administrative team was my first teacher in the ways of Ellsworth High School; their relationships with and beliefs about teachers became mine, for the most part. Two important consequences emerged from this fact. First, I developed an immediate, close working relationship with this specialized staff of four people. Second, I suspect that teachers first saw me as a strong administration man, as someone who was influenced strongly by counselors', the assistant principal's, and even the secretary's beliefs about them as teachers. This administrative posture created (and recreated) stereotypical distances between teacher and principal. Armed with the advice and perspectives of central staff, I largely became acquainted with teachers as I approached them to resolve management problems. I spoke directly with them in faculty meetings, in monthly department head meetings, or when I had a need to approach them: "Any problems with your class lists?" "Did Peter make the add/drop deadline?" "I'm missing your sixth period attendance sheet."

As I recall it, I did not do much to shift this primarily business tone in my relationships with staff. I was, for one thing, wary of forming any potential alignment with individuals or groups that might later compromise my access to and objectivity with them all. Thus I attempted to present major school concerns to *everyone* and called regular staff meetings for that purpose. I watched carefully to avoid forming an in-group of confidants—and an out-group with whom I would later have to deal. My work with department heads did little to build a positive relationship. These six senior teachers were a paid subgroup with vaguely defined responsibilities; we met monthly, but departments themselves met only intermittently so that any teamwork we could muster as a department head group had little direct chance of carrying over to the rest of the faculty. These predictably bureaucratic contact patterns were no substitute for individual associations with teachers. Sensing this, I called each teacher in and met with each department in the first four months to discuss program and individual concerns. But what relationship was I building by calling in teachers to interview them?

As time passed, some of the starch went out of my relationship with some staff. I think an important contributor to this process was the willingness of some teachers to ask questions and my growing willingness to foster open discussion. As noted in Part I, I often felt barraged with the question, "How do you want this done, Mr. Donaldson?" Not only did teachers look to the new principal for direction, but my preoccupation with organization and management (and perhaps my doctorate from Harvard) likely encouraged it. As a novice, however, my immediate objective was to continue existing practices just to place the school in motion. So I asked questions: "How have you done this before?" "What's the purpose of doing this?" "Who is usually involved in this group?" Gradually, through lots of individual conversations and even in some of the formal meetings, I believe I communicated the idea that I was interested in preserving past practice and in entertaining teachers' opinions. I recall being heartened by the news from the superintendent during that first winter that some faculty felt I was fair and reasonable. Indeed, more teachers began to approach me as time went by.

My early relationship with faculty, then, was colored by the pall of bureaucracy and tradition, but there were increasing opportunities, for some at least, to come to know me more personally. I tried to make these individual contacts, providing time did not force them to be all business, increasingly open-ended and two-way. As I felt more comfortable with the routines of the school and more confident that the building might just run smoothly of its own accord, I sought out opportunities to converse with faculty. It is probably significant, however, that I never thought of having a relaxed faculty coffee or an informal gathering after hours for this purpose. For whatever reason, I simply did not think of that sort of contact as important to my job or my personal goals. (From where I sit now, I believe such a step would be an extraordinarily valuable one for a new principal to take with his or her faculty.)

Against this backdrop, a number of early episodes—later to become part of a lore about my principalship—shaped my image and my future relationships as part of the culture of my leadership (Schein, 1985). My active pursuit of smokers and skippers and a confrontation with a group threatening to walk out were communicated widely and, I suspect, formed the basic outlines of my leadership profile in the minds of many staff. Similarly, my first formal speeches in faculty meetings and assemblies outlined a business-first platform in which I placed learning and teaching at the top of our collective agenda. But it was my response to the first major *faculty* challenges that, I sense in retrospect, molded my character in the minds of teachers and therefore the relationships between us.

Some of these challenges established my philosophical position. One, for example, dealt with the system for reporting grades and pupil progress to parents: I endorsed the concerns of some that we did a poor job of early warning and that our report cards gave parents and students inadequate information for them to use in developing a strategy for improvement. A second challenge was arena scheduling: I began an evaluation of its effects that led to the conclusion that, despite faculty support, it was a selective scheduling procedure open to misuse and that it neglected the scheduling priorities of low-track students. A third issue was the absence of organized purpose and sequence in the school's curriculum. We began in the winter a citizen review of the substance and sequence of each department's course offerings. These issues had kicked around EHS for a number of years, but I chose to attend to them and to address them in faculty and department head meetings. Hence, I presented my value system by focusing us all on some matters of practice *I* viewed as significant. We became acquainted over professional discussion and disagreement that showed how others thought and felt about these issues and their underlying value systems. As teachers, staff, parents, and students listened in on these discussions, they learned that Donaldson was serious about curriculum, student placement, and communication to parents. They began to establish a basis on which to agree or disagree with me, to support or undercut me, to trust or distrust my leadership.

More significant than these early positions I took, however, was my handling of the first few conflicts among faculty. These marked the true end to the honeymoon in which I could make decisions or take stands that did not directly offend anyone. Within six weeks of the beginning of school, faculty and staff began to bring to me issues on which staff disagreed. Typically, a teacher, counselor, or staff member would come to me seeking my judgment and direction. After listening and perhaps talking to other concerned staff, I would learn that the proposed resolution of the issue would satisfy the complainant but dissatisfy others. Actions I took to resolve issues of this sort seldom made everyone—and at times anyone—content.

As I handled each of these first interstaff differences, I learned that our staff was webbed by long-standing divisions that, in the mid-1970s, had been exacerbated by inflamed management relations in the district. At first I thought these staff differences were only characteristic of my school. I tried to handle them as best I could, hoping that I would not permanently offend any staff or faculty and damage my budding relationship with them all. I suspect that I learned rapidly to equivocate: I examined conflicting concerns through questioning the relative merits of various arguments, sought alternative and nonpolarized options, and, when backed to the wall, chose one side or the other. Later, I discovered that these episodes are a part of every leader's work and that, importantly, how one responds to them is perhaps the most powerful way that a leader communicates who he or she is and what he or she stands for.

One of these first interpersonal issues centered on whether it was permissible to purchase new cross-country track uniforms. The two coaches held one position, the athletic director the other. It took me several conversations even to discover the nature and extent of the difference. After learning bits and pieces of the matter in these brief on-the-fly discussions over a week's time, I found myself supporting the argument put forward by the coaches. Intending to meet and discuss my leanings with the athletic director prior to finalizing my position, I was jolted by his agitated entry into my office. He had heard from the coaches that I favored their request and he did not like it. He was upset not only that I did not agree with his position but that the coaches, not he, had succeeded in getting to me. My desire to be objective and open to all views contravened the protocols of line-staff relationships, at least as the athletic director perceived them. Needless to say, this was my introduction to many subsequent events in which I felt forced to choose between what seemed right and what seemed bureaucratically proper. Welcome to the principalship, Donaldson! And welcome to stage two in your relationship with staff, a stage in which frictions and jagged communications increased with some staff—and uniformly pleasant interchanges were replaced by innuendos and sidelong glances.

Entrance upon this stage of increasingly differentiated and complex relationships seems inextricably linked to my increasing contact with staff individually. As I came to know teachers through individual discussion about their work and their views on the school's needs, I naturally collected increasingly varied perspectives. That these conflicted with one another should be no surprise, nor should the fact that staff would openly disagree when an issue arose that drew upon these conflicting views. What was surprising to me was the unforgiving quality of the conflict in some instances. Some staff seemed hardened into antagonisms on a personal level that prohibited open discussion on the merits of the issue alone. No amount of professionally objective discussion about an issue of education, it seemed, could cork the vinegar bottle. Ironically, the more open and frequent were my contacts with staff, the more they seemed likely to tap staff hostilities and complaints and to spill some vinegar. Once spilled, my quandary was what to do with the sour emotional mess. To act upon it invited open upheaval and accusations of partisanship even while it promised the chance of resolution. To ignore it permitted the continuation of hostilities as permanent impediments to staff solidarity and progress on a professional mission. The interplay of approach and avoidance over such delicate staff matters left me sitting on the fence—both philosophically and interpersonally—more often than I liked.

As my first years passed, I found my approach to these messy personnel issues to contrast more and more with my approach to management details. I took a rather stiff-lipped approach to such office procedures as attendance, data-gathering from homerooms, disciplinary steps, and student activity finances. These were matters of administrative prerogative; they were open to suggestion by anyone involved, but they were the bailiwick of the principal and central staff. I took this view partly because I believed inordinate amounts of time could be wasted in discussion of procedures and that divisions over such mundane issues would needlessly impede our work in more important areas. And partly I was convinced that such procedures will work most effectively when centrally coordinated and mandated. This approach to procedural activities seemed to some staff to contradict my more participatory approach to curricular and philosophical matters. While some teachers criticized my choice of procedures (such as extended homeroom periods for student council or office purposes cutting into teaching time), others seemed upset by the inconsistency in leadership styles. These friction points made their mark on my relationship with teachers: to some I thankfully was in charge; to others I was unbending on management and procedures; to others I was attentive and concerned; to yet others I was wishy-washy and capricious.

These, then, were the elements of my early experiences with faculty: formal business meetings, frequent individual contacts of a managerial nature, and, in growing frequency, individual and small group discussion over issues arising in daily operations—issues that increasingly involved staff disagreements. Stylistically, I mixed a directive and task-oriented approach to procedural matters with a receptive, questioning manner on policy and staffing issues. As time passed, several changes came over my patterns of staff contacts. Some led me toward more open and mutual relationships with some staff and toward more formal and stiff one-sided relationships with others. Some affected greater solidarity among most staff while apparently driving the remainder to feel increasingly outcast.

In general, the more my associations with staff diversified, the more I attempted to clarify and explain our collective professional goals and procedures. Mysteriously, the stronger my need to establish a clear, unified purpose became, the more reason some faculty had to disagree and even to build interpersonal hostility toward me and toward other teachers. I rather naively believed that professional integrity and clear vision would provide the rallying point for us all to team up and make Ellsworth High School a truly superior institution (and, indeed, it did for some). But without solid relationships to build on, they only seemed to drive my relationships with other staff into a downward spiral.

THE MIDDLE PERIOD

How did my patterns of contact with faculty evolve into stable forms in my middle years as a principal? And what were the impacts of this evolution on the group of us and on the school? One major pattern was my immersion in curricular planning and student placement, an involvement that established a proactive character to my relationship with staff. In my first years, the school faced important curricular decisions and related to them were issues of staffing, of student placement, and of faculty and public confidence.

I became involved in these kinds of issues in my first months on the job, in part because our guidance director retired in December, in part because I saw them as a way to assert my ambition to be an educator's principal. I learned quickly a great deal about what courses our students were taking, how those courses were being determined in the first place, and how teachers were assigned to teach them. I felt increasing need to pose two questions about these practices: Are they effective for our students? How can they be improved? These basic queries led me and teachers to questions of curricular rationale and planning. They as well implied questions about teacher competency and the appropriateness of their teaching assignments. As anyone familiar with high schools might guess, this approach constituted something of an intrusion on traditional "teacher territory." My hands-on approach to scheduling and to student placement only exacerbated this sensitivity.

Initial teacher reactions to this activity, I imagine, were apprehensive: what is this new principal driving at that he is mucking around with my assignments and questioning student placements? Gradually, however, some staff welcomed my active involvement in this critical interface between curriculum, teacher, and student. They began seeking me out with problems and suggestions concerning individual students and, increasingly, concerning what and how we were teaching. My involvement in these matters gave these staff a chance to clarify their niche in our school's work and to team with me on important professional issues. Some staff seemed rather neutral about the entire matter, taking what came from me without much reaction. Others persisted in their apprehension. These faculty resisted my attempts to clarify what their courses were about, for which group of students the courses were designed, and whether or not Carl or Jill belonged with them. Conflicts with teachers arose annually over specific students and curricular units. I was practically always involved with these, inevitably in a decisive and controversial sense in some cases, and this led to a division in staff with regard to their judgments of me.

Throughout my principalship, I was heavily involved in these programmatic activities, although I sought to engage guidance personnel in them as well. This investment gave me a crucial knowledge base for making decisions that affected teacher and student life alike. Later, it provided a foundation on which we could evaluate and alter curriculum, giving me a hand in decisions ranging from textbook selection to the scope and sequence of curriculum. These activities put me in contact with staff individually and in department meetings, and it did so in a proactive manner (creating the perception that I was academically goal-driven as we have seen). Over time, however, I found that approaching whole departments with concerns brought little real change (though distinct cosmetic changes in some instances). Departments, in fact, seemed to balkanize the faculty to resist changes and to rigidify principal-faculty relationships. Eventually, I concluded that the most productive forum for such considerations was conversation with individual teachers or discussion in small groups of concerned teachers assembled for the purpose.

Two other major activity patterns in this middle period intensified my individual relationship with faculty: the formal observation of teachers and my role with "special case" students. As I have mentioned earlier, I came to my work as a principal convinced of the value of professional criticism and the productive potential of clinical supervision. The procedure I followed with increasing refinement over my seven years began with a preobservation conference, moved to observation of teaching, followed with a postobservation conference, and ended with a written statement of the observation and what it revealed about the teacher's performance. The sequence exposed teachers repeatedly; it was a process fraught with anxious moments and it fostered a sense of vulnerability. That I pressed each teacher into this experience within the first six months of my arrival generated a flood of varying reactions: "Who was Donaldson to suggest that I need to be professionally monitored?" "What does he mean I must state clearer objectives?" "Why did he ask *me* what I thought of the class? *He's* the evaluator!" "He must have been hired to clean house!" Some teachers even appreciated my paying attention to what they did *inside* their classrooms.

My relationship to teachers took a quantum leap with my initial supervisory experiences and my persistence at the activity. In retrospect, I believe I was somewhat clumsy early on, particularly in not clearly explaining the process I intended to follow and the aspects of teaching I was going to focus on. Thus, there was ample room for teachers to feel offended (and my original round of off-the-record evaluations in December of my first year certainly was offensive). Nevertheless, observations and especially the conferences provided moments of one-to-one contact for me and each teacher in which we had to converse about professional *and* personal aspects of teachers' work. It seems only natural that these moments would crystallize the relationship between us and, not surprisingly, those relationships turned out to run the gamut of trust, honesty, respect, and professional productivity. My pursuit of teacher observations gave my relationship with each teacher a character and vividness; I was not going to be viewed by anyone as a colorless or neutral manager.

My relationship to individual teachers began to vary as I observed teachers with uneven frequency. The assistant principal and I could not evaluate all teachers more than twice in a year, despite the need of some for feedback and monitoring. So we set priorities: we would be sure to observe teachers about whom we had doubts so that we could be sure to create a documentary history of their performance; we would cover all new teachers in order to establish a firm basis for our professional relationship and tenure judgments; and we would observe the rest as we could. The unfortunate consequence of this strategy was that I spent less time observing and encouraging teachers with whom I had a more productive relationship. Conversely, I could be seen as continually exacerbating already irritated relationships with others. No doubt, this pattern of activities deepened poor relations with a group of teachers, a trend that produced its own crop of conflicts and tightened the spiral of hostilities.

My ongoing involvement with special-case students also gave my relationships an intrusive quality. I dealt daily with many students: repeating discipline cases, habitually tardy or absent students, student leaders, special education students, heavy participators in activities. Some of these students, the special education and discipline kids, became the focus of repeated contacts with teachers, providing avenues for me and individual teachers to discuss student needs, curriculum, teaching methods, and extra services. These daily interchanges with teachers about individual students through corridor conversations, notes, and classroom or teacher room discussion inserted me in another way into the teacher's business. My advocacy for individualizing student services was symbolized most by my role in special education screening and placement (the Pupil Evaluation Team or PET). I was a member and part-time leader of the team composed of teachers, guidance personnel, and the parent and student in question. As the PET screening, diagnosis, program planning, and student evaluation process grew during my tenure, I came increasingly to see it as the approach we should take to all students and all matters of educational planning. We should start by assessing students' capabilities and interests: establish learning and behavior needs, plan teaching to match these needs, and evaluate to determine effects.

My role as leader and especially enforcer of the PET process and decisions engaged me in numerous discussions with teachers about what was called for in their dealings with individual students. My use of the diagnostic/prescriptive framework sent messages to all staff that this was to be their approach as well and that individual students were to be the unit of all of our attentions. My advocacy of such an approach was the source of continuing frustration for some if not all teachers; with their daily loads of five or six classes and from 90 to 120 students, I was heaping on questions about specific students, implying a need for individual attention. Each time I asked about individual students, I had the sense that I was encouraging healthy tendencies in most teachers, but creating dissonances in their daily routines as well.

My involvement with student issues—and the issues of teacher competence that were never far behind—created, I suspect, somewhat conflicted relationships between me and most teachers. I was the principal who asked idealistic questions that tended to gnaw at one's teaching conscience: Am I reaching all the kids? Are they all getting a fair shake? Is everyone working hard enough? Are they making progress? While I knew that I created discomfort in approaching teachers with such questions, I believed this to be important to maintaining a proper perspective on our work. We needed to fight the tendency to fulfill the demands of routine, simply to survive the day and go through the motions. So I began trying to offset the discomfort by offering encouragement, generalizing teachers' needs and seeking in-service activities to mitigate them, and trying to pool resources and thinking into common solutions.

This led to a fourth pattern that affected our relationship: individual and small-group problem-solving. I gradually learned a strategy that resolved individual student problems and, in the best cases, gave groups of faculty a greater sense of efficacy and colleagueship with one another and with me. I began by pooling similar teacher concerns that seemed to crop up over time, perhaps from supervisory conferences, from departmental reviews, or from casual conversation. I then invited commentary on the concern in a group setting or two in which discussion focused on brainstorming causes and possible solutions. Eventually, interested teachers, counselors, and we principals made changes—often small ones—at the conclusion of the cycle.

For example, we experienced a rash of failures among freshmen one year. Individual discussions with teachers led to a group meeting that identified poor study habits as a common problem. This led to faculty investigation into study skills curricula and to communication with eighth grade teachers about curricular and skills expectations. This one series of discussions fueled several years of self-evaluation and resulted in curriculum planning and even some meager attempts at interschool coordination. The same sequence occurred with increasing frequency through the seven years I was in Ellsworth, and covered a range of issues from junior proms to drug-free graduation parties to the introduction of computers and new course sequences for vocational students. As long as I could bring episodes of this sort to a conclusion for the group, it seemed both that individual teachers felt better about their difficulties and that the group relationship strengthened.

I devised a number of formats to encourage and permit such an evolution of thinking to occur among staff. We began voluntary staff coffees, held after school with specified topics that had come to my or a teacher's attention, to explore and to feed each other's thinking. I also asked each department to do an annual review of all aspects of its work—courses, teacher assignments, student loads, materials, space, equipment—and to make this an active process. This then plugged into my annual review of all our offerings, of student needs, and of our budgetary needs. It was a process that asked each teacher to make recommendations about his or her students and to generate new curricular suggestions. I also attempted to build into our in-service and workshop activities topics that arose from these kinds of reviews and discussions as well as from my individual dealings with teachers about students or a classroom observation. I attempted to sponsor programs of in-service designed to provide sustained attention to one aspect of our work (teaching methodology, writing instruction, health and safety training, for example). Finally, I grew increasingly to value informal gatherings of teachers, such as coffee and danish at 7:15 a.m., as means of both pulling us together for pleasant contact and listening to what staff seemed most concerned about.

These efforts at taking staff's professional and personal issues and building them, where possible, into changes in our operation met with mixed success. I expected that ideas from the ground up would receive a better welcome and more support at the implementation stage than top-down. In the final analysis, this may have been the case as both our plans *and* our relationships were strengthened by pursuing bottom-up concerns and ideas. The process, however, was not smooth. My memory is clogged with discussions among faculty in which the idea or proposal, though originating among staff, was buffeted by assailing argument and criticism. I seldom witnessed clear consensus of our faculty. Regardless of the amount of research or logical argument lying behind a position, it seemed that any idea or proposal received some vocal opposition, some private advocacy, and a lot of silence. A good number of the changes we made in the school in my later years were the result of quick hearings and quiet implementation engineered by me and the teachers involved. Groundswells of school improvements, fed by joyful consensus, did not sweep through my high school faculty meetings.

Whether this organizational constipation was created by union-management hostilities, by teacher burnout, by departmental fragmentation, or by personality frictions, it seems characteristic of many high schools. I was constantly frustrated by it, wanting on the one hand to have teachers' professional advice and consent (and thus, I assumed, their willing participation) while on the other discovering repeatedly that the teachers did not exist as a single-minded body. I increasingly saw teachers alone or in small groups, sought consensus in their perspectives and their insights on student and school needs, and formulated proposals or topics for their collective analysis. Shying away from faculty meetings, I resorted to memos describing the issue, asking for written feedback, and announcing an open discussion on the topic. After running the cycle through, I figured everyone had had their chance to offer criticism and suggestions, so we could proceed with the action phase. It took a while to discover and then accept the fact that flak and noncompliance were going to come regardless of what I had done to include people.

As I grew comfortable with my role and as I came to understand the limits to my ambitions, I found myself attending increasingly to the social dimensions of my relationships. The first three or four years were a time of great activity and purpose for me; I suspect I was viewed as a driver despite my attempts to listen and consult. But learning that some faculty resisted me and perhaps resented me and that others simply could not respond to my vision brought me up short. Was it worthwhile alienating staff in order to maintain my own vision and sense of direction? Some relationships had in fact deteriorated to a point where some teachers and at least one department were very difficult for me to work with (and vice versa). Conversely, I found myself more and more relaxed with most other teachers and our communication became increasingly free.

With all teachers, I spent more time on pleasantries and relationship maintenance than at the start. Although I tried not to drop the professional agenda from our conversations, I shared with the majority more personal and social information, giving the tone and flow of our discussions a breadth and natural quality they had lacked earlier. Our comfort levels with one another grew, separating professional concerns we each had from our feelings about one another to some extent. With some of these teachers, friendships developed that extended beyond school and to our families. With regard to the minority with whom this social ease and mutual respect did not develop, however, professional issues became even more difficult to resolve because of the interpersonal static. As time went by and my relationships seemed to solidify, they also polarized; a clear group of about 20% dug their heels in at everything I said or did. They were the source of my greatest sense of failure and frustration in the later years.

THE FINAL POSTURE

In my final years at Ellsworth High School the social and interpersonal developments of the previous years had worked their effects. My capabilities as a principal had increasingly come to be enhanced or limited by the relationships I had fallen into. Despite my desire to be on good terms with everyone, I ended up on *different* terms with everyone. My abilities to guide, shape, direct, and encourage the whole staff uniformly were, I felt, nonexistent except in cursory managerial terms. I grew increasingly hopeless about my potential to be a good principal with some staff with whom it seemed every interaction was stiff, guarded, or hostile. I came to ignore and avoid them except when business with them was unavoidable. I tended more to the majority, with whom affairs were brighter, more open, and even self-sustaining in ways I had not even considered at the start of my principalship. It was this cohort that made Ellsworth High School more than an average school and that made my work as a principal professionally fulfilling.

The prominent feature of my final relationship with faculty was its differentiation and scattered quality. While it was easy-going, open, and frank with some teachers, it was anxious, guarded, and even evasive with others. In my early years I tried to approach faculty consistently as a group and to seek consensus, but after perhaps the third year I was inflicted by a growing sense of the futility of this approach. When addressing the entire group, I could not free myself from the knowledge that, in some teachers' minds, much of what I was saying was a joke; it neither inspired them to act nor scared them to comply. So I fell back to a differentiated approach: I sought out the inspired hard workers increasingly for their opinions and help while avoiding the pockets of grumblers. I sponsored voluntary faculty discussions (with coffee and goodies) to provide a collegial forum for myself and for those staff who could feed off open discussion of our work. By contrast, formal faculty meetings decreased in frequency and in breadth of topic; they became perfunctory business meetings to handle the necessities of the day (and without coffee and goodies). Further, I found myself dealing increasingly with individual teachers or in small groups assembled to deal with a specific issue.

A consequence of this posture was that my relationship to teachers tended both to solidify on an individual basis and to become less noteworthy to the staff as a whole. As I dealt individually with a teacher, he or she built with me a quite concrete series of experiences that tended to shape a clear perspective between us. For some, I tended repeatedly to seek changes or even corrections in practice and the relationship froze into a boss-employee framework. For others, I rarely sought changes in individual performance but requested help for my leadership or in running a schoolwide event. With these teachers, I increasingly gave (and wrote) commendations; our relationship tended toward open, mutually respectful involvement. Other relationships evolved to states somewhere between these two. Perhaps more significantly, however, my common definition as a leader became blurred in this process. I was different things to different people. As I became increasingly hesitant to appeal to the faculty in toto (encouraged by the expansion of my job to the vocational school), I suspect the profile I cut as a school leader became increasingly enigmatic.

I carry with me a sense of failure in this regard. When compared to the current blueprints of the strong instructional leader in the effective school, I do not view my later years as principal to stack up well. In a sense, I gave up trying to unify the faculty. I had taken a high road with everyone by appealing to their professional consciences to improve the school. Some had responded and some had not. Through teacher evaluations and supervisory interventions each year, I had confronted weak and disharmonious practices and behaviors. The result was that we all had to live with the interpersonal discomforts of working daily with those who either could not adjust to my demands or, more typically, did adjust but forever resented me. These forays into pressuring recalcitrant teachers to improve cast a pall on some who were not recalcitrant. This was not the kind of professional leadership they hoped for and that would inspire them; the aftershocks of my confrontations with staff seemed to depress everyone for a while. With each incident, I tended to back away a bit more from believing that confrontation was good for us, despite the fairly consistent support of the superintendent to the contrary.

I felt caught in a conundrum, squeezed as a leader between responsive and unresponsive teachers, between capable staff and marginal staff, and above all between the expectation that I form one happy, motivated staff and the reality that I could not. Later on, I often felt reduced to frustrated inaction. This sense of powerlessness led me to seek small successes in individual relationships and to push ahead with programs and people who could succeed. It meant leaving the ill-begotten to die on the vine. As long as I could look at the majority of the staff and see the possibility of both forward movement for students and the school and a degree of personal openness and support, I could justify my presence as the principal. But it also meant that I had accommodated to attitudes and even practices with which I was not comfortable.

In the final analysis, I found myself talking and feeling like many high school principals I knew then and have met since. Their perspectives reflect the same disjunction between desired staff relationships and actual experiences. Their expectations as leaders and educators also seem derailed by the divisions and disharmonies of their faculties. They also seem somewhat paralyzed by the perpetual conflicts of teachers' association and management, of their evolving need to hold teachers and others accountable, and of the interpersonal scars that mount from these activities. The active life of a high school principal, fractured as it is by so many student activities and faculty specialties, complicates the matter further. While fighting brushfires on four fronts, it seems nearly impossible to maintain perspective on the whole staff, the whole institution, and the relationships one needs to preserve to encourage improvement. The sheer weight of business, as well as the wearying drag of disaffected students and faculty, conspire to keep all but the most energetic, self-confident, and powerful principals from staying atop the job.

As I look back, I am stunned by one aspect of this picture of myself: I was operating largely on assumptions about faculty perceptions of me and my leadership, not on direct feedback from them. Of course, the leader who feels even somewhat embattled finds it more difficult to ask for such feedback than does the leader who is riding high. Did I paint myself into a corner by assuming that faculty had lost confidence in me? How do busy principals really know how faculty view them? How sure are they that their readings of teachers' motives and feelings are accurate?

Most principals are like me, I think. We plunge into our busy days and weeks, assuming that what we perceive is true. In doing so, we are probably *reinforcing* the negative and positive relationships we imagine and contributing ourselves to the division of the group and the fragmentation of our leadership. I have had the unusual opportunity to listen to a large number of teachers and other staff with whom I worked and have found that their views of me were surprisingly different from my views of myself. As will become clear in Chapters 8 and 9, I have learned that this matter of clarifying expectations and impressions of one another is an essential and continuing requirement for healthy leadership.

Chapter 8

The Principal from the Faculty Perspective

> Principals frequently are expected to be all things to all people, to do all things and to do them well. This might have been a reasonable expectation in days gone by, but it is no longer realistic given the increasing complexity of the role and its demands.
> (Blumberg and Greenfield, 1980, p. 16)

How did the faculty at Ellsworth High School view me? This chapter explores staff descriptions and evaluations not only of me as a principal but of me as a person. On the questionnaire described in Chapter 4, I asked staff to reflect on my tenure at the school on a variety of instruments and open-ended items. From these, I have drawn a series of observations about how I appeared to staff as a co-worker and leader and, as I will discuss in Chapter 9, what their views of our relationship were. This chapter begins with staff descriptions of me and moves to their evaluations of me. I wanted to find out first how staff depicted me as a person, focusing particularly on relational aspects of that profile. Then, by asking them to evaluate the effects of my style and activities on the school, I sought to assess the extent to which our relationships were tied in their minds to beneficial or deleterious outcomes.

MY LEADERSHIP STYLE

In Chapter 4 I reported faculty and staff perceptions of my activity, my patterns of contact with them, and the goals I pursued. Most teachers found me energetic, difficult to stay in touch with, and driven by good intentions. My profile was peripatetic; I appeared, as I felt, anxious to be on top of everything, to see that all parts of the school functioned well. One section of the questionnaire gave me a chance to learn how staff understood these activities as a leadership style. I used Fiedler's Least Preferred Coworker Scale (LPCS) (Fiedler, 1967) to obtain a general description of this style. I asked staff to "describe Gordon as you remember him at school" and provided the sixteen scales from Fiedler's LPCS for them to use. The results permitted me to examine the extent to which staff found me concerned with group-leader relations as opposed to task accomplishment. Further, it depicted for me the sorts of relationship characteristics they assigned to my leadership.

Table 5 summarizes these perceptions. Most EHS staff described my leadership as focused on creating group and interpersonal bonds (on the scale of 1 to 8, my overall mean score for all sixteen items was 6.5, where 8 represents "very concerned with establishing good relations"). With one or two exceptions, staff saw me as a leader who, in Fiedler's words, "was more concerned with establishing good interpersonal relations [and as] more considerate than low-LPCS leaders." As the table indicates, practically all staff rated me above 4 on all scales. Although I found these observations by staff heartening because they confirmed my own self-perceptions as a person who values positive interpersonal relationships, they were more informative when examined more closely. In particular, I was drawn to examine two aspects of the table: the relative position of each quality and the scattering of people who rated me as "not considerate" (1 to 4 range) on some items.

How did the relative ranking of the sixteen characteristics help me understand my professional personality? Staff seemed to agree most that I was "pleasant" and "friendly," as practically nobody rated me below a 5 and upwards of 80% rated me in the top two categories. Only slightly weaker majorities than this also rated me "helpful," "supportive," and "cooperative"; and a similar number saw me as "enthusiastic" and "cheerful." That is, I was outgoing and pleasant to nearly everyone; but I was not viewed as helpful, enthusiastic, and upbeat by all those who felt I was pleasant with them.

In fact, other items suggested that some staff found me hard to read and even "distant" despite my "pleasant" and "friendly" exterior. These data seemed incongruous. I tried hard to present myself to staff as willing to listen and anxious to maintain open communication and trust, even when I did not trust or support some individuals. The questionnaire seems to indicate that my true feelings came through. Nearly a dozen of those who responded saw me as "guarded" and "distant" and some also found me to be "rejecting," "frustrating," and "cold." Clearly, my staff could see through my visibly friendly approach to people and discern that I might

Table 5
Staff Perceptions of My Personal Style: Fiedler's Least Preferred Coworker Scale*
(distribution of staff responses by percent; N = 54)

Describe Gordon <u>as you remember him at school</u> by circling the appropriate number between each pair of terms.

	1	2	3	4	5	6	7	8	
Unpleasant				2%	2%	6%	38%	52%	Pleasant
Unfriendly				2	2	12	28	56	Friendly
Rejecting			6		6	22	22	26	18	Accepting
Frustrating		2	2	6	8	10	36	36	Helpful
Unenthusiastic			2		20	20	40	18	Enthusiastic
Tense		2		10	18	22	34	14	Relaxed
Distant	2	2	10	8	22	32	16	8	Close
Cold	2		2	8	16	32	28	12	Warm
Uncooperative		2	2	2	18	16	30	30	Cooperative
Hostile		2		2	12	12	28	44	Supportive
Boring	2	2		6	22	16	32	20	Interesting
Quarrelsome			2	2	20	20	42	14	Harmonious
Hesitant	2		4	2	8	10	36	38	Self-Assured
Inefficient	2		2	4	16	10	32	34	Efficient
Gloomy					18	14	45	23	Cheerful
Guarded			6	4	18	10	14	24	24	Open

Mean score, all items: 6.48

*Some scales have been reversed here to align positive and negative attributes.

really be coming from somewhere else. While I was encouraged to learn that a clear majority saw me in very positive light interpersonally, an identifiable minority had serious questions about my openness, helpfulness, and acceptance of them or other staff. These staff saw me as I saw myself in this respect.

I isolated those characteristics on which the fewest staff rated me in the 7 and 8 range because I felt these might tell me which of my interpersonal dimensions staff had most doubts about. These included "relaxed," "warm," "open," "close," and "accepting." While most staff found me more like each of these terms than their opposites, I was struck by the increased uncertainty in their minds about these aspects of my leadership. They seemed to be saying that I was pleasant, friendly, and cheerful, but that I was not all that easy to get to know. I was a bit uptight, on edge, and reserved. I was discriminating to a degree, not unconditionally supporting and "accepting" everyone in everything they did. The reader, I suspect, will see here some confirmation of my own views as I described them in Chapter 7.

Overall, the LPCS has helped me understand myself as a leader who might appear easy to talk to and approach but who, to some at least, was not that easy to trust or work with. Considering the fact that 19% of the staff who received surveys did not return them and that some of these were probably hostile to me, I believe the picture painted by the LPCS is more positive than the reality was by a small margin at least. Nevertheless, most staff saw me as a principal who wanted to work with them, who aspired to support and encourage them to do their work and to feel positively about their role as members of the staff. I established a positive relationship with many staff and my leadership style emphasized the value of this relationship for most.

I learned a bit more about these perceptions of me from staff comments on the questionnaire. Twenty-three of the fifty-four respondents volunteered brief descriptions of "an aspect of Gordon's work—either positive or negative" in response to an open-ended item on the descriptive portion of the questionnaire (see Appendix). These comments sorted into three domains: Six dealt with areas of need, seven were offered with value neutrality, and sixteen indicated areas of strength.

The first set of comments all focused on inadequacies in my communication with and handling of people. To one person, I needed "to learn how to make people *want* to follow [my] lead." To another, I "needed to expand [my] political awareness in regards to [my] teachers." Yet another cited "poor communication" between both principals at the high school and the staff and, to one teacher, I was simply an "inept speaker." In the most detailed comment, a staff member provided some useful analysis of my "trying to do too many things at once" and explained how this led to an absence of follow-through and an indefinite quality in my purposes and expectations of others. This staffer suggested that my "leadership abilities would have been more successful if [I] had been a little more precise and demanding."

Some staff who volunteered descriptions of areas of strength identified this same quality, but saw it as positive. They seemed to view my indistinct expectations as a vote of confidence. One noted my ability to "understand" that staff could work "without much direct supervision" and commended me for "allowing this [self-direction] to develop." Another concluded a description of the indistinctness of my leadership by writing, "all in all, things ran smoothly and he gave us a good feeling about ourselves and our teaching efforts." These remarks remind me of the dictums of situational leadership and the leader's challenge to shape his or her approach to followers according to the needs and expectations they have. Clearly, some staff wanted more direction from me and were dissatisfied with merely a congenial and supportive posture, while others found this posture to free them to do what they felt was best.

Many of the comments noting areas of strength addressed my willingness to help staff. The phrase "always willing" appeared three times in relation to providing time, effort, and "optimism." Further, one teacher noted that I was "always aware as an administrator [that] it was sometimes too easy to lose the perspective of the classroom teacher." Two staff members, in this same vein, commended my ability to consult with teachers and to be decisive. Others commented on my interpersonal success with the public, parents, and the school board. I was described as "adept at dealing with the politics involved with [my] job" and as having "a great deal of polish and tact when it came to dealing with parents in parent-teacher conferences." A third staffer reinforced this point by writing that I was "the only educator, on any level, I've met who realizes there is a world outside of a school building."

A theme in these comments also identified me as someone who was driven by ideas and good intentions. Although these are vague descriptors, they suggest to me that some staff wanted a principal who did more than provide a congenial environment. Four teachers attributed to me "good ideas," "intelligence," "knowledge" of students and teaching, and "sincerity." Several saw me simply as "professional" (and one even went so far as to label me "a professional's professional"). All these remarks left me with a sense that some staff respected my technical proficiency, my background, and my bearing as a professional, with its suggestion that I was motivated by more than merely personal or interpersonal ends.

Finally, the value-neutral comments offered a new angle on my principalship. Two staffers wrote at length about the conditions surrounding my tenure at EHS, in effect portraying my leadership as seriously constrained by outside forces. One wrote that I was "hampered by a job description impossible to become thoroughly successful with—lack[ing] authority to *push* for a more enthusiastic and capable faculty in some areas." The other saw me in my "early years at EHS, [as] an idealist and [as] very positive in his relationships with faculty and students, but the situation he was in changed him. It changed all of us." I remain intrigued by the insights of these two faculty members, as they suggest that some staff viewed my work not merely in terms of my own character and capabilities but in terms of broader organizational and even political dynamics. I was especially impressed that some believed that my success as a leader hinged on the quality of person on the staff (a lesson I took a long time to learn).

Three remarks began to identify another aspect of my character, that of a self-initiating and action-oriented person. They echo some of the comments noted above portraying me as an "idea" person, but add a measure of impatience to that persona. One felt I had "courage": "I never doubted Gordon's supply of guts. He might blunder upon occasion, but he did it with gusto." In a remark that uncannily complements this view, another staff member noted that I "often led by example rather than through directive and sometimes not everyone got the same message." Another wrote that I "did not hesitate to make the *final* decision" and added that this contributed to the sometimes controversial nature of my leadership. These remarks confirmed my own sense of mission and my desire to have an impact as a principal. Futhermore, some teachers understood that this drive can disrupt happy, supportive, and open relationships with staff, that I could neither avoid "blundering upon occasion" nor having out-and-out confrontations with staff.

All in all, the descriptions of me contained in the LPCS and these volunteered comments provide a beginning portrait of staff views and beliefs about me that are vital to my understanding of my relationship to staff. Viewed as pleasant and friendly by most, I was at the same time seen as interpersonally effective by most—and ineffective by a half dozen or so staffers. Many saw me as well intentioned and capable of acting to put my intentions to work, but some felt I was uncooperative and even inept at handling people. Most who returned the questionnaire believed that my positive qualities outweighed my negative and, in balance, that provides the essence of a working relationship: mutual regard. In the next section, we turn to staff evaluations of my success, where I will examine how productive staff believed I really was.

WAS I EFFECTIVE, OR WAS I NOT?

The LPCS demonstrated staff's understanding of me as a person and as a co-worker. While the nature of our relationship is hinted at in these data, it comes into greater focus in another set of data from the questionnaire. I constructed a scale that asked staff to evaluate "What Gordon was like in his contacts *with me*." They responded to eighteen descriptors of principal behaviors, some clearly positive (e.g., "helpful to my teaching skills"), some clearly negative ("close-minded to my views"), and some ambiguous ("hard to satisfy"). Each descriptor was derived from some body of research or description of principals where it was associated with positive or negative performance. Staff ranked a Likert scale for each descriptor, from strongly agree to strongly disagree, thus evaluating aspects of my relationship to them.

Reading assessments of my work and relationships directly from the pens and pencils of two-thirds of my staff was a sobering experience. I had never asked for feedback that was so final and that was offered with so few strings attached. I read these in two ways. First, I took each descriptor at face value and combined them for a profile of the staff's assessment of me. What attributes did most staff agree described me? Were they good or bad? I used their mean scores for this purpose, looking at their rating on the scale of 1 (low or negative) to 4 (high or positive), after reversing negative items to align numerical values. Second, I examined the distribution of individual staff scores for each descriptor because this gave me a better understanding of how divided their evaluations of me were on certain aspects of my performance. These I considered useful profiles of my relationship with staff. How many, for example, found me "helpful to their teaching skills" and how many did not?

Table 6 displays the eighteen descriptors in rank order according to mean scores, accompanied by the distribution of responses for each. I have separated the scores into four quartiles (strongly agree, agree, disagree, strongly disagree) for ease of interpretation. Two sets of descriptors clearly cluster at the top (3.25–4.00, strongly agree and at the bottom 1.00–1.75, strongly disagree). Considering that four other descriptors fall within .04 of these cutoffs, fifteen of the eighteen were ranked well toward the extremes. These data appear to offer some fairly clean evaluative statements of my profile as a principal.

I was most surprised by the interpersonal cast evident in the "strongly agree" cluster. Staff, by and large, saw me as "relaxed and friendly," "encouraging," "trusting and accepting," and "supportive in tight spots." Reflecting responses on the LPCS, staff again saw my direct personal contacts with them as more oriented toward maintaining good relationships than they were toward being "all business." Confirming this view, they ranked "not concerned with me personally" and "aloof and distant" in the lowest quartile. A large majority of responding staff also described me as "professional" in my contacts with them. This heartened me as it confirms my success at maintaining ambitions for the organization while simultaneously supporting warm relationships with staff. The term "professional" suggests success in keeping the purposes and mission of the school in focus even as I was "relaxed and friendly" and "trusting and accepting." Similarly, many staff rated me "fair," implying that relationships, either per-

Table 6
Staff Evaluations of My Personal Effectiveness with Them
(frequency distributions, rank ordered by mean; N=54)

In his contacts <u>with me</u>, Gordon was:

Attribute	% Staff Assigning:				Mean Effectiveness Rating
	1	2	3	4*	
A professional	0%	6%	15%	79%	3.73
Relaxed and friendly	2	2	38	59	3.52
Fair	10	2	17	71	3.50
Encouraging	4	6	26	64	3.50
Trusting and Accepting	4	7	40	49	3.34
Supportive in tight spots	6	11	36	47	3.24
Helpful to my teaching skills	4	15	36	47	3.23
An effective motivator	2	15	53	30	3.11
Mainly concerned about my work	4	23	53	21	2.90
Guarded in expressing himself	26	32	28	13	2.29
Hard to satisfy	43	38	15	4	1.79
Difficult to understand	47	34	13	6	1.78
Critical of my performance	56	19	23	2	1.72
Close-minded to my views	53	30	11	6	1.70
Not concerned with me personally	60	23	8	9	1.66
Not a significant force	47	45	4	4	1.65
Aloof and distant	68	23	8	2	1.44
Impatient	68	28	4	0	1.36

*4 = <u>strongly agree</u> (mean scores 3.25-4.0)
 3 = <u>agree</u> (mean scores 2.50-3.25)
 2 = <u>disagree</u> (mean scores 1.75-2.50)
 1 = <u>strongly disagree</u> (mean scores 1.0-1.75)

sonal or political, did not cloud my judgment heavily. Reinforcing this perception was strong disagreement that I was "close-minded to [their] views" and "not a significant force."

On the other hand, staff were not so certain that I performed two critical school leadership tasks. Most agreed that I was "helpful to [their] teaching skills," but the strength of this agreement was considerably lower than for interpersonal attributes noted above. They were yet less certain that I was "an effective motivator," as only 30% of the group "strongly agreed" with this descriptor. Staff appear to have viewed me as an interpersonally adept but "professional" educator who did assist them in their work as teachers. But they also found me not to be the inspiring motivator that I believe strong leaders are. Along these lines, I was perplexed by the fact that many did not think I was "hard to satisfy" or "critical of [their] performance." As I have mentioned in earlier chapters, I felt a lot of the time that I was pushing staff, holding them up to standards that they did not feel comfortable with. This feedback suggests that I may have been doing this for a minority only (20 to 25%).

I have written in earlier chapters about a dissident minority of staff with whom I could not maintain at times even a civil relationship. From these data (recalling that they do not include some staff who I suspect would rate me low), it appears that roughly 10–15% of the staff make up a minority who found me "unfair," "discouraging," not "trusting and accepting," not "supportive," and not particularly "helpful to [their] teaching." These are, I suspect, many of the people who agreed with some of the bottom quartile descriptors: "critical of my performance," "closed-minded to my views," "not concerned with me personally," and "aloof and distant." Noting that the mean scores for the high school staff tend to be more moderate than for the entire respondent group, it becomes obvious that the bulk of this disapproving group were at the high school. My guess is that they were some of those teachers whom I found nettlesome and unprofessional and whom, as they rightly observed, I could not convince myself to like or respect.

So, what have I learned about my relationship with staff from these data? First, I have been surprised by the unanimity expressed by these fifty-four staffers. They saw me in largely similar ways, as someone who approached them in a healthy and open manner. Further, they saw me as a professional, as an educator who kept business before him and them and who respected their integrity and the rules of fair play. I do not appear to have been the leader many of these staffers would follow into battle, however. As a motivator and even as a person, I was viewed in more ambiguous terms. Close to half the group found me to be "mainly concerned about my work" and "guarded in expressing [myself]"; I suspect that these folks felt less sure about my motives and my acceptance of them than did the other half. Reinforcing this point, perhaps, is the fact that half the group expressed something less than strong disagreement with the statements that I was "closed-minded to [their] views" and "not concerned with [them] personally."

All in all, I am intrigued by how positively these assessments of me came out. Certainly they are more positive than they would be had all staff responded; and I suspect they are more positive than they would have been were they collected while I still served as principal. Curiously, they reflected a more positive view of me than I often felt existed. I saw myself as more of a "driver" of staff than as a "truster" and "supporter." I felt like a constant intruder into teachers' rooms, curriculum, and student relationships, a perpetual balancer and evaluator of staff and practices. Although I appeared relaxed and friendly, I was always somewhat anxious that my efforts and personality were not what the school needed in order to make strides. The dissidents—sniping, complaining, and generally dragging their feet—wore away at me, sapping my energies and more importantly my optimism to the point where it took all I had to be optimistic with others. This may account for staff's low rating of me as a motivator. It is a story of the tail wagging the dog, to some extent. I would guess it is a common one in the annals of high school leadership.

MY SUCCESS AT REACHING MY GOALS

Staff were asked to rate my success, from "no success" to "high success," on the same list of twenty-three goals presented in Chapter 4. My strategy was first to obtain a measure of my effectiveness at a variety of activities and then to build a basis for comparing what I valued with what I accomplished. Table 7 displays the distribution of ratings for each goal and presents the goals in rank order according to mean scores. I will use mean scores in this discussion.

I was most impressed by the fact that the staff thought, on average, that I neither "very successfully" nor "very unsuccessfully" accomplished any of the goals. Mean scores clustered in the middle half of the continuum, with no scores in the "unsuccessful" quartile and only two on the borderline between the "successful" and "high success" quartiles. This pattern suggests several explanations. First, it might be that staff did not view me as notably outstanding in any area. Second, it could also be that staff felt unprepared to evaluate me, given the brevity and lack of specificity in each goal statement. Third, staff might have found it unreasonable to evaluate my "success at accomplishing each of these activities" because most activities are not the singular domain of the principal; that is, to evaluate how well the principal does at many of these activities involves separating the principal's effects from the respondent's own effects and those of other respondents. As will become evident, each of these possibilities probably operated to some degree.

How did my staff rate my success? Within the middle two quartiles, nineteen of the twenty-three goals lay in the third or "good success" region, suggesting that the staff attributed to me a generally high level of efficacy on the job. The four goals that fell in the "slight" success or second quartile—"leading Ellsworth out of the Dark Ages," "forcing" students and teachers, and keeping people "on the defensive"—are messianic, coercive, and disharmonious, implying patterns of authoritarian and capricious activity. Staffers on the whole did not apply this image to me. However, some members of the group did feel that aspects of the image *did* apply to me. In particular, some 44% felt that my work did "lead Ellsworth out of the Dark Ages." Similarly, 43% felt I was successful at using force to get students to behave. Regarding the more authoritarian and manipulative activities with adults, all but about 25% staffers saw me as unsuccessful (perhaps because, as Chapter 4 reports, many viewed these as not goals that I embraced).

What were the goals that staff believed I had "good" success with? These nineteen goals may be examined in clusters according to their mean ratings. At the low end were three: "to create a cooperative faculty team," "to befriend staff," and "to use staff for his purposes." The first and second of these reflect directly my success at establishing productive relationships. Some 61% of the staff believed I had "good" or "high" success "creating a cooperative faculty team" and 52% that I "befriended staff." In contrast to the LPCS results where I was viewed as friendly and outgoing *in relation to the staff member him or herself,* here my friendliness and cooperative relationships *with staff in general* are considerably less apparent. This equivocation is no doubt caused by the obvious conflicts I had with some faculty and the perception of many that I was "distant." Fifty-six percent of respondents rated me with "good success" on the third goal in this cluster—"to use staff for his purposes"—suggesting that many staff saw me as capable of masterminding strategies, making decisions, and taking action based on my own reasoning and goals, not necessarily on those of the faculty. I am intrigued that this perception of me was juxtaposed with perceptions of my friendliness and cooperative spirit: can a principal both manipulate staff for his or her own purposes and be viewed as a friendly team-builder?

Fourteen goals were packed into a narrow range of .28 points in the upper middle of the "good success" quartile. These break down conceptually into several groups. Bracketing the range were "to make school run smoothly and quietly" and "to make school comfortable for staff and students." Over 75% of staff felt I had "good" or "high" success with these managerial and relationship-oriented goals. These reinforced other data from the survey depicting my leadership as interpersonally attuned and managerially deliberate.

A second set of goals receiving "good success" ratings were those deal-

Table 7
Staff Perceptions of My Goal Attainment
(frequency distributions, rank ordered by mean; N = 54)

Indicate your evaluation of Gordon's success at accomplishing each of these activities.

	% Staff Assigning:				Mean Importance Rating
	1	2	3	4*	
to work his way up the job ladder	2%	14%	40%	44%	3.26
to make fair decisions, treat everyone fairly	4	11	43	43	3.24
to make school run smoothly and quietly	0	11	67	22	3.11
to create public support for school	0	15	61	24	3.09
to involve students actively in school	0	23	45	32	3.09
to earn a good income	8	18	34	40	3.06
to raise student performance	0	21	53	26	3.06
to implement management's desires	2	14	67	14	3.00
to inspire students to achieve and behave	4	17	56	24	3.00
to make the school its best	0	22	61	17	2.94
to befriend students	2	28	46	24	2.93
to exercise his authority	4	17	64	15	2.90
to encourage staff creativity	4	19	65	13	2.87

ing with students. Except for "force students to behave," all other student-labeled goals fell very close to one another within this cluster. These four addressed the matters of active student involvement in school, raising student achievement, inspiring students to achieve and behave, and befriending students. Altogether, staff seem to have seen me as directly responsible for student effects. These data were particularly gratifying, as my attention to student outcomes, curriculum, and socioemotional needs dictated so much of what I did. It was to this rather idealistic commitment to students, too, that I turned when I faced conflicts with staff, parents, board, and others.

Table 7 (Continued)

Indicate <u>your evaluation of Gordon's</u> success at accomplishing each of these activities.

	% Staff Assigning:				Mean Importance Rating
	1	2	3	4*	
to make teachers accountable for teaching	2	25	59	15	2.87
to put his own ideas to work	2	24	61	13	2.85
to make school comfortable for staff and students	4	22	61	13	2.83
to create cooperative faculty team	7	32	50	11	2.65
to use staff for his purposes	10	29	56	4	2.54
to befriend staff	7	41	43	9	2.54
**to lead the district out of the Dark Ages	14	41	31	14	2.54
to force students to behave	17	39	37	7	2.33
**to keep everyone on the defensive	35	44	16	5	1.91
**to force some teachers out	42	40	9	9	1.86

**11 or 12 nonresponses

*4 = <u>of utmost importance</u> to him (mean scores 3.25-4.0)
 3 = <u>quite important</u> to him   (mean scores 2.50-3.25)
 2 = <u>slightly important</u> to him (mean scores 1.75-2.50)
 1 = <u>no importance</u> to him   (mean scores 1.0-1.75)

So it was doubly pleasing to see that staff in general felt I had made a difference with kids.

A third set of goals provided a variation on the above themes. These dealt not with goals that affected the school's positive performance but with goals that met my personal or managerial needs. These were "to earn a good income," "to implement management's desires," "to exercise his authority," and "to put his own ideas to work." Here, staff indicated that I successfully looked out for myself: I satisfied the desires of the superintendent and board and made a good living doing it. Furthermore, I exercised my own authority and was not bashful about asserting goals and practices that were my own. Clearly, I was viewed as a principal who had both an agenda for himself and the school and the intention of pushing that agenda. Staff rated me as a principal, then, with some self-assurance and some success at shaping others' work to my goals.

The two remaining goals in this cluster were broadly stated and covered a multitude of activities: "to create public support for school" and "to make the school its best." More than any other goals, these seemed to reflect grand summaries of my activity. They each portrayed a major aspect of the typical principal's responsibility: dealing with the publics of the school and establishing an atmosphere of restive aspiration for everyone concerned with the school. Not only was I rated high in both areas but I also received "no success" ratings from nobody. I was viewed as the successful politician and image-maker for the school. My success at "making school its best" evidences the staff's judgment that I was in my position for basically altruistic purposes. It will be important to pursue this finding, for heated debates rage over perceived conflicts between administrative means and ends. If I am serving the purposes of students and doing "the best" for the school, is it admissable for me to use "authority," "manipulation," and even "force" in the service of those ends? We will pick up these themes repeatedly in later chapters.

The intertwining of an altruistic bent and a self-serving agenda was highlighted in the two goals on which I was rated most successful: "to work his way up the job ladder" and "to make fair decisions, treat everyone fairly." These were, along with "to earn a good income," the only goals that 40–44% of the staff judged me "highly successful" at accomplishing. No doubt the two dealing with income and career are placed so high because they were relatively easily measured and difficult to refute. My income was high for the area; I did move "up" to the university from the principalship and, during my tenure at Ellsworth, I moved "up" to increasingly wider circles of responsibility. While a high rating on these self-serving goals alone would embarrass me, staff judgment that "fairness" was an overriding accomplishment reassured me. This evaluation counterbalanced the suggestion found in several lower ranking goals that I was perhaps exercising power for my own personal ends. An administrator who is viewed as "fair," and particularly one who works to make the "best" school, is unlikely to be seen as one who has hidden personal motives and agendas. I was, to most respondents at least, a principal who formed judgments and made decisions not on the basis of who would like him or whether the outcome would discomfort someone, but on the basis of what was best for the school.

In sum, the fifty-four staffers who responded to the survey believed as a group that I was moderately to quite successful at attaining many goals. These include management and personal career ends that, as we saw in

Chapter 4, were considered less important to me than instructional goals. Significantly, the instructional goals were among the most successful as well, suggesting that the purposeful steps I took to promote academic and social growth were perceived by many to achieve results. Interestingly, a clear minority believed that I succeeded at manipulative and power activities. Practically all respondents, however, agreed that I "treated everyone fairly" and "made fair decisions."

IMPLICATIONS: SO, WHAT WAS OUR RELATIONSHIP?

These faculty and staff evaluations of my style, activities, and goal attainment permit me only to conjecture about my relationships with other adults in the schools. As I have examined the variety of responses to each item, I have become more aware of the diversity of individual evaluations and impressions of me. Therein lies an important lesson: among busy teachers and staff in a typically fragmented U.S. high school, unanimity about the principal's character, talents, and accomplishments may be extraordinarily hard to develop. Interestingly, these data demonstrate that Ellsworth faculty and staff agreed more about my style and character than about my accomplishments. My interpersonal manner and the persona I presented seem to have been more easily assessed than were the outcomes of my work.

This observation suggests that the principal-staff relationship may be both more obvious and more important to staff and faculty than the principal's effects on school outcomes. Teachers knew my interpersonal style and my character from direct contact (and most commonly through social interchanges). These attributes of my leadership, as well, may have mattered the most to teachers and staff. When compared to judging whether I caused the school to improve (an admittedly complex and contestable activity, at best), staff seemed more comfortable judging me on the basis of how I worked with them. I think it likely, too, that they saw themselves as the people most responsible for the achievements and failures of the school, not the principal. In short, staff looked to me not so much to make single-handedly the school succeed as to establish a climate in which *they* could accomplish that difficult goal.

Based on these evaluations of me and my work, then, teachers and staff primarily saw me as someone who was pleasant, friendly, and fair. I was, as well, a bit distant and emotionally reserved; I was to most "mainly concerned about my work," a "professional" who was somewhat guarded in his ways and discriminating in his judgment. To about 20% of the staff, I was hard to satisfy, critical, and "not concerned about me personally." Clearly, my relationships with faculty and staff varied. Not only did they view their relationships to me differently, but the criteria they used to understand and evaluate me did not seem constant from person to person.

More often than not, their views of me fell to the positive side of most scales, but seldom did more than 30% rate me in the most positive category. It seems that I had a faithful minority who evaluated my style and success very positively, a persistent minority who were unsure or negative, and roughly half the staff who were positive, but with reservations. (I was unable to determine if individual staff consistently rated me positively or negatively, but it seems likely, given the high reliability scores for most sections of the instrument, that they did respond in such patterns. Further refinement of the research procedures in this regard would be most useful.)

Beyond these item-level observations, three themes play through these data that seem to characterize staff views of our relationships. Faculty and staff, on a variety of items, believed that my intentions for the school were professionally unassailable, that I had a propensity for acting on those ideals even when it meant crossing people, and that I was willing to "get along" with everyone interpersonally despite personal or political frictions. I think most believed that I would put the school's interests (as I interpreted them) before my personal relationship with any staff member. Our relationships were friendly but professional; I wanted to build a "cooperative faculty team" but not at the expense of "putting some of my own ideas to work" or "moving up the career ladder." In the final analysis, I was anxious to see things happen, to accomplish all those goals, and my relationship to any given faculty or staff member was not going to stand in my way. It may have been just this view that led many staffers to rate less positively my success at creating a cooperative faculty team, at motivating staff, and at making the school its best.

This characterization suggests that staffers on the whole may have approached me with some hesitancy because *I* had an agenda. Thus, my purposes defined for staff and faculty what we all were to do, to an extent; and my sense of mission gave our relationships a dynamic and directed quality. Leadership, to the extent that I provided it, was I suspect tied in faculty minds to the fact that I possessed this agenda and the will to act on it. I was authoritative, not merely responsive. As we will see in Chapter 9, my agenda and sense of mission interfered with my ability fully to satisfy staff's—and my own—expectations of me as a leader.

Chapter 9

Leadership Within a Shifting Complex of Views

> Gordon was an ineffective principal. He was idealistic but did not know how to gain support for his ideas or how to generate enthusiasm. . . . He was a nice guy, but not a leader.
>
> (An Ellsworth Teacher)
>
> Even though we may disagree on the merits of [his initiatives], Gordon carried them out with diplomacy and professionalism. He is my model of the professional educator.
>
> (Another Ellsworth Teacher)

My relationship to faculty and staff was neither simple nor stable over time. When we read about the importance to successful leadership of establishing a good working relationship with faculty, we are frequently unaware of the dynamic nature of this activity. As staff evaluations of me attest, I was neither universally liked nor unanimously considered successful. I, in turn, purposefully differentiated among faculty in both my regard for their professionalism and my personal comfort doing business with them. Our views of one another and, inevitably, the relationships they shaped evolved with the months we were together. Indeed, the uneven quality of my relationship with staff seems only natural: who could expect to hire a principal who would form open, productive, and permanent relationships with all the adults working in a school?

But can the principal establish a *good enough* working relationship with all staff to permit each person to feel motivated to work well? Or, conversely, do the interpersonal and professional skills and characteristics of the principal interfere with staff members' abilities to perform their jobs well? In Ellsworth, the majority of my staff reported positive views of me and these views were reciprocated. However, between 20 and 25% of staff questioned my regard for them and my motives as leader; others acknowledged these poor relationships and commented that they affected everyone's ability to succeed. In my own reflections, I despaired that I could not revive open communication and mutual respect with these teachers. In the end, I have concluded that the principal who does his or her job as leader and evaluator is unlikely to generate fruitful relationships with all faculty and staff. The successful principal must establish a baseline of support, respect, and open communication with most faculty and staff. (A clear two-thirds majority would, I believe, be considered very successful in this regard.)

In this chapter, I explore through faculty and staff comments about me and my leadership how my relationships to many others confounded my relationship and success to each staffer. In these written comments emerged the intensity and the gradations of feeling that enlivened the web of my relationships with staff, superintendent, board, students, and public. As will become clear, the strands in this web interacted, creating the relational context in which I functioned. At the end of the chapter, I identify four dynamic themes in this context that have application to the work of other principals.

IN THEIR OWN WORDS

Forty-two teachers and staff members wrote comments in response to the survey prompt, "In summary, state briefly your overall assessment of Gordon's work in Ellsworth as principal. Feel free to use the reverse side as well." My analysis of these written comments has sorted them according to evaluative conclusions about my leadership, observations about my relationships, and statements on my style and activities. Interestingly, staff comments tended to focus on aspects of my style and manner, rather than on concrete actions or philosophical or programmatic stances. Descriptors emphasized *how* I presented myself and *how* I did things, rather than *what* I did. They tended to assess my performance as it affected them and other staff, rather than as it affected students, the public, or other specific populations. These patterns suggest, as we saw in Chapter 8, a preeminent concern on faculty and staff's parts with the principal's relationships and his or her treatment of them personally.

Four types of statement recurred in these data: Those explaining what I did or did not choose to do; what I did or did not do because of external circumstances; what kind of person I was, in both personal and professional terms; and finally what I accomplished (a category that, as I mentioned, was sparse, but that is central to my search for lessons about my effectiveness). I examine each category in the following pages.

What I (Willfully) Did or Did Not Choose to Do

One set of comments describing activities clustered around the idea that I worked hard at what I did. Typical of these were descriptions of high-minded educational activity: I was "solidifying goals and functions," "making Ellsworth a fine educational institution," "constantly striving to improve the quality of secondary education," "[establishing] 'projects' for teachers' meetings and workshops," and "being visible." Offered in a laudatory vein, these comments depicted me working to see that professional ambitions came to fruition. Though agreeing that I worked hard, however, three staff remarked that my well-intended efforts failed because I did not direct them at the "tough" problems. One wrote: "Excellent job as principal. Could have made some lasting and important contributions if he had been willing to address the issues that constantly created turmoil in Ellsworth."

A second large set of comments addressed my supportiveness with regard to teachers' activities. These specified "help in the classroom," "backing me up in critical situations," and being "positive and offering his help." One teacher noted that "Gordon was supportive and encouraging to teachers in their first year at Ellsworth. His support seemed to wane in the second and successive years." Another teacher noted a balance in my approach to helping staff: "Gordon was mostly fair and pertinent in his criticism and mostly generous and appreciative in his praise/recognition." While most staff made reference to my supportiveness in these rather unspecified ways, at least one saw as my major failure my inability to build mutually supportive relationships with staff over their professional agendas:

Gordon was an ineffective principal. He was idealistic, but did not know how to gain support for his ideas or how to generate enthusiasm. He kept trying, but that only led to antagonistic attitudes toward him. It was often mentioned that he did not listen to other people's ideas, even if *he* asked for them. Gordon lacked a professional attitude. He often wrote notes on torn pieces of scrap paper, asking for a response. Personally, I ignored them and he never followed through. He lacked organization. Sometimes events were planned the same day of their occurence. His priorities seemed to lie in satisfying the Superintendent's whims (and boy is he whimsical), rather than trying to meet the needs of students and teachers. He's a nice guy, but not a leader.

Several respondents saw the focus of my activities inclining heavily toward students and academics. As one put it, I was "very concerned about the well-being of students' needs and educational goals." Another saw me as "very creative and very perceptive in his approach to problem situations. He was a positive force in making EHS what it is, especially in academics." Yet another saw me as "very strongly pulled toward educational philosophies applied in the classroom." While this orientation perhaps accounts for the "idealistic" label in the lengthy quote above, it also seems to have created the clear impression that a primary concern for me was what happened inside the classroom.

This observation is reinforced by the number of general references to my focus on "improving the quality of secondary education" and doing "what he felt was the best for the improvement of EHS and its faculty and students." In contrast, a few staff suggested that I had little concrete focus of any kind, let alone a focus on academics and students. In a comment reflective of the building-hopping I did in my last three years, one staffer noted that "Gordon spent most of his time outside the high school and nobody knew where." And my favorite: "Gordon never did figure out what he was supposed to be doing. His handling of personnel was a disaster."

What emerges from these comments is perhaps less important than what does not emerge. The majority of staff made reference to activities they clearly related to positive performance on my part. Yet the absence of detail about these plagues their assessments; it seems that staff were hard-pressed to find the words and the conceptions of the principal's function necessary to explain what activities I was engaged in that were productive. On the opposite side of the ledger, a half dozen staff were apparently more prepared to describe what I had *not* done (e.g., written "professional" notes or handled "personnel" properly). Indeed, my behavior to some was adequately inexplicable that they could only see me as a principal who did not know what to do.

Staff, it seems, want principals with a sense of their own agency and effectiveness. Unless the principal helps them understand specifically his or her ambitions and strategies, they will be at a loss for criteria to judge his or her effects. For staff with whom relationships are weak, this vagueness provides an opportunity to see the principal as confused and even unfit. This was, I suspect, the case for me. Staff with whom I established a solid professional relationship tended to articulate in a general way what I *did* well; those with whom I had less productive relationships perseverated on what I *did not do* well and my own overcommitment and vagueness of focus gave them plenty of room to document their case.

What Impact Circumstances Had on What I Did or Did Not Do

Teachers and staff can choose to understand the principal's effects not so much as his or her own, but as shaped to a degree by external factors.

In discussing my performance, twelve staff identified conditions and the people who created them as significant influences on my effectiveness. These sorts of comments fell into three categories. In the first set, staff saw me in conflict with the cultural/political/historical context in which I was operating. For example, one staff member saw me as "out of his element, somewhat . . . very intelligent but this doesn't always mean success in rural coastal Maine when you're from 'Beacon Hill.' " Others saw me confronted with "a poor political situation," "a very conservative/reactionary area," and a "period of transition . . . entering a 'back to basics' period, having abandoned our feeble attempts to encourage a certain degree of student initiative in the educational process."

Importantly, those who chose this historical/political interpretation of my success also concluded that, in general, I had done "an excellent job" and had "carried [the job] out with diplomacy and professionalism" despite circumstances. Filling out the picture was the staffer who saw me as a welcome relief from some of these forces: "Gordon was like a breath of fresh air . . . but many were locked inside with the doors and windows tightly shut." For a number of these staff, I seem to have brought energy and optimism to the leadership of a school that had only a dim chance of innovating or improving.

A second set of remarks saw my performance hopelessly intertwined with administrative problems facing Ellsworth. Some of these dealt directly with the superintendent: "Gordon got caught up in the superintendent's 'administrative team' and he couldn't really be his own man working for that 'power monger.' " More frequently, staff noted the lack of clarity about my job and the extensive demands it placed on me. One writer linked this to the upper administration's failure to empower me, but also included the demands of running the building: "If given more power to make decisions and implement programs, Gordon could have been more effective. . . . He was caught up in the day-to-day operations and the administrative paperwork, giving him less time to work as a change agent." Several others echoed the sentiment that I was overextended. As one put it, "he was spread *too* thin . . . I would love to have worked with him in a less 'hopeless' capacity (hopeless in his job description)." One person drew on a business management paradigm to imply shortcomings: "Gordon was sincere and honest. . . . Unfortunately, school administration is like a business and sincerity and honesty are not always the only qualities needed."

Finally, three staff ascribed difficulties I had to poor relationships with staff. These echo the staffer who stated that "my handling of personnel was a disaster," but do not conclude, as he or she did, that it spelled failure for my leadership. Rather, they recognized that conflicts existed between me and some staff and went on to suggest that these were not entirely my doing and may indeed have been unavoidable: "Some teachers liked his approach, some did not. With the staff at EHS, no one could change that. It is not an easy job, not even a pleasant one at times." While one writer suggested that my "young age and excessive education" may explain such abrasive relationships, it was more common to see them in terms of a complex of factors:

> [The fact that] his relationship with . . . staff was strained [was] not solely his doing. Disunity and lack of cooperation grew; instituting programs became increasingly difficult and programs which could have been initiated never came to fruition. He relied upon a few to cooperate but could not motivate the staff as a whole.

It may be no coincidence that this rather hopeless rendition of my situation seemed the most familiar to my own thinking during the last year or two of my work. Importantly, all these comments portrayed me as somewhat powerless and I am inclined to think that, for most teachers, having a principal whose hands were tied was not comfortable. To a degree, it implied that they were organizationally powerless as well.

What Kind of Person I Was

The most frequent comment about my performance was couched in terms of my personal qualities, as distinguished from my professional actions or accomplishments. Twenty-one staff and faculty described my personality and character directly, often using salutary adjectives such as "outstanding," "model," "excellent," "successful," "Ellsworth's loss."

One common focus of staff descriptions was my "concern about what was happening in school—to both the students and the faculty." To this group, integrity and sincerity were important:

> An outstanding quality of Gordon's was his integrity. Also, I found him very supportive of me, not only in my classroom but in my personal life as well. He was always concerned, and genuinely so, about how things were going. . . . I was sad to see him leave for another job.

Concern and dedication seemed, as well, expressions of the amount of effort and time I put into my work, an attribute of my work style, which no one questioned in any way in the survey. Many associated the term "professional" with this general orientation: "[Gordon was] a true professional, interested in children and education."

A second theme in these descriptions ran tangentially to the first; it dealt with my concern for "improvement," for "quality," for "standards." For one staffer, I was "an outstanding educator . . . dedicated and constantly striving to improve the quality of secondary education." To others I was "very sincere in [my] efforts at improving education at EHS [as evidenced in my focus on] academic planning." One teacher wrote that "[Gordon was] fair minded; very strongly pulled toward educational philosophies applied in classrooms; strong-willed." As indicated elsewhere on the survey, I had an agenda for myself and for my school; I came to Ellsworth, as one person put it, "with many good ideas" and these propelled my approach to my work and the work staff was to do.

A third theme focused on my personal relationship with staff. While most of these comments were positive, several were pointedly negative. Terms such as "supportive," "willing to help," "encouraging," "good to work with," "friendly," and "positive" were mentioned repeatedly (three to eight times each). Many of those who used such terms also attributed to me an "ability to deal with people" in a "sincere, honest, and fair" manner. And some noted that I was "positive and offered help [even though the teacher] may not always have agreed with [me]." These staff appreciated my directness and my ability to overlook personal differences and conflicts in order to keep functioning. One teacher explained that

I enjoyed my association with Gordon very much. There were times when we both frustrated one another. I would rate Gordon's overall job on a 1–5 scale as a 4 or 5–on the good side. There were times when he might be a bit aloof and shoot down a series of requests with a chuckle of sarcasm (light-hearted) as if to say, "Are you serious?"

A guidance counselor alluded to this ability to remain engaged interpersonally despite professional differences: "It [would have been] easy to treat others impersonally, especially when dealing with a number of inept or incompetent so-called professional teachers and administrators. (I did not feel one of them nor did he try to impart such feelings)."

In contrast with these laudatory views of relational abilities, others pinpointed my interpersonal skills as my major failing. Several staff identified conflicts with others as a recurring dimension of my work. While several of these noted that they "still don't understand why" these developed, one teacher gave the following analysis:

Gordon's interpersonal skills were somewhat lacking. He knew how to use the people he liked and valued, but didn't always know (it seemed) how to give the positive strokes to those people who needed them to keep going. . . . He was unable to read the moods of his staff, which often led to unpleasant situations which might have been avoided if he had a better handle on what was going on with his staff (professionally, emotionally, and privately). . . . Politically and organizationally, Gordon was much stronger than he was (is) on a human level. His interpersonal skills are there, but are not consistent.

Other staff implied that my inability to "handle staff" was a constant issue, though one that reared its head at odd times, against a backdrop of generally friendly, positive, and supportive relations with most. In this light, it may be the inconsistency of my performance that caused the most consternation. This attribute, among others, may be what led one respondent to conclude that "I have enjoyed other principals much more during my teaching career."

A final theme was composed of remarks about my treatment of the writer. They suggested strongly that it was their own relationships with me and their direct experience with my personal qualities, not my "accomplishments," that determined my value as principal. "As a principal and friend, I enjoyed him very much" typified several comments. Conversely, two noted that "I did not feel valued [by Gordon]." How we got along and stylistic aspects of my daily presence in the buildings shaped my success most. In this regard, statements of our personal relationship were offered as evidence of my "professionalism," of my "dedication to education," or contrarily of my ineptness. A number of these writers seemed to feel a need for me to be close, constantly reinforcing, and a source of strength to them. For those with whom I developed such a bond, I was a successful principal and for those with whom I did not, I was a failure (and for many others, our relationship lay somewhere between these two). Success, in the eyes of most staff, was very much a matter of who I was.

What I Accomplished

Our field has been criticized for generations for its inability to agree on and use outcome measures. We have not wholly endorsed management or teaching by objectives, nor have we, in recent years, successfully reduced teacher or student evaluation to concrete, measurable terms. We resist this tendency. So it is perhaps not surprising that staff neither readily use outcome measures nor appear to agree on many such measures when they have the opportunity to evaluate a principal. The following comments will serve to indicate the types of comments staff made infrequently about the "final effects" I had on the schools while I was principal.

Several staff cited my effects on students. I was, according to one, "a visible principal . . . which I think is a positive situation for the students." Another noted that "students seemed to like and respect him." Several staff saw "students at the center of his concern" and clearly implied that a measure of my success lay in my ability to operate successfully in the realm of student management and motivation. As one put it, "Ellsworth will regret that he resigned. . . . The city and the students were the losers." Once again, no details were included to relate my performance directly to effects on students.

A second series of remarks made similarly general connections between my work and the school's condition. For example, one staff member noted that "[Gordon] maintained [Ellsworth's academic reputation for excellence] during his administration. This is the primary purpose of a principal." Reiterating this theme, another wrote that "Gordon was quite a positive force in making EHS what it is—especially in the area of academics. He seemed to be very creative and very perceptive in his approach to problem situations." A central ingredient of my performance in this vein was a willful optimism: "I feel Gordon was an *excellent* administrator at Ellsworth. He had high expectations of his staff and students. This is good, it encouraged everyone to better themselves." To at least one teacher, my accomplishments were part of a rightward swing:

Gordon assumed the principalship of EHS during a period of transition—we were entering a "back-to-basics" period having abandoned our feeble attempts to encourage a certain degree of student initiative in the educational process. Even though I feel we may disagree philosophically on the merits of such changes, I feel Gordon carried them out with diplomacy and professionalism. He is my model of the professional educator.

The list of accomplishments in the interpersonal dimension of my work was the longest and most mixed. In previous sections of this discussion, we have seen references to my support of staff "in critical times," my "fair-mindedness," and my "good rapport with staff." While most staff supported this general view, a number noted that later in my tenure I had allowed the staff to become divided at the high school. As one put it, "disunity and lack of cooperation grew [as] his relationship with staff became strained." Two others opined that I "didn't know how to gain support for [my] ideas or to generate enthusiasm. . . . He kept trying . . . but there were antagonistic attitudes toward him." The most direct of these comments barred no holds: "Gordon never did figure out what he was supposed to be doing. His handling of personnel was a disaster. He has no capacity for leadership." Although these opinions lay in the minority, their presence was reinforced by other staff who noted that "some teachers liked his approach, some did not."

Several staff took a more global view of my effects. One of these reiterated the theme of my "diplomatic" and "political" savvy: "Gordon had great respect from the community, as indicated by the school board's desire to find a 'twin'-type replacement when he left." Another noted that "he did work hard and effectively to solidify the goals and functions of primary and secondary education in Ellsworth." Numerous references to my accomplishments were so vague that it is impossible to tell what I accomplished: "Gordon was *good* for education in Ellsworth"; "he seemed to accomplish a great deal with the school system." It may be that staff ignorance of my activities and the dispersal of my work into three buildings in later years gave no staff member a clear idea of what I did. Also, some felt I neglected them, not so much intentionally as because my energies and focus were diverted elsewhere: "Given the magnitude of his challenge at EHS, I can understand why he appeared to place my department in lower priority."

Finally, two staff commented that a noteworthy outcome of my years in Ellsworth was career advancement. As one put it, "Gordon sees his future as an ever-ascending staircase." A second began his or her remarks as follows: "I never felt that Gordon intended to remain in the Ellsworth system for an extended period of time. He seems to be gaining experience necessary for his progressing with the educational system in general."

In sum, these open-ended staff evaluations of me cluster around five themes. First, I was generally commended for hard work, good intentions, and a professional bearing. Second, most staff found my interpersonal skills and my personality the easiest attributes to describe as they sought a terminology for more specifically lauding my work. Third, comments notably neglected descriptions of my accomplishments, perhaps reflecting uncertainties about what in fact I did or was supposed to do. Fourth, a cluster of six staff specified shortcomings in my performance, articulately finding me lacking in interpersonal and leadership arenas. Finally, a number of staff chose to evaluate me in the context of the town, the administration, the faculty, and the times, providing a view in which my specific competencies and characteristics and the purposeful directions I set played second fiddle to these stronger external influences. The following section examines this fifth theme in greater detail.

THE IMPACTS OF EXTERNAL CIRCUMSTANCES

No individual operates in a vacuum. Principals are sometimes inclined to think, as other leaders are, that their willful purposes flow directly into the trunk line for action. Clearly, the school environment and the community environment beyond it mediate the effects of the principal. Understanding the context is integral to understanding the impacts of the individual.

I included a second open-ended question in the survey to capture the highlights of my work context: "If you are aware of any circumstances affecting Gordon's performance that were beyond his control while working in Ellsworth, briefly note them below." I provided two columns on the last half page of the survey, the first labeled "Circumstance," the second "Effects on Gordon." Twenty-five staff responded. In contrast to the generally glowing evaluations made on the preceding open-ended item, these comments tended to describe factors that constrained my performance and pointed to the failures in my principalship. With one exception, those who responded perceived the general environment in which I worked as a difficult one.

The administration of the school system was noted as a significant factor by ten staff (the largest single set of comments). While one person viewed the relationship of principal to superintendent/school board as "naturally political," most respondents characterized these effects much more strongly. For them, the primary consideration in thinking about circumstantial dynamics was that the administration was "antagonistic," "conservative," "adversarial to faculty," and generally "not held in high esteem." The superintendent was described as one who used "power plays" and who "sought to elevate his own ego and public image"; one teacher called him "oppressive."

The staff who made these comments described the effects of this condition on me in a variety of ways. One teacher thought it created a situation in which I was conflicted, echoing several others who noted my "frustration" with it:

Circumstance: Hostile relationship between faculty and superintendent/school board

Effects on Gordon: He had to either walk a middle road or choose sides. Unfortunately, he made the wrong choice. A faculty that is supported and encouraged by its principal will do the same in the classroom. I'm not sure if he actually *sided* with the superintendent, but his hands were never dirtied in the murky waters of conflict.

Others noted, in a similar vein, that the character of the "top administration [failed to] lend positive enthusiasm to many positive ideas which Gordon tried to implement." Several saw my association with the administration as the kiss of death, viewing the administration's low esteem as "rubbing off on him" and leading to an overly "cautious" attitude on my part. At least one staff member saw the incompatibility between me and "higher management" this way: "His intelligence was so far above the local management it was hard for him to achieve his goals for himself, the school and the community."

A second group of responses focused on the community and the general conditions one might find in a rural area. Those who identified such circumstances tended to play on the "conservatism" and "small town" nature of the people. One described our circumstances this way: "Provinciality of the community, typically downeast, Maine; small, not visionary or educationally oriented or quickly receptive to changes in direction or point of view." Another was blunter:

I do know that Gordon had to work within a situation that had more than its share of individual personal vendetta/prejudices. . . . Real small town, back-biting. . . . A lot of this kind of crap got directed toward Gordon, not because of what he did but in a lot of ways because of who he is—Harvard educated, sophisticated, a bit distant, not one of the boys, etc.

The effects on me noted by staff tend to follow the flow of this last comment. Like the drag on my work some felt the administration caused, the "provinciality" of the area

slowed down the progress that Gordon's potential leadership could accomplish in raising the level of instruction and educational achievement. Many teachers reflected that provinciality and thus retarded progress available to Ellsworth's schools through Gordon's leadership ability and training. Gordon must often have been discouraged. . . .

Lending voice to this general view of the "hog-tied Gordon" was a third group of comments that centered on the staff of the schools. Five respondents remarked on the "entrenchment" of teachers or singled out specific teachers or groups who resisted my efforts. One teacher saw these teachers as "firmly entrenched high school heroes." Another saw blockages caused by a "lack of strong department heads in certain areas" and "weak departments" in others. Yet another perceived "certain senior staff members undermining most of Gordon's work at EHS." A fourth saw "local teachers with reputations from past accomplishments (political alliances that were entrenched)" as the cause of troubles for me. This staff group was also viewed as "a small group of malcontent teachers who would not accept *anyone* as their superior [causing] a bit of an undercurrent in the staff. They did it before Gordon and they carry on now that he is gone."

Most staff who wrote about this faculty factor predictably saw it as a source of frustration and professional sabotage. One teacher noted that "[firmly entrenched high school heroes] stabbed him in the back in public affairs. [They] tried to thwart the class programs of Gordon's they had agreed to implement." Another noted that these circumstances "frustrated" me, while a third presented these effects as inhibitors to my "innovative" programs and leadership: "[They made it] difficult to create a cooperative teaching staff. . . . Some departments had only one strong individual, others didn't even have that, therefore innovative curriculum changes were almost non-existent because certain staff members refused to cooperate." One teacher, in a more optimistic vein, felt that faculty opposition had "slight" impact on me "as was justified."

A fourth series of remarks described the nature of my job as an important factor in my performance. Most of these referred to the vagueness of the position I held in the last three years (the one most recent in respondents' memories). As one put it, I had "too many students . . . and too many teachers and too many grades 7–12 . . . to be responsible for. Summing up, [he had] too many hats to wear." Two others noted that I worked in a situation where there was "no clear chain-of-command" and that, with "two principals" at the high school, "the faculty was unsure of just who to talk to about what." As might be expected, this condition created ambiguity both for me and for staff. Without a clear position and a clear role, my abilities to direct and influence were seriously curtailed. One staff member described these effects simply by writing, "He never knew who he was or what he was supposed to be doing."

Two staff, however, saw a different side to the situation. One noted that my position as supervising principal "gave him authority to be where he wanted and to do special things that got other teachers upset." Although I am interpolating, this remark implies a sort of administrator-with-portfolio status that allowed me to apply pressure where and when I wanted (as well as, I assume, give support in the same fashion). Interestingly, these were the only comments that described circumstances advantageous to me and my performance.

A final set of circumstances dealt with who I was. Although rarest in number (four comments), these tended to see my background, personality, and style as important intervening factors in my performance. Two noted my "Harvard Ph.D.," one my youth, and one my "limited teaching experience" (despite the fact that it was longer than the median for the high school). In the most detailed description of this kind, one teacher wrote: "My overall impression of Gordon was at first one of misunderstanding. He has a habit of sometimes talking down or over people's heads. Later as I got to know him, that didn't bother me. I felt that he could *effectively* handle most problems that were thrown *at him*." Here is the suggestion that communication skills and perhaps personality infringed on my desire to reach clear understandings with staff about their and my functions. As one might expect, most writers saw these personal factors limiting my performance. My doctorate "put some teachers on the defensive immediately. Those people decided early on that they were going to do little to cooperate or make his job easier." My background caused "resentment by some long-term staff," so that I "had to talk to a stone wall that was unwilling to listen to new ideas. Therefore, many of his proposals were not given consideration by staff because they were from him." Youth and "limited" teaching undercut my "credibility," particularly with reference to my "classroom expertise."

A final note to these responses will serve to summarize them. I select it because it resonates most with my own recollection of my circumstances. One teacher began his or her comment by noting that I came to a district "already characterized by strong adversarial feelings between staff and administration." The teacher went on to say that the stresses of my position were not all the result of these feelings: "In constantly attempting to be scrupulously fair to everyone, he was occasionally very unfair to some members of staff who were receptive to *his goals*." This insightful remark captures precisely the conflict I felt in striving for a "just environment" for staff and students within a context that seemed to undermine trust. What I find most poignant is the observation that my "scrupulous fairness" actually *created* unfair conditions for those who were ready to follow my lead. In the following section of this book, I will discuss at length this conundrum, for I feel it is one of the most common for principals and for managers of all types.

What I learned from staff descriptions of the "circumstances" in which I worked was most enlightening. In concert with earlier comments, they helped me see how environmental factors shaped my success, both directly and indirectly as they affected staff and faculty beliefs in my capabilities as a leader. That most viewed me as constrained suggests a range of new explanations for why I did my job as I did it (these will be the topic of the following chapters). Viewed as firsthand evidence of participants' beliefs about their workplace, these comments also revealed a staff and faculty who saw the deck significantly stacked against them. To the extent that they saw me lacking the potential to offset higher administration or the rural mindset, for example, these staff had more or less reason to be optimistic about the system's—and their own—efficacy.

In the final analysis, I was viewed by most as a good person and committed professional who was only moderately successful because circumstances were beyond my control. This conclusion says a lot about me, but it implies a lot as well about those important faculty and staff who wanted our schools to improve. Most believed that I was successful at reaching a number of goals, but I was most successful at establishing a positive personal style and at obtaining my own personal advancement. Teachers and staff, however, needed more than that. The same environmental chemistries that muted my success muted theirs. As several staff pointed out, my tenure as principal would have been much more noteworthy had I handled the forces that wore away at *their own* effectiveness with students.

MAKING SOME SENSE OF OUR RELATIONSHIP

The reader no doubt feels as dazed by this whirlwind of perceptions as I did in my job. Not only did individual staff members hold differing views of me, but these views were sometimes expressed with great conviction. I have struggled to make sense of all these perspectives in order to reach some conclusions about my effectiveness as a principal. What constitutes a good working relationship between principal and teachers? Must it include mutual admiration and respect? Must it be free of anxiety? Does it need to be friendly? How do the principal's many relationships with faculty precipitate out to one leadership style or one faculty-principal relationship? In the ensuing pages, I share four lessons from my experience that have helped me begin to answer these questions.

The first lesson is that *individual relationships matter, but they are not enough* to establish a firm leader-follower relationship. I enjoyed high positive regard from most respondents when they evaluated my individual rapport with them on the LPCS and on other scales. Open-ended comments also reflected staffers' general appreciation of my interpersonal style with them individually. Their evaluation of my work with the faculty in general, however, was not so positive. Many noted the difficulties I had with other teachers and some commented on the negative pull on them all that resulted from these failures. I was viewed as a person with integrity and direction and I was respected for that. But when assessing my performance as a principal, these did not necessarily equate in staffers' minds to a strongly successful leadership rating. In the final analysis, it seems, teachers and other staff want their principal to work well with them individually but also well enough with everyone else that the staff group is not continually experiencing interpersonal stresses.

This is a tall order, perhaps especially tall in a high school. Certainly, my self-evaluation in earlier chapters documents the doubts and problems I experienced trying to lead the faculty as a group. In fact, I practically stopped trying, over the years moving more and more toward individual and small group contacts and away from faculty meetings and consensus building. As I reread faculty comments, I see that they recognized my loss of faith in them as a group. As I increasingly avoided attempting to shape them into a working group, they seemed increasingly to feel that the possibility of working as a unified team slipped further and further away. I now believe that a principal who loses faith in faculty as a team cannot be highly successful as a principal in the eyes of most faculty. He or she will have failed to sustain a belief essential to the teacherhood that the teachers in each school building constitute a professional society. The principal, as the formal leader, is first among equals in this professional society; he or she functions symbolically as keeper of the faith and instrumentally as unifier of the team. As I found, this requires considerable skill, optimism, and faith.

The second of my lessons is that *respect for the principal begins with respect for the person and respect for his or her professional integrity*. This conclusion may not be a startling one, but it nevertheless needs repeating among administrators. In a school the size of Ellsworth, respect does not follow from the accoutrements of the position: authority, organizational power, and access to information. Rather, it must be earned among the educators whom one leads. Indeed, traditional accoutrements actually hinder this process. My staff feedback highlighted two qualities that I believe were central to my ability to fashion this respect: My "fairness" and my "professional" commitment. "Being fair," I suspect, meant that I was able personally to accept each person I dealt with on his or her own merits and to avoid being influenced by others' preconceptions or biases. "Being professional" reflected my success at putting students, teaching, and the school's interests above my own or those of any pressure group.

Certainly, not every staff member believed that I was fair and professional all the time. But the vast majority from whom I heard seldom questioned my integrity in these regards and, as I see it, this provided the important groundwork on which we could establish mutual respect. Oddly, some equated my professional commitment with "idealism" and even with "naivete" while others expressed frustration with my inability to "play politics" and "take sides" against negative influences (was this "fairness" taken to the extreme?). But most staff felt as I did that maintaining focus on the fundamental goals of the school rather than on political or intermediate goals exerted a steadying influence. To most, I suspect, the knowledge that I would give them a fair hearing was most important because it meant that I could freely advocate for programs and issues and develop my own professional plank without repressing them or their ideas. This goal orientation and interpersonal security were necessary to the development of teachers' faith in our professional relationship and, consequently, in me as a leader.

The third lesson is that *most principals will fail to develop positive relationships with some portion of their faculties, but this need not lead to failure as principal.* This was my hardest lesson because I wanted very much to succeed with everyone. Clearly, I did not. But this was not my greatest failing; what hurt my leadership most was my preoccupation with the recalcitrant group. Conflicts over procedure, disagreements over philosophy and programs, and fundamental incompatibilities in personality between principal and teacher cause strife and impede the important work of schools. Some of that is inevitable and some is necessary (especially where the principal has a strong mission and must work with staff he or she has not hired). We multiply the hazards of conflict, however, when we worry excessively over it and it affects our approach to *all* teachers and staff. As occurred to a degree in my case, small failures can create a downward spiral in which the principal gradually ceases to build positive relationships with the entire faculty and the group comes treacherously close to ceasing operation.

Interestingly, the faculty and staff comments convinced me of the inevitability of failed relationships in school leadership. Many staffers understood the constraints within which I worked: higher administration did not support positive staff relationships; the community did not value some of the broad educational goals I espoused; some staff colleagues were, plain and simple, unworthy of anyone's respect. In the view of many staff, it would have been a miracle if I had established a warm collective spirit among the whole staff and forged a consensual effort among them to move the institution along. So most teachers understood me and my work *in their collective context* and they were willing to give me credit for doing as well as I could given the circumstances. Nevertheless, the bulk of the staff wanted a leader who could keep them and the collective institution in which they worked moving forward and feeling positive *despite* these failed relationships. I sensed that they wanted me to seal off these dysfunctional appendages and to keep the group unified and professionally productive. If I had done this, my success would not have been limited to being well-intentioned and friendly, to handling people well, or to my ability to get the most out of limited opportunities. Teachers and staff—and I think community and students—would have more convincingly seen me as a principal who made the learning and growth of students and staff improve.

The fourth and final lesson is simple: *The principal who is successful at building staff relationships must be capable of addressing interpersonal concerns involving himself or herself.* In looking back at the evolution of my approach to staff, I now see that my tendency toward individual contacts and working mostly with "the willing" was not healthy for me or for the high school. I think I knew that at the time, but I was unable to do anything about it. I now believe that I needed skills and support that were missing. I needed to learn how to voice interpersonal concerns of my own and to encourage others to voice theirs. I needed encouragement to deal with the fallout that accompanies such activities. If I could have put my concerns about the dysfunction of our faculty group on the table, I believe the group itself could have acted to improve how it worked, how it felt about itself, and its general morale. Failure to help a working group confront its failures, I have concluded, constitutes an abrogation of leadership. Avoidance of the hard questions surrounding faculty teamwork suggests that the principal does not care about that teamwork, that he or she devalues the cooperative aspects of professional education.

I suspect that I needed more support and more skills than I had to pull this off with the faculty and staff at Ellsworth. Such skills involve sensitivity to group process, comfort with discussing feelings (particularly anger), and negotiating interpersonal working agreements. More importantly, I needed to know how to initiate direct discussion of team morale and shared responsibility *when I was myself one of the essential parties involved.* I have, as do many principals, extensive experience in negotiation, conflict management, and facilitating groups in which students, teachers, parents, and matters of curriculum and policy are at stake. But these skills become somewhat useless when I am part of the problem that the group is struggling to resolve, as was the case in my leadership at Ellsworth. Clearly, principals need better facilitation skills and a better support network to give them perspective on their relationships with faculty. They also need on some occasions outside assistance to help them and their staffs confront the tough but pervasive problems of functioning as responsible units in a very important field.

These four lessons leave me with quite a different perspective on the principal's relationship-building function than the one I began with. No longer do I expect the principal to be solely responsible for the success of his or her working relationship with staff and faculty. No longer do I expect relationships to be uniformly smooth and positive in all well-functioning schools. I now see the principal's task centering on doing the best with what he or she has. The principal has two major resources in this relationship-building work: him- or herself and the staff. Both resources have their special talents and capacities and both have their natural limitations. It is unlikely that any two schools will have similar-looking principal-staff relationships, yet they could both be maximally functioning schools.

Most importantly, I have come to understand the utter impossibility that the principal can shape the best relationship with his or her staff without some assistance. Clearly, such assistance can come from insiders—from teachers and staff who will provide feedback like that I received. But assistance from the outside has special value, as it is not muddied by participants' ideas and feelings. I had little opportunity to benefit from observations of the school, the staff, and my relationship (despite an occasional insightful discourse from the superintendent). Yet I believe trusted colleagues from other schools, the superintendent, and perceptive organizational consultants can provide such observations and the means to reflect on them. Just as any professional needs to gain perspective and distance on his or her work, principals who are surrounded by people with hope and expectations for them need periodic opportunities to understand how those hopes and expectations are shaping their beliefs about themselves and their actions. Ultimately, the productive faculty need to feel that their principal consciously nurtures their mutual relationship, not that he or she is consumed by it.

PART IV

THE IMPACTS OF PRINCIPALS: HOW DO THEY MAKE A DIFFERENCE?

As I have explored the secondary principalship through my own experience, I have constantly teetered between oversimplifying the realities of school leadership and burying the reader in detail and conflict. I chose to structure the exploration by function, starting with the principal's choice of activity patterns, moving to his or her understanding and deployment of people, and concluding with the establishment of relationships. These three functions have not been presented prescriptively, since I do not intend to instruct principals in "how to" lead. Rather, they are offered as an easily remembered guide to three aspects of principals' work that have major impacts on their success as school leaders.

Every principal has an activity pattern, just as every principal makes judgments about students, faculty, and community and establishes a relationship with staff. In illustrating what my activity patterns were, how I understood the people in the school, and established relationships with staff, I hoped to convince the reader of the need for all principals to monitor their functioning in these three important areas. One important question remains: what evidence do I have that principals can make the difference in schools that I claim they can? If a principal monitors his or her functioning in the ways I have illustrated, what makes me think he or she will be a better principal than if he or she does not? I have no evidence other than what I have learned firsthand from my experience; secondhand from other principals, teachers, and superintendents; and thirdhand from the writings of Gerald Grant, Roland Barth, Ann Lieberman, and Kenneth Leithwood. Indeed, this accumulating wisdom is substantial and it has gradually nursed into life a new understanding of principals' impacts in and on their schools. It is to this understanding that I devote the remaining chapters of this book.

We labor under some misconceptions about principals' effects and it will be my contention that these misconceptions seriously impair principals' self-concepts and their success. The most egregious of these is that principals largely operate as agents of a bureaucratic hierarchy. In this view, we can expect principals to "cause" the production of learning through structuring learning situations, scheduling, supervising and evaluating teachers, and directly influencing students. Principals, by virtue of their position, training, and proximity to the central office and school board, are seen as essential middle managers in an organization designed to assure that students learn and prepare for work and citizenship. A second misconception, arising from the instructional leadership movement, is that principals can have many of these same impacts on student learning if they simply reduce their bureaucratic managerial activities and become "teachers of teachers." By paying greater attention to curriculum, to student assessment and placement, and to matching instructional strategies to student needs, the principal can boost the entire school to a new level of pedagogical performance—causing achievement scores and teacher satisfaction to rise and everyone to be pleased.

These two misconceptions share the common belief that the principal occupies a singularly pivotal role in the school's performance. I do not disagree that principals play a central role in the creation of good schools. I contend, however, that the principal's effects are *never* single-handed; we can never credit the principal alone with causing educational gains. As we view the principal's role in schooling, we must not be misled into thinking that a good principal can "turn that school around" or that "education has gone to hell at that school since the principal left." Instead, we must encourage everyone—school boards, superintendents, parents, students, and most of all teachers and principals—to understand the principal's effects *interactively*. The principal does not act in a static environment, but in a constantly changing envelope of motives, moods, interests, human capabilities, and events. As Sergiovanni puts it, school leadership operates more like the surfer choosing a wave to ride than it does like the pitcher controlling the pace and direction of a baseball game (Sergiovanni and Moore, 1989).

Chapter 10

Taking Activities, Partners, and Relationships from Intention to Impact

> Those who lionize leadership miss important behind-the-scenes aspects of day-to-day leadership. They depict the grand designs without the niggling problems. They assume that leadership is the exclusive preserve of the heroic boss.
>
> (Murphy, 1988, p. 655)

Principals often embody the hopes, dreams, and purposes of the people they work for and with. What the school board, the central office, the parents, the teachers, and the students want for their school they expect and hope the principal can deliver. Riding on the principal's shoulders is an expectation that what he or she intends to have happen will happen. For those around the principal, making what *they* want to happen then becomes a matter of getting the principal to agree, endorse, and execute. The principalship is the receptacle for many, many intentions.

But, as my case has amply illustrated, the world of schools is vastly more complex than many think. This chapter draws some lessons from the preceding parts of the book about the principal's capacity to have clear impacts on a school. The issue of one's ability to take an intention (yours, mine, or anyone's) and realize it in action is a central issue of my principalship and a central issue underlying school improvement efforts. I conclude that it is indeed possible for principals to lead—that is, to help a school realize its good intentions. Such leadership, for most of us, however, will not and should not resemble the models of "heroic" leaders that so imbue Western culture.

In brief, my approach in this chapter is to revisit the three major functions of the principal's leadership: (1) committing time, energy, and attention to *activities* that advance most the purposes of the school; (2) identifying and involving capable *people* in such essential activities and providing for their success; (3) understanding and developing *relationships* with them that maximize everyone's success. I draw lessons from my experience and reading about each of these three functions that encapsulate the essential aspects of the principal's leadership. I hope to illustrate how the Functional Approach can help principals to understand and improve their own leadership and others to analyze and plan school improvement initiatives.

THE PRINCIPAL'S ACTIVITIES MUST SERVE THE SCHOOL'S PURPOSES

Principals are inundated with activity. Part I of this book has cataloged the many people, questions, procedures, events, and agendas that swirled around me as I was in charge of the school. I often felt swamped by these activities, not merely because they were so numerous and relentless but because I found many of them compelling business for me. Each request, each complaint, each celebration had people attached to it who were clients of my school. As one who views education as a service profession, my impulse was to respond to each activity by involving myself and, to a degree, being in charge of what happened as it played out.

Many leaders drown in the maelstrom they invite when they cannot resist this "I'm essential" syndrome. As my profile of activities demonstrated, I could not be all places at all times or all things to all people. The trick was to learn to select which activities required direct involvement and how to remove myself respectfully from the many others I could not or should not have a direct hand in. Some view this problem as a matter of time management, but that is only the manifestation of the real issue: discerning which opportunities for action hold the most promise for making significant impacts on the intellectual, social, and moral development of students. Out of my self-reflection have emerged three lessons in this regard.

Persist in Activities Central to Children's Learning

The principal's influence over a school and community is as much symbolic as it is direct. To the staff I worked with, it was the issues they saw and heard me articulate and where they saw me "doing my business" that created the most powerful image for them of what I stood for. They recalled most often having contact with me in the halls and on the fly and from this many deduced that managerial and procedural goals were very important to me. I dealt with them over student placement and raised curricular questions in faculty meetings and department meetings; so, many teachers believed that professional and academic goals were foremost for me. They saw, heard, and interacted with me about particular kinds of school issues—organizational procedures, student behavior, curriculum, and teaching—and these set the priorities for my tenure as principal. Despite the fact that these priorities did not agree totally with my own, my activities conveyed my real priorities.

Managing my work activity so that instructional priorities stayed uppermost was a constant challenge. My divergent activities, harried looks, and forgetful manner no doubt evidenced to some a diffusion of focus and, to others, a confusion of purposes. In fact, my approach to faculty was not wholly coherent: I was good at verbalizing appropriate instructional and curricular ideas but, when it came to putting them into action, I sometimes felt unsure, hesitant, and awkward about the best interpersonal approach to take with my bumptious staff. This has only strengthened my belief in the importance of holding some clear, fundamental convictions about how learning should take place and of making those transparent to teachers, staff, students, and community. Most importantly, this clarity of conviction needs not only to be in the principal's head, but in the principal's activities, for that is the medium that communicates most strongly what the principal values.

For high school principals, attaining this clarity of mission is especially important because the functions of secondary schools are so diverse. High schools in the United States are beset with conflicting agendas, ranging from academics to athletics, from social integration to vocational training, from survival to restructuring. The high school principal is inevitably drawn to those activities that are most public: athletics and discipline. Indeed, the principal must have some role in these; but to apparently overcommit his or her time and energies to them often leads both the principal and the school into a downward spiral academically. So the challenge is to develop ways of regularly attending to questions of curriculum, of pedagogy, of scheduling, and of student assessment and progress and, most importantly, to do so in a fashion that publicly demonstrates the principal's interest, involvement, and capabilities. Persisting in such activity will assure the school's and the community's focus on student learning as well as on social and physical development.

Make Activities Public and Make Them Positive

A number of researchers have noted that the successful principal is the visible principal (Blumberg and Greenfield, 1980; Persell and Cookson, 1982). I concur, but with a caveat: visibility alone will not make the leader of a strong school. Two conditions must apply. First, as noted above, the principal's priorities must clearly endorse the educational purposes of the school as opposed to only its social or community functions. Second, the principal's public presentation must be positive in tone; it must convey to others the principal's belief that the school is a healthy place for all its students and yet that it can improve.

I mean by "public" the corridors, classrooms, and meeting rooms of the school as well as the usual forums outside the school. In the later years of my tenure in Ellsworth, I found myself working a lot in committees and through consultation with individual teachers. I was shocked to discover that recently hired staff in those years had very little idea of what I did or stood for. Veteran teachers whom I knew well also began to complain about an absence of leadership. Yet here I was in *more* meetings than ever and more heavily involved in academic issues than ever. My problem was that I had allowed my activity—not so much myself—to slip from view and staff were losing the benchmark for the school's value system and direction that I had provided, however ambiguously, before. Faculty and staff, at least in schools the size of the three in Ellsworth, need to hear, see, and feel the principal's optimism and energy directly.

Making one's work public and ensuring that it carries a positive, optimistic tone are very difficult tasks. Many of us, myself included, are not inclined to be public figures, even within our schools. Or we do not feel secure enough about what we believe and think to go public with plans and ideas. Faculty divisions, administration-faculty conflicts, and local politics sometimes make public leadership a hazardous activity, constantly open to carping from one corner or another. If my experience was indicative of others', principals must not be deterred by such influences. They must grow comfortable with the skills and postures inherent in being public figures and rally the important supports for themselves to maintain optimism.

Use Activities to Demonstrate a Sound Value System

Teachers, students, and parents watch principals as much to learn how they will treat them as to understand what principals stand for. Most staff I worked with valued my even-handedness, my commitment to fair treatment, and my faith in the goodness of kids even while some disagreed with me and questioned my leadership. I tried always to make my conversations and my decisions about students and staff demonstrate my respect for them as individuals. Given the tremendous amount of my time that was devoted to face-to-face interactions, the opportunity for me to convey the fundamental personal values so important to a school was ever-present. As I concluded in Part III, this relational aspect of my work was extremely important to staff and faculty. My success at the most basic level hung more on the ways I treated students, staff, and parents than on any curriculum, teaching, or organizational ideas.

Principals' behaviors are more potent than their ideas. Their treatment of students and staff establishes their ethical virtue and the trustworthiness of leadership for the school. The school leader handles discipline and meets parents and evaluates teachers. But as he or she conducts these activities, he or she sends verbal and nonverbal messages to students, parents, and teachers about their value, their role in educational decisions, and their capacity to grow and learn. The principal's activities have a norm-setting power that can establish the school as a place that respects people, their views, and their aspirations regardless of how unorthodox or ill-informed those activities may be.

Events continually tested my belief in the goodness of people. Some kids were outright disrespectful of me and others. A few faculty showed disdain for me, for other administrators, and for each other. Some even gave up on certain students early in the year. On occasion, dealing with some of these people and with others, I lost patience, said things I later regretted, and behaved in ways I regarded as unprofessional. The job can do that to the most positive of people, I would guess. But that does not excuse such lapses, nor does it make it possible to recover from them (and staff comments about my leadership demonstrate that I did not). Principals need some supportive means to help keep the keel of their value systems even, for it steadies the interpersonal world and ethical mission of the entire school.

THE PRINCIPAL MUST ATTRACT AND SUPPORT CAPABLE PEOPLE

The best solution to the problem of the overburdened principal is to find and support good partners. This lesson took me at least five years to learn. Beginning as I did as a raw recruit with no history at Ellsworth High School, my tendency was to try to provide all the leadership and the follow-through in all areas of the school's mission myself. This was not only foolhardy but it inhibited the development of a professional climate of responsibility and efficacy.

Leadership in a high school *is* dispersed. Teachers, students, and parents have vast influence over the outcomes of schooling and their leadership must be harnessed and coordinated. So, too, counselors, specialists, secretaries, coaches, and janitors significantly determine the quality of student and adult life. To bring intentions into practice, the principal constantly confronts the task of forming these people into teams with coherent visions and plans for making them work. This task is never accomplished, as new needs continually arise and new staff are always coming on board to help with new and old needs. Three lessons were valuable to me as I worked to improve at this task.

Understand Staff as Partners, Not as Vehicles or Instruments

When I started out in Ellsworth, I had high ambitions for the school. A good part of me believed that I was going to succeed because I could direct, cajole, and manipulate staff to work within my design to accomplish these ambitions. After a few months, I discovered that teachers, secretaries, janitors, and others were unlikely to change their behaviors and attitudes just because I presented a compelling argument or issued a memo. A vast and mysterious territory of motives—from philosophical conviction to interpersonal fear to union membership—stood in my way. The greatest frustration and source of stress in my principalship was my inability to understand why I could not make the faculty a cohesive unit to execute practices that fit my vision of an improved Ellsworth High.

I think, now, that an important flaw in my approach was the belief that staff were vehicles and instruments for my design rather than partners in designing. The staff questionnaires have convinced me that leadership is a reciprocal process: faculty who saw me as a partner to their efforts were the very teachers whom I viewed as my partners; conversely, those teachers I was unable to see as partners undoubtedly reciprocated. Those faculty who constantly resisted me were faculty whom I believed needed changing. The harder I tried to pressure, cajole, and confine them to my vision of their work, the less they viewed me as their leader. In the end, they were responsible for my feeling that I had failed to bring together a faculty in a manner I feel is essential for making major school improvement.

Clearly, the principal cannot dictate who his or her staff is. Inevitably some will not merit full partnership status because they lack basic competencies, interpersonal skills, and appropriate values. Edwin Bridges (1986) has estimated that between 5 and 15% of schoolteachers in the United States might fall into this category. Further, events in a school year and the dynamics of union-management relationships will lead others to behave in ways that may not endear them to the principal. I contend, however, that these facts do not justify the principal's adoption of an instrumental attitude toward faculty for, once that attitude emanates from the leader, all staff have reason to doubt the leader's motives toward and respect for them. Professional organizations such as schools whose purpose is to respect and nurture children can ill-afford to have workers who do not feel respected and nurtured themselves. This requires the principal to prepare a philosophically sound approach to staff and faculty that respects their integrity, intelligence, good intentions, and will to improve. Only when facts demonstrate that this good faith has been ill-placed in one individual may the principal take another approach, and then only toward that individual.

Hire the Best, Accept the Rest (at least at first)

The new principal must work with the staff he or she inherits. Staff must be approached with the good faith assumption that they are all capable and committed. Clearly, to do anything from the outset but accept them in this manner would be to flirt with immediate disaster. I have learned, however, that such acceptance cannot be blind. The principal must actively work to know his or her staff, their pleasures and gripes, their attitudes, their capacities, and their aspirations for the school. Far from sitting back and assuming everyone is doing a bang-up job, the principal must be interviewing, discussing, observing, and providing consultative feedback in order to learn how the team of his or her partners functions.

I did not take the time to do this early in my tenure at Ellsworth, but as I began observing teachers' classrooms and attending department meetings I quickly began developing an objective basis for understanding my partners. This process took years and never really ended. The generally high regard that staff held for me professionally, I believe, resulted from my efforts to know what they did and to open discussion about how well they were doing (despite the fact that this was a frightful experience for most of us at the start). I bear some scars from having to impel myself into the private life of the teachers; for some teachers, this invasion was the proof that I was too pushy and interested in my own agenda to be their leader. But I can see no good rationale for not becoming as thoroughly acquainted as possible with these key people and especially with their professional problems and successes.

I found that the best means of developing a team of partners, other than working hard to know staff who were there, was to hire aggressively. Over my seven years at Ellsworth, I had a hand in hiring 25 teachers, counselors, and auxiliary staff. By exercising my hand in the recruitment, interviewing, selection, and induction of new staff, I found I could not only bring on people with an interest in being active partners but start them out in a more open, co-equal relationship with me. I also learned how difficult it was to hire proven teachers but, on the other hand, how easy it was to attract teachers with an interest in taking part in school decisions and working hard. I did not always hire "winners," as Ken Blanchard would put it, but I could usually hire people who wanted to win and thus who could develop the skills to be winners in most cases.

Foster Continuing Examination of Practice

High schools offer many subjects, cultivate dreams for many futures, and respond to the varied melange of personalities, temperaments, and social divisions typical of adolescents. For this reason, high schools must employ a variety of staff. That variety must not simply be academic, it must as well be in pedagogical styles, personality types, cocurricular interests, and personal backgrounds. A central purpose of the principal should be to foster this diversity so that students, as they meander their ways along increasingly separate paths, have compatible, sympathetic, flexible adults to accompany them.

I made the mistake early of believing that teachers should conform to a single pedagogical style, that a single set of interests were desirable in a teacher, and even that certain personality types were effective while others were not. Thanks to some brave teachers at Ellsworth, my fairly narrow conception of the "good teacher" broadened and I came to see the desirability of a greater variety of styles, personalities, and curricular subjects. In the place of this original narrow standard for teaching performance, I developed another. Instead of centering on one or two "ideal" classroom performance types, my new standard grew around the conviction that all teachers should be self-critical; they should be willing and able to seek constant improvement in their teaching and their handling of children. As long as a teacher can demonstrate in student growth the merits of his or her practice and as long as a teacher remains open to continuous examination of practice, the particular style or approach he or she uses is of little concern.

This discovery took me out of a supervisory mode in which I felt I had to correct misguided pedagogical and student management practices (a posture that conveyed the impression that I knew it all and that, again, teachers were vehicles and instruments). Moreover, it permitted me to approach teachers more as coach-critic. My function grew to that of observer, reflector-on-practice, and, in the best relationships, co-discussant on issues of professional improvement. These are the activities that Roland Barth (1990), Ann Lieberman (1988a), and Judith Warren-Little (1985) have described as the elements of the community of learners that schools can become. Although my relationship did not mature with all faculty and staff to permit such open discourse and to support such diversity, where it did it was most fulfilling for me and for the staff member. We made only small inroads on creating an ethos in which teachers might begin to do this with one another.

The principal's "people" function must include fostering this kind of professional self-examination if the staff and school are to improve in all ways. This requires hiring teachers with a self-confident disposition toward reflection but it also requires the principal personally to take part in mutual feedback with teachers. In a word, the principal must be prepared to model self-growth practices as well as to lead and reward them in others. The longer I was in Ellsworth, the better I became at these activities with many teachers. I believe this challenge-and-support approach led many staff both to respect my professional integrity and to welcome, in most cases, my supervisory and curricular conferences and meetings.

THE PRINCIPAL MUST DEVELOP CONSTRUCTIVE RELATIONSHIPS WITH STAFF

As I have read and reread the preceding chapters, the pervasiveness of my concern with staff relationships has impressed me. Stories of incidents from Ellsworth end in explanations of my interplay with one or two teachers. Characterizations of periods in my principalship revolve around descriptions of my relationships with teachers (my "committee period," for example). My recollections of how I felt on the job and about the job seem largely to hinge on incidents with specific teachers, administrators, or support staff in which the interpersonal fallout was most noteworthy. This has led me to wonder if I was overly sensitive to this relationship dimension of the job—and even to wonder if that made me unsuitable for the high school principalship. Perhaps only thick-skinned people make successful high school principals.

But I have concluded otherwise. With a growing number of writers about the principalship, I now believe that focusing on principals' relationship-building capabilities is one of the keys to high school improvement. Despite the volumes written on the relational aspects of leadership, we know desperately little about the unique characteristics of relationship-building between principals and their staffs, particularly in high schools. Four lessons of my experience may seed our future knowledge in this respect.

Approach Every Staff Member Believing He or She Can Do the Job

If the principal holds the beliefs about people summarized in the previous section, he or she will have faith in staff. Demonstrating this faith so that the staff member finds it credible in a fast-moving, compartmentalized high school, however, is an extraordinarily difficult task. The fragmentation of activity and time, the separation of faculty into departmental fiefdoms, the sheer size of high school faculties, and the presence of unions can erode both the principal's faith in staff and the opportunity to demonstrate that faith. I came to the job in Ellsworth with a strong belief that competent, creative teachers are the linchpin of the high-performing high school. I encountered, however, a steady stream of incidents and information that raised questions about specific Ellsworth faculty members. One did not show up for work, another seldom took attendance, another spoke of students in a degrading manner, and others showed little interest in formalizing their curriculum—the list goes on and on. Further, other administrators, parents, counselors, and even board members as much as told me to watch out for so-and-so. Many people and many events conspired to make me see my faith in teachers as naive and premature.

I learned, however, the exceptional importance of giving each teacher, counselor, secretary, and janitor the chance to prove that my faith in them and their abilities was warranted. In some of the cases where I was encouraged to be guarded with a staff member, my faith did in fact prove ill-placed; but in some others it did not and a constructive (though not always smooth) relationship developed. When I came to doubt a teacher's worth to the school, I know he or she soon felt that doubt and a hesitancy and wariness colored our relationships. My observations of the teacher and interchanges with him or her, in turn, tended to confirm my doubts and the relationship began a self-reinforcing, downwardly spiralling path. If I had lost faith in every teacher who made a mistake, with whom I disagreed, or about whom somebody complained, I would have found myself in a deep collective spiral from the start.

Separate the Relationship from the Evaluation of Performance

Some will read the above paragraphs and conclude that I believe principals should have blind faith in their staffs and that staffs, consequently, will run wild, with no "quality control." As a principal, I was constantly concerned with this bifurcation of trust and accountability: to monitor and evaluate staff implies distrust, does it not? I have learned, however, that the principal can build a healthy professional relationship with a staff member while simultaneously fully performing the evaluation and feedback functions of the supervisor. I would even venture that the strongest professional relationships between principal and teacher grow *because* the principal is serious about and competent at evaluation and feedback.

The strength of the professional relationship between the principal and a staff member cannot be measured by how positively or negatively the principal rates the staff member's performance. To give feedback on weaknesses in performance does not consign the relationship to failure. Conversely, strong professional relationships are not built by giving staff members unequivocally positive feedback. The principal must understand that the professional relationship hinges on the credoes of the previous section of this chapter: faith in children's and staff's abilities to learn and improve; a belief that teachers, coaches, and staff of all types hold the key to the school's performance; a belief that scrutiny of practice is important to teachers', staff's, and administrators' improvement. The ability to separate the person from the performance permits the principal and the staff member to retain and nurture these fundamental faiths while at the same time working on specific acts, behaviors, and skills that will improve performance.

My most fulfilling moments with staff were those when we could join in critical discussion about our work, have that discussion lead to plans for improvement and growth, and feel that a spirit of trust and mutual ambition undergirded the interchange. The important conditions for such discussions were two: the relationship between us was trusting and collaborative; and the information about our performance was accurate (whether positive or negative). In these situations, both parties took as premises that we each had the best interests of the school at heart and that each was willing to improve. From there, we could mutually collect and use evidence of our strengths and our flaws to build goals and a plan for improvement on individual, group, and institutional levels. In these cases, I believe we managed to separate the assurance of our worth as people and professionals from the specific data of our particular acts and contributions. Significantly, when this relationship developed, I felt as comfortable receiving feedback on my performance as I did giving it.

Clearly, I did not attain this understanding or such open relationships with all staff. In fact, my need to address problems in the practice of some staff did not permit the trust and assurance of worth to develop. Before it could, I came across as the boss telling the staffer that he or she was not working to expectations; behind my advances was an implied threat: improve or I will terminate employment. With some staff, too, it was not so much my feedback on performance that stunted the relationship as it was a basic incompatibility of personality, background, or professional orientation. Herein lies the third lesson.

The Principal's Relationships Will Not Be Uniform

I made the mistake early in my tenure of thinking that a measure of my success would be the extent to which I had strong, positive relationships with all staff. I would have faith in them, they would have faith in me; I would like working with them, they would like working with me; we would be one happy family, working toward common ends. I learned that this vision of the successful principal, as pleasing as it might be, is unrealistic. Teachers, counselors, coaches, secretaries, janitors, and other staff come in too many stripes for one person to ever form uniformly strong working relationships with them all. Add to this the busy nonroutines of a high school and it becomes clear that the principal has neither the time nor the occasion to build and maintain such relationships with such a wide variety of people.

A minimal relationship, however, must be established with each staffer. That relationship must carry enough mutual understanding that frank, accurate communication about the important business of the school can take place. This basic communicative relationship looked different and worked differently with each staff member but it existed with almost everyone. Most importantly, this relationship was not formed on the basis of personal likes or dislikes or interpersonal compatibilities. I tried to keep open channels with all staff *despite the fact* that in some cases we did not like or perhaps even respect one another. I was civil and pleasant with everyone and made a point of making contact frequently. I insisted that we keep talking with one another, if only about nonprofessional matters. Although this required extraordinary effort with some staff, to cease direct, personal communication would have consigned some teachers to professional Siberia—at full pay. Worse, failure to insist on a minimal professional relationship would signal that I had given up believing that the faculty needed to work as an integrated unit.

Strong Working Relationships Don't Happen; They Evolve

My final lesson is the most powerful one. I started in Ellsworth by attending to managerial tasks; I was going to set the school on a steady, efficient course and *then* attend to the interpersonal climate, the curriculum, and the professional ethos. When I got around to these apparently less urgent agendas, I discovered that I had already established myself as a businesslike manager, much in the mold of the traditional high school administrator. I had already sown the seeds of a typically bureaucratic ethos. The task that lay ahead of me was not just showing that I had a mellower and more collaborative side but actually *undoing* the traditional principal-teacher relationships that I had unwittingly built.

I learned to see our "getting along with one another" as a long-term, evolutionary process. Incidents in the early days, such as confronting student misbehavior in the cafeteria, running interference for students with teachers, or docking a teacher's pay set up my image in the minds of staff. It was not until years later that I understood how these acts led to discussions among teachers about me that in turn disposed them in certain ways toward me in our interactions. I discovered that as long as I dealt with the faculty as a whole group on important issues, I was likely to reinforce certain aspects of my personality that inhibited the development of positive relationships with some faculty. Conversely, the more individual and small group contact I had with some faculty, the greater were our chances to see strengths in each other, to develop a common core of values and goals, and to confirm our relationship through working together productively on a problem. In the final analysis, forming healthy working relationships hinged on my perceiving the differing interpersonal modes in which staff preferred to form relationships and my understanding how time and personal contacts created conditions in which those relationships evolved.

I have characterized my tenure by the phases of interpersonal mode through which I approached staff: I began dealing with them often as a whole faculty, then moved to more departmental and ad hoc groups to accomplish our ends, and finally found myself working most often with individual faculty. Each of these played an important role in determining my final effectiveness as a principal. One of my greatest mistakes was not realizing the need to be working in all three modes continuously. I too easily gave up calling meetings of the whole faculty and some formal committees, such as the department chair group, and took the path of least resistance, working increasingly with the willing staff and writing off the unwilling and unable. Instead, I should have realized the interplay of the three modes; better faculty meetings, for example, can be created through stronger individual relationships with faculty. One mode should not be pursued to the neglect of the others.

As time passes and patterns of contact with individual staff form, relationships evolve. This is a natural and inevitable evolution; it occurs whether we as leaders mean it to occur or not. If I neglected a teacher either willfully or because I was too heavily involved with others, it affected our relationship, it sent messages to that person about his or her importance to me, and it influenced his or her sense of purpose and significance to the school. Principals, whether they are loved or hated, respected or disdained, are part of a personal and professional tapestry of relationships that affects staff and the adult ethos of the school. Principals must understand this fundamental fact, must learn to interpret their behaviors and attitudes in light of it, and come to assess their effectiveness by frankly examining their staff relationships—whether they turned out as they intended or not. The feedback from my colleagues at Ellsworth opened my eyes to this fact in ways that my busy schedule, my need to explain faculty deviance, and my own self-doubts never permitted during my tenure.

A FINAL NOTE ABOUT THE PRINCIPAL'S INTENTIONS

I began this chapter questioning the conventional view of the high school principal as an executive with directive authority. The lessons I have explicated portray the principal's power as circuitous and indirect and the principal's effects as somewhat mysterious and indistinct. High school principals do not provide leadership the way generals direct military campaigns. They lead, instead, through a myriad of directives, conversations, public postures, and behind-the-scenes decisions. Above all, they lead in the important arenas of student life—curricular and cocurricular—through the leadership of those other adults in the school who deal constantly with students. For that reason, the relationships formed between principal and teachers, counselors, coaches, librarians, aides, secretaries, and all other adults are a medium vital to the principal's success and the school's performance.

These observations may make it appear that the principal's intentions for the school, for staff, and for his or her own activities are less significant than is commonly believed. If the principal's effects are not direct, one might argue, then must the principal have clearly formed ambitions at all? They will only be altered and even derailed by all those people and all those relationships. Obviously, principals must have intentions for themselves, their schools and students, and their staffs. But they must realize that only *some* of their acts and decisions will directly affect outcomes implicit in these intentions. For example, my work as a disciplinarian gave me the daily chance to shape individual student behavior and the climate of the school; similarly, making a ruling on the time of an athletic event gave me the chance to communicate my priorities for athletics and academics. But all too often my decisions and acts were either so short-term or so intertwined with faculty consultation and issues of compliance that they had no perceptible immediate effects. The net result, as Roland Barth has put it, is that I, as many principals do, continually felt that I had "more than enough responsibility but less than enough authority" (1979).

I believe that many high school principals discover this fact and retreat from having clear intentions for pedagogical and curricular performance, where the realization of those intentions is so hard to discern. Instead, they focus on two areas in which they can have some direct influence: cocurricular activities and student management. The worlds of sport, music, and drama offer principals concrete, public opportunities to put an undisputably good face on their schools. Even if they fail, the effort to support students in these activities will always be appreciated by their parents, the community, and the media. Similarly, student management provides an immediate arena of daily activity through which the principals can communicate their will. Few choose to question principals' rights to act autocratically in this arena and, as long as they succeed at it, they—and their superiors—can always be satisfied that they "made the school run quietly and smoothly." Unfortunately, this syndrome can drain the leadership, and eventually the life, from the academic program in a high school. In no small part, this may have created the conditions we now find in U.S. secondary education (Sizer, 1983).

Principals must feel that their intentions for their schools make a difference. In high schools with their large and complex programs, student bodies, and faculties, principals must develop conceptions of their purposes and powers that are vastly more sophisticated than the military or "great man" models. I suggest that high school principals' effects are most potent in two senses: figuratively and operationally. Beyond those rare occasions when the principal acts single-handedly and influences the behaviors of the school directly, his or her acts and the intentions behind them are diffused by teachers, students, time, distance, and hearsay. My case amply illustrates the fact that a principal's effects are a mixture of what he or she wants to have happen, many others' *interpretations* of those intentions, and the beliefs and opinions of those other people about the principal as a person.

Consequently, the principal's symbolic presence and activities, his or her opportunities figuratively to shape what others think their purposes and activities should be in school, have tremendous potential impact. Principals must be skilled at identifying and using public forums, collective decision-making processes, and crises to demonstrate their values and goals for the school. These are opportunities to put many people on the same wave length, to assert a common vision, and move everyone toward understanding their common mission. Bennis and Nanus (1985) describe this as directing the organization's "attention."

Complementing this figurative shaping of attention is the integration of broad intentions into daily interactions. Most teachers, students, and parents learn about the principal's intentions from the many seemingly insignificant daily contacts they have with him or her. Rather than viewing these as mindless and bothersome, the principal must understand these contacts as opportunities to demonstrate and practice his or her intentions, as occasions to make the philosophy and goals he or she stands for operational. Of utmost importance is that the principal's actions and words in everyday school business speak louder than the routine policy statements and pontifications for which high schools are infamous. These smaller and quieter decisions *show* people firsthand who the principal is and what he or she stands for. As my own case illustrates, this direct contact shapes and reshapes a relationship that establishes the character of the principal's leadership.

Dave Parker, a baseball player, once described his leadership of the Milwaukee Brewers by saying, "I just came here and tried to be me. Some people think that provides leadership." Many principals are inclined to feel just as lost as Parker at explaining and understanding their leadership largely because they cannot see their intentions being enacted. Rather than conclude that they have failed as leaders because their platforms have not been realized, they mystify the notion of leadership, seeing it as an effect of their personality or measuring it in terms of who is happy with them. In contrast, I argue that we must learn to understand the principal's effectiveness as a mix of intentional and unintentional effects. Principals must learn that their acts and decisions will have important value-setting and priority-defining powers, but that the people with whom they work and the students and families who ultimately must be affected by those acts and decisions will give them shape and purpose as well. For that reason, principals must learn to work through people, a complex task that revolves around their abilities to understand and form relationships with a wide variety of those people.

Chapter 11

Paradoxes of the Principalship

> When a man's vision of order, of a pure and painless life, has been defeated by a social world too complex to be disciplined, the man isn't defeated, only his belief in his own omnipotence is. . . . However, losing the feeling of being omnipotent is the birth of feeling personally strong in another way.
>
> (Sennett, 1970, p. 116)

School critics and reformers alike have heralded the principal as the new savior of the American school. The "effective schools" movement, stressing instructional leadership over management, has given the principalship newfound prominence as the keystone to student achievement (Brookover and Lezotte, 1979; Edmonds and Frederiksen, 1978). The principal literature has shifted its focus toward the instructional leadership model, accentuating teacher supervision and evaluation, curriculum planning and student assessment, and setting a strong mission and climate for learning (DeBevoise, 1984; Persell and Cookson, 1982). These initiatives, motivated as they are by good intentions, project the power to change schools onto the principal, raising expectations and, I believe, promoting the unreasonable notion that principals should single-handedly turn schools around.

My experience as a principal substantially belies this trend. I entered the principalship with high ambitions for affecting the academic, social, and moral education of children. I took steps to insert myself into the classroom business of the schools in Ellsworth. I did not, however, discover an overtly influential or immediately rewarding role for myself there, nor did

I see evidence, even over the long term, that my presence had an impact on students. Although I believe heartily in the precepts of instructional leadership, I did not find that providing such leadership came as simply as the effective schools formulae suggested.

The reasons for this might be several. The model of the instructional leader proposed from much of the "effectiveness" research has derived from research in elementary schools. We have made little effort to relate it to high schools where departmental fiefdoms, procedural calcification, and large enrollments present sharply different realities. Ellsworth High, furthermore, might be regarded as inhospitable to the role for a variety of reasons—from understaffing to politics to morale—touched upon by the staff in the open-ended survey items. The instructional leadership model, too, might be viewed as the pipe dream of professors and frustrated principals, a construction of the school leadership function that ignores the realities of unions, management, and the nitty-gritty of school-building supervision. Finally, however, I submit that the instructional leadership model suffers from the malady that has beset much administrative theory from its beginning sixty years ago: it was conceived in a relative vacuum of practice and became oversimplified as it was set forth in the literature.

Simple explanations and straightforward how-to models for the secondary principalship explain only a fraction of what I have experienced and what I see other principals experiencing. High schools do not respond any more cleanly to Management by Objectives, to Strategic Planning, or to management technologies than they do to instructional leadership. Each principal must take the nub of these good ideas and mold them to the character of his or her faculty and the flow of life in the school. My principalship and my continuing work with principals show the principalship to be dynamic, characterized by the ambiguities of many competing and often irrational forces. It is a role requiring the constant use of discretion, not formulae. Success hinges more on management of oneself and one's relationships than it does on management of bricks, budgets, and boys and girls.

In this chapter, I draw on both my direct experience in Ellsworth and my associations with principals in the Maine Principals' Academy to describe the principalship in a new way. (I will use anecdotal notes and written evaluations of the Academy since 1980 to illustrate points.) The conception of the principalship that emerges portrays the principal's work not in neat, methodical terms but as paradoxical. For each well-intentioned strategy principals devise to make their leadership effective, countervailing forces—many legitimate and wholesome in their own right—set up difficult choices. Obtaining the benefits of one strategy often involves sacrificing the benefits of an alternative strategy. Each new solution proposed by the principal is likely to do damage to some element of the status quo, alienating some person, placing stress on some resource, giving birth to an opposing rationale and strategy. This win-lose quality of school leadership makes the role complex, challenging, and often stressful. To succeed at it requires principals who are perceptive, conceptually adept, and interpersonally attuned.

Five major paradoxes shadowed my work as principal. They recur with pesky consistency for other Maine principals as well. For us all, the challenge presented by these double binds was to learn to acknowledge them and their nonrational qualities and to divert the conflicting energies they created toward beneficial ends.

THE HIGH EXPECTATIONS PARADOX: PROMOTE CLEAR, UNASSAILABLE GOALS FOR STUDENTS *BUT* BE RESPONSIVE TO THEIR NEEDS AND IDIOSYNCRACIES

The principal who is actively involved in instruction can proudly point to the ascending pedagogical priorities of the school (what the effective schools movement called "setting high expectations for achievement"). That principal, however, cannot raise learning standards and become engaged in the school's instructional problems without encountering the uncertainties and complexities of the classroom (Bacharach and Conley, 1989; Shulman, 1989). As I, like many of my peers, conducted more classroom observations, initiated more curriculum reviews, and became more involved with difficult-to-teach students, I admitted to my already uncertain and complex world a sea of new and even less manageable problems. We could raise standards easily on paper and in faculty meetings, but improving the learning of students—more of whom were now *below* the new high standards—was a Herculean task. Each student, each group we now had labels to identify, had idiosyncracies we could not adjust to; and each kid's ego was increasingly vulnerable to deflation as we upped the achievement ante. As we led the way into instructional improvement, we increasingly placed ourselves in a position to "put up or shut up," as one principal at the Academy put it. Another wondered, "How can I argue for better teaching, get into those classrooms more, and then not help teachers solve the tough questions they face there?"

Here is the rub. Many principals believe that "the strong leader" should solve the problems laid at his or her feet by staff, parent, or superior. The self-ascribed "instructional leaders" believe they must be experts on instruction; their success in their own eyes and especially in the eyes of their teachers to a large degree rides on their ability to aid teachers with their pedagogical challenges. Hence, the stakes are even higher for the principal than for the teacher: inheriting a problem from a teacher or creating one through instructional innovation, the principal must wrestle with age-old (and probably insoluble) learning conundrums in a very *public* arena. His or her competence as a problem-solver and pedagogical analyst is on display.

I and many of my colleagues found this dilemma especially vexing in our frequent dealings with "less able" students. Once called upon to handle behavior problems, we now were confronted with students who either could not or would not learn. What were we to do when presented with a student who could not or would not rise to meet those high expectations? What recourse did the principal have? All too often, we had no easy answers or instant resources. This High Expectations Paradox confronted us constantly, evoking the feeling of high-wire walking. With almost hourly frequency, we dealt with students and staff on issues involving student failure to adhere to expectations, rules, or goals and all too frequently it was the student's self-respect and sense of personal integrity that hung in the balance. When we set high ambitions for students, we automatically engaged ourselves in the risk of failure. Told that we were to develop a student climate in which students were to achieve *and* feel valued, we found ourselves serving as figureheads for a system of learning that threatened vicariously to dissemble students' self-respect.

For a number of us at the Academy during the 1980s, the High Expectations Paradox created a feeling of heightened vulnerability. Whether creating the master schedule in a high school, designing a new language arts curriculum, or doubling their time supervising teachers, these principals felt the pinch of those higher expectations. One middle school principal said:

How can I preach to my teachers one minute that we should be jacking up our goals for the kids and the next minute telling them that I can't help them with the fallout? I mean, if we do this [instructional leadership business] we've got to be ready to back up what we say. I'm not sure . . . I *know* I'm not ready to individualize our curriculum and grouping so that we can deliver.

Others noted that they could no longer apply policies to students so consistently if they had to begin considering individual differences. Although ready to seek ways to consider those differences, some principals (and I among them) were very concerned that doing so might bring down the wrath of some teachers who wanted them to be "consistent." Others were simply afraid that they could not find the time to give consideration to those differences.

Some principals, of course, do not feel the conflicts raised by the High Expectations Paradox. Some of my Academy colleagues thrived on their new charge to reset the goals and purposes of school. They were eager to learn goal-setting techniques and to borrow new instructional programs to implement. But they did not consider it their responsibility to share in the difficult pedagogical problem-solving of their teachers. That remained the teachers' territory; that was what they were hired for. I imagine that the teachers in these principals' schools neither felt supported in their efforts to change nor believed that their principals would follow through on their exhortations to higher performance. In the typically departmentalized high school led by the managerially focused principal, simply setting higher expectations cannot succeed in raising student achievement. To the contrary, it is most likely to lower teachers' feelings of efficacy and, ultimately, their confidence in their principal.

THE ACCOUNTABILITY PARADOX: SET AND USE HIGH PROFESSIONAL STANDARDS FOR FACULTY *BUT* CREATE STRONG MORALE AND TEACHER PARTICIPATION

The Accountability Paradox may be seen as the staff corrollary of the High Expectations Paradox. It pits concerns for quality performance against concerns for the interpersonal and emotional climate among professional employees. At the root of this Accountability Paradox are two premises, both of which were very real for me and many Academy participants. First, most of us who aspired to instructional leadership believed that as professionals we and our teachers could—and should—constantly improve our performance. Of our practices, our personnel, and ourselves, we routinely asked, "How could we do this better?" We assumed that we were not performing all functions as well as we could, much less should.

The second premise was that we principals knew about some practices and staff in our schools that should be removed. Some programs were minimally effective; some staff were deadwood. Yet our evaluation procedures and our political positions were not good enough to document these conditions and forthwith to remove them. Through the 1980s, mounting criticism of teachers only exacerbated these conditions: the more the public called for improvement, the more we Maine principals felt the need to identify practices and people in our schools that needed to change—or to be removed.

Against this growing clamor for accountability, reinforced as it was by our own internal standards and evaluations of weak practices, stood the paradoxical call for "positive faculty morale and climate." As one Maine elementary principal said, "They want us to fire the lousy teachers on the spot but not have it destroy the 'warm fuzzy feeling' we're supposed to create [among the faculty and staff]. . . . Good luck!" Pressures for the principal to lead faculty in an open, supportive, and participative manner have grown in professional literature, the workshop circuit, and graduate coursework. But many Maine principals find it extraordinarily difficult to approach this style of leadership while raising performance standards for all teachers *and* pressuring marginal teachers to improve or resign. On one hand, we hear that we should involve teachers in significant decisions, supervise "for professional growth," and nurture the faculty to build cooperatively a productive climate. On the other, we hear (in the words of one principal) "that we should be leaning all over [the teachers] like a drill sergeant, making them shape up or ship out."

The Accountability Paradox came home to me and my Maine colleagues in a number of circumstances. We saw in the course of our daily rounds ways that the school could improve: the troubled students, the complaint from the science teacher, the suggestion from the school board member, the question from the superintendent, the report from the janitor, the proposal from the student council. The improvement implied the presence of an inadequate practice or person. But we felt simultaneously from teachers the pressure to believe that *they* were competent. Interpreting calls for improvement as indirect criticism or direct insult, teachers could readily conclude that the principal had lost faith in them—or that he or she never had any in the first place. As in my case, in these situations resistance can flare, morale dips, and frequently staff themselves become divided. Ironically, the principal's active attention to improvement, often in the form of efforts to be responsive to suggestions and complaints, engages the risk of faculty discontent and resistance. As one high school principal put it:

They've got us over a barrel. I know where our program is weak, I even know what teachers have retired on the job. But the moment I start talking reform, I've got them in my face saying, "You don't trust us? You don't support me!" I can't improve the school alone!

THE AGENDA PARADOX:
BE ACCESSIBLE, RESPONSIVE AND INFORMED *BUT* ESTABLISH AND MAINTAIN MISSION AND AN EFFICIENT ORGANIZATION

The crux of this paradox is time. The expectations for principals themselves are now stretched in so many ways that the normal ten- or eleven-hour day is insufficient. Leadership literature tells principals to be visible, be accessible, and be informed about all aspects of their buildings (Blumberg and Greenfield, 1980; Hallinger and Murphy, 1987). At the same time, principals feel the traditional press to run a tight ship "from the helm," the position of control and of maximum perspective on the ship's movement. Often these produced a lively contest for Maine principals' time and energy:

Part of me says I should be seeing students, teachers, and classroom teaching; I should be walking the halls, solving problems and keeping in touch with everyone. Another part, though, says I need to collect my thoughts alone, to sort out what's happening, to assure the community and superintendent everything's running according to Hoyle. I constantly feel as if I cannot do both.

It is a contest not only of time but of focus and of activity type, built into the nature of principals' work.

The paradox is the product of mixed agendas. My work in Ellsworth was not clearly defined by anyone, nor was that of many other principals in Maine. We felt it was left to us to run the school, to do all that is required to make the school successful. For some principals, this might be viewed as an invitation to a pleasure cruise: at one level, at least, it is not difficult simply to run a school. For some who aspired to grander accomplishments as I did, however, it caused problems. It meant satisfying a range of agendas, some real and many only imagined. American parents, as John Goodlad (1983) found, want the school to "do it all" for their children; these principals felt it was up to them to see that the school delivered "it all." For us, this was the Agenda Paradox: will I be a visible manager and friendly facilitator or will I direct the school program through deliberate policies and decisions aimed at fulfilling the mission of the school? While these may not seem incompatible from a distance, they were often in conflict for me and for many others as we contemplated putting these ambitions to work.

In asserting an efficient, goal-directed organization, we ran up against the loosely coupled nature of U.S. schools. As the outside called for strong mission and guaranteed outputs, the inside—the curriculum, the kids, and the teachers—refused to be organized quickly or uniformly. One high school principal said, "I can make the best damn master schedule, institute competency testing, and rewrite the curriculum to match, but it won't amount to a hill of beans if I can't sell it to the staff and deliver some front-line assistance to them day in and day out." Many of us felt compelled to reorganize staff and curriculum, to reestablish mission, and to hold endless meetings to pull this off. But we were visited constantly by the specter of our distance from the action and the enormous energy it would take to close that distance. One principal wrote:

How can I learn about this complicated and extensive organization if I am not out in it constantly. But when I am out in it constantly, I hear all these immediate demands to solve short-term problems. When I become involved in those, I've lost contact with the grand plan and perspective on where we're going.

In short, we principals frequently felt out of control.

Others expressed the Agenda Paradox as a conflict of managerial concerns and programmatic concerns. Does this school need most a leader who is visible, whose personal presence will foster an interpersonal environment conducive to the social and citizenship goals of school, and whose model is essential to the faculty and staff? Or does this school need most a leader who can chart a course for the students and faculty, who can reorganize the school to set it on that course, and who can stay the course through the normal meteorological cycles of the school year? Many Maine principals voiced the opinion that "I cannot go in so many directions and be in so many places *and* feel I'm leading this school toward improvement."

Recognizing that both kinds of behavior are viewed as leadership behaviors, the principal's paradox is only deepened. Many of us could not exclude either, so strived to provide both kinds of leadership. This strategy served often to tax our time, wit, patience, energies, and grasp of the school and its overall direction. It was apparent from many Academy discussions that this paradox of leadership priorities made many principals feel that they were not wholly successful at any form of leadership.

THE AUTHORITY PARADOX:
AUTHORITY—NOW YOU HAVE IT, NOW YOU DON'T

Most principals are familiar with the Authority Paradox. By dint of their positions, principals are thought to have authority by the public, their superiors, and varying numbers of staff and students, but they work in environments in which the authority to affect significantly the school and the educational process must always be earned. Here lies a crucial distinction between the power that is ascribed to principals and the authority they need to lead effectively. The paradox involves the two and the confusions that arise when, as they often do, people interchange them: ascribed power often inhibits the earning of authority.

As I and Maine colleagues attempted to lead our schools toward greater instructional effectiveness, we met head-on this Authority Paradox. One Maine principal described our plight as follows: "I'm not at all sure how I'll convince the teachers that I'm credible [about instructional matters] when some of them won't even follow my directions [in managerial matters]." The separation of the educational function and the administrative function is apparent and, in spite of recent attempts to join the two, well entrenched. The principal's ascribed authority—hierarchical power—is best defined *not* in terms of educational matters but in terms of managerial details: setting duty rosters, monitoring attendance, leading public functions, scheduling classes, making policies regarding extracurricular life. The tough assignment for aspiring instructional leaders is to establish a positive authority for themselves in the pedagogical and curricular realms when, historically and perhaps ideologically, that authority is assumed *not* to exist.

This problem is a steady theme in this book, as it often was at the Principals' Academy. We often found ourselves operating with complete autonomy and faculty compliance in the managerial realm only to find ourselves, within the next half hour, sweating to be listened to by those same teachers as we operated in the instructional realm. I can recall, within a single conversation with a teacher, the topic shifting from a procedural concern (student tardiness, for example) to a pedagogical concern (a classroom motivation technique). In the first matter, I was assumed to have the power and authority; in the second matter, the teacher was. For many of us, the power of the position may seem relatively constant; but in reality, authority is evanescent. Now you have it, now you don't.

This paradox was bothersome to Maine principals not because we wanted power in all realms, but because we needed to learn, sometimes for the first time, how to build professional authority. A third-year principal put it as follows:

I don't want the teachers to do what I say. I don't feel I know what exactly to do in most situations. In fact, I need them to help me understand what the details are so I can have a better idea what to do. What *I* want is for them to see me as a teacher too. . . . That's what I am, really. I want them to respect me for what I know about kids and teaching.

The dilemma caused by this paradox did not exist for a lot of us until the instructional leadership movement came along. Now, encouraged to take a more active role in the instructional realm, we found some teachers suspicious, some eager to have us involved, and a number simply disbelieving. One principal said, "I feel like I've got to somehow show them that I'm not coming into their classrooms to blow them away. I'm not the same person who rags them about lunchroom duty when I'm discussing curriculum with them. I'm more of a colleague."

Clearly, the major question for many of us was how we could change our relationships with our teachers, how we could persuade faculty that we were not "top-down" managers but "collaborative" leaders. Most were finding this vastly easier to articulate than to pull off. Not only did the history of principal-teacher relationships prevent this evolution, but union-management divisions, personality differences, and faculty subdivisions threw obstacles constantly in the way. Expectations from the superintendent and school board and parental opinion sometimes made the costs of such a change too great. Said one exasperated principal:

Frankly, I don't know if it's worth it [to try to build a more collaborative relationship around instructional issues]. My boss wants me to kick ass, the parents keep hounding me to solve their problems [with teachers], and the older teachers just pay lip service [to my approaches].

Struggling with the Authority Paradox has deepened my appreciation for the difference between power and authority. In Ellsworth I discovered that my relationships with individual teachers, staff, students, parents and board members were influenced heavily by their needs to understand their leader as a wielder of power and a developer of authority. Most significantly, these needs varied extraordinarily from person to person. Some expected to see authority earned through the development of mutual respect and the sharing of important powers within the school. Others seemed to *want* to see power exercised, needing the feeling that someone was firmly in charge in order to respect my authority. Still others would not allow power to be used freely without their open review; they wanted, it seemed, explicitly to vest authority in me themselves. And some seemed to need the principal to have power or authority largely because they needed to fight it, sidestep it, or prove that it was unjust; they resisted assigning authority to me entirely.

The Authority Paradox is not only a function of the principal's middle management position but it is inevitable for anyone who must lead others. Authority not only has a temporal dimension—now you have it, now you don't—but it also has an interpersonal dimension—you have it with John, but not with Sally. For principals who seek to engage with their faculties in a partnership around instruction, a sensitivity to these fine distinctions and a comfort with the ambiguities this introduces to their relationships are a necessity.

THE SUCCESS PARADOX: BE A SUCCESSFUL PRINCIPAL . . . *BUT* WE WON'T TELL YOU WHAT THAT MEANS

The final paradox is a natural extension of the Agenda and Authority Paradoxes. It arises from the fact that teachers, students, supervisors, parents, and board want the principal to succeed but they frequently view the principal's success in different ways. More fundamentally, it arises from the difficulties everyone has defining how success can be measured and documented. The principal comes to the job with the hopes of many people riding on his or her ability to make the school function. The Success Paradox emerges from the fact that principals must operate within this cloud of expectations without specific definition or feedback on performance.

The Success Paradox ironically plagued most those Maine principals seeking new and more effective roles. We did not conform to the "old style" principal who was better known to parents, kids, and board members than the new. Pursuing the "new style" principalship risked not only appearing to ignore some of the old model but also actually spending time and energy on activities that many saw as "not what principals do." This was particularly troublesome for some principals who felt that the old model was more easily defined and more publicly observable than instructional leadership:

When I came here, the expectations for me were clear. The kids wanted someone who was friendly, the parents wanted someone who was firm and who would advocate for them, and the board wanted the school to look good and give the kids plenty of work. Since I've been spending more time on curriculum and supervising teachers, I've been less available for some of these things. I know they want me to do these [instructional] things, but I wonder sometimes if they really understand them. Will they count [when I'm up for a new contract]?

The Success Paradox for this principal, as it was for me and others, hinged on whether we could afford to deflect energies and time from "what most people expect" to the activities we professionally were committed to. For me, it meant establishing myself as a capable traditionalist, then gradually shifting the patterns of my activities and relationships, a strategy that required more time and energy than I often had.

While community forces tended to define success in traditional terms, other professionals—and especially teachers—were frequently sources of support for change. One elementary principal noted that "I've got some crackerjack teachers who *thank* me for taking the time to sit down with them and work out problems." The reader will recall that groups of teachers at Ellsworth found my involvement both supportive and heartening. Particularly at the elementary level, my Maine colleagues felt that their interest and participation in classroom and grade-level problem-solving and planning reassured teachers that "I am more one of them than I am an administrator." Importantly, some principals also felt that the superintendent encouraged their instructional involvement. The fact that the Ellsworth superintendent clearly wanted me involved in teachers' classrooms and leading programmatic decisions freed me to set these kinds of new activities as priorities.

Ultimately, most principals burdened by paradoxical standards relied for support and guidance on their own internal compasses and on one another (particularly as the Academy grew and principals' associations increasingly professionalized). I worried in my first years in Ellsworth that my interests and goals would be so incompatible with those of the opinion-setters in Ellsworth that I might find myself without a job if I were not careful. So I tried to cover the conventional bases while also following my own inclinations. Although I was later able to delegate some of the old in order to build on my success at the new, I nevertheless found myself intellectually, philosophically, and interpersonally so diffused by multiple agendas and clienteles that I often felt directionless. My evaluations from staff demonstrate my scattershot pattern of success, attesting not only to the variety of targets I *aimed* at but also to the variety that staff and faculty carried for me. Clearly, a score on one target often meant a miss on another.

The only resolution to the Agenda Paradox that finally comforted me was to aim at—and hit—the targets dictated by my own goals and professional conscience. My principal colleagues in neighboring districts and the professional society-building nurtured by the Maine Principals' Academy were instrumental in helping me articulate and stand behind my own standards.

IMPLICATIONS FOR PRACTICE AND TRAINING

Lightfoot (1983, p. 309), in concluding her impressive study of six high schools, wrote that "a consciousness about imperfections, and the willingness to admit them and search for their origins and solutions is one of the important ingredients of goodness in schools." The paradoxes in my work and colleagues' work capture the essence of these "imperfections of goodness." As we attempted to think and behave more as instructional leaders in our schools, we not only encountered these five unruly dilemmas but we often felt that we were responsible for creating them. Particularly as they played out in interpersonal relationships with staff, the win-lose nature of the paradoxes had a discouraging effect on principals trying to do their jobs in new and purportedly more effective ways. We saw that it was easier to back off from new initiatives in curriculum, instruction, supervision, or grouping than to insist upon them because backing off would actually make the school *more* orderly and our jobs *more* manageable. In the face of this fact, it is remarkable that principals are mounting the efforts at instructional leadership and school improvement that they are.

What might assist them in this effort? I can suggest three initiatives. One speaks to the way we educate principals about the role. The second addresses how schools as workplaces may need to change. The third advocates for a continuous forum to which principals like the ones I have cited here can go to gather support and critical perspective to continue their work.

Regarding the preparation of principals, most of those with whom I have worked at the Principals' Academy have said in one way or another that their preparation was too prescriptive, that it did not focus enough on the nature of the job and of schools as complex organizations. They found texts and professors too ready to proffer logically coherent, orderly profiles of "how schools ought to be." In doing so, they violated what these principals came to see as the disorder and illogic of their experience. In particular, the paradoxes explored here were nowhere on the horizon in the preparation programs of many of these principals. In taking their first positions, they anticipated finding clear expectations for themselves, the time to build "clear missions" and "strong relationships with faculty," and to have the ear of the faculty and parents in moving the school forward. Many were shocked to find that the tasks conflicted with one another and that few initiatives went without calls for a counterinitiative, few investments in one direction came without a cost in another.

The greatest challenge may be to help future principals understand that competing claims on their agendas, time, energies, and value systems need not be resolved by opting for one or another alternative. Each paradox may break down into two major contending forces; for example, the instructional agenda or the managerial agenda, the public's expectations or the profession's, high expectations for achievement or high expectations for discipline and order. It is important to resist this simplified "either-or" resolution, to struggle instead to appreciate the value of the competing forces, and to come to understand how both might need to exist in opposition to one another if the school is to do its job.

High schools in the United States will continue to pursue varied goals for students. As long as they do, the principal's success will hang to a degree on his or her ability to juggle these competing agendas, standards, and tasks. Preparation programs and literature must not mislead future principals with tidy prescriptions—either for management activities or for instructional leadership. We must make better use of practicing principals' craft knowledge (Blumberg, 1989) and of the growing literature on the nonrational dimensions of leadership (Cousins, 1988; Leithwood, 1988; McPherson, Crowson, and Pitner, 1986).

This observation leads to a suggestion for those who can shape the workplace of principals: teachers, superintendents, and school boards. If principals are to become constructively involved in instruction, they will need training, guidance, and support. Most principals operate in widely varying schools and staff milieus; most feel that they are in it alone. As they strive for a greater share of influence in the instructional realm, they encounter obstacles at most every turn but feel that they have little natural support. Clearly, some spadework needs to be done with teachers, superintendents and boards in order to acquaint these important actors with the paradoxes faced by the middle managers in their schools.

Such preparation should not simply carve out new responsibilities for the principal. That has been done, and that is what has led to the Accountability, High Expectations, and Agenda Paradoxes. Instead, teachers and superintendents need to negotiate with principals a working agreement about the principal's activities in the instructional realm so that the emerging relationship includes shared responsibilities for instructional initiatives and outcomes. Such negotiation should include discussion of the goals of the instructional program, the nature of the curriculum, the evaluation criteria and procedures to be used to judge performance and outcomes, and the designation of responsibilities for these key instructional functions. Discussions and decisions in these realms would have alleviated much of the ambiguity experienced by the principals with whom I have worked.

Finally, these paradoxes are not merely the product of the instructional leadership focus of recent years. They are more fundamentally the dilemmas of any leader of an organization as complex and dynamic as a secondary or elementary school. Leaders will seldom have smooth worklives in these places where the work is not predictable, where emotional and psychological factors intervene in the production of outcomes, and where monitoring and correcting practice are problematic. They need opportunities to review and sort out both their schools' experience and their own experience. Cooper's (1988) study demonstrates that principals, like teachers, cannot understand the evolving needs of students and their learning without some mechanism to promote analysis and sense-making within their own professional routines.

For principals in Maine, the Academy provided that opportunity, albeit not continuously enough to sustain them. Principals' centers and academies in other locations have succeeded more at this than we have (National Network of Principals' Centers, 1986–1989). It is encouraging to see growing interest in "schools as communities of learners" (Goldman and O'Shea, 1990; Lieberman, 1988b) and in applying reflective practice in all educational roles (Schon, 1983). Where busy principals confront paradoxes in practice, they will need more than an infrequent conference or course to understand those paradoxes and then to develop effective means of working within them. Principals can benefit from both the literature of organizational change and the accumulating wisdom about change agency (e.g., Fullan, 1982; Shepard, 1985).

Chapter 12

Capacities and Qualities for High School Leadership

> Whether we will be able to move to the next stage [of change toward schools that work better for students and adults] . . . will depend on our collective ability to think in new ways about the meanings and responsibilities of shared leadership. . . . Teachers and principals can hold leadership roles and, working together, they can help the schools build a professional culture.
>
> (A. Lieberman, 1988b, p. 653)

Over the past fifteen years, I have been engrossed in the pleasures and problems of high school administration. Most teachers, parents, and school board members I have talked with viewed their high school principals with slightly jaundiced eyes. They never seemed quite sure what to expect of them, and never seemed fully satisfied with what they did. Similarly, most of the high school principals I know have felt like warriors, first in the battle to bring order to schools in the late 1970s and later, in the 1980s, to ride (and survive) the waves of school reform. Except in rare cases, my principal acquaintances have felt, as I did toward the end of my tenure at Ellsworth, resigned to their inability to fulfill the expectations that others—and they themselves—held for their schools.

As I have read over the material in the foregoing chapters, I find that much of it seems an explanation for this failure. Although I was successful in some of the interpersonal and image-setting activities of the principalship, I left the job feeling that I had failed to form the high school faculty into a team. My motives for writing this book have been rooted in this problem. As I have explored the three major functions of the principalship, I have turned one eye on myself and how I might have been the cause of my own failure; and the other eye has been trained on the position itself. With the assistance of staff feedback, I have learned how some aspects of my leadership may have contributed to the faculty's lack of integration. But, as one might suspect, I have also learned that my concept of the principalship, and the concepts of it that others hold, may have been more at fault. This book, as Roland Barth notes in the Foreword, is about my struggle to conceive a new role for the high school principal that squares with my own value system as an educator and a person.

What would make someone an effective high school principal? This is the essential question for every principal, teacher, and superintendent as it is for educators of principals. The question has no simple, uniform answer. Every new theory about high schools and their improvement tempts us to reconstrue our understanding of the principal's competencies and personal qualities. From my tenure at Ellsworth, in a high school typical in size and I believe in culture of most U.S. high schools, I learned what worked and did not work for me. In the following pages, I share the lessons that have shaped my new conception of the high school principal.

I identify two sorts of personal characteristic that help make a principal successful: capacities and personal qualities. The difference is important. By "capacity" I mean the individual's general ability to perform a given function; clusters of skills combine synergistically to compose the capacity. I believe these skills, as well as their integration with one another, can be learned and honed. I use the term "personal quality" to identify an enduring human attribute that appears essential to successful principal practice. These are not skills so much as they are traits of personality and temperament. They are rooted more permanently in the person than are capacities. I believe, nevertheless, that a principal, through regular feedback and reflection, can accommodate his or her practice to them. In this regard, they give shape to the principal's style.

A CAPACITY TO UNDERSTAND THE GOALS OF THE SCHOOL

Each high school's goals for students must direct the actions and decisions of educators and the school's success must be measured against those goals. The principal is uniquely placed in the typical high school structure to see that this goal-directed function of the school is fulfilled. The principal, as the school's ritual leader, is expected to know the school's goals and to see that the school's activities meet those goals. This function does not, as we used to think, simply require a philosophical choice followed by the execution of directives. As is apparent from this book and others such as *The Good High School* (Lightfoot, 1983) and *The Shopping Mall*

High School (Powell, Farrar, and Cohen, 1985), numerous and conflicting forces buffet the secondary school, its directions, and its staff and principal. High school leadership is not methodically sequential but paradoxical and episodic. At sea amid the demands of people, programs, and paper, the principal is a navigator and crew manager, a problem-solver and sail-trimmer more than a firm-handed helmsperson. The weight of daily and weekly exigencies works ponderously to decenter and dull the school's mission. The principal guides and shifts these weights to keep energies and activities revolving smoothly around the school's core purposes.

To fulfill this function, the high school principal must have the capacity to articulate purposes for his or her school, a capacity requiring intellectual, philosophical, and interpersonal abilities. The capacity draws ideas and information continually from the principal's pursuit of knowledge about adolescents, the educative process, and socioeconomic and political conditions. Goals must be jointly set by staff and community, a complicated and periodic process that demands of the principal conceptual and interpersonal adeptness based on this knowledge. Once consensus exists to support a manageable number of clearly written purposes, they must be commonly understood and continually related to the work and decisions of students, staff, and administration. In a word, they must be purposes that can be transposed into working principles that will guide the activities and decisions of all people who have expectations of the school.

This capacity to articulate purposes and to stay the course grows from the convergence of four skills. First, the principal needs to *understand the purposes U.S. high schools have served and might serve*. This understanding derives from experience, reading, and reflecting; it requires a studious interest in schools as organizations. The principal's knowledge about high school purposes gives him or her a vocabulary for discussing the goals of his or her own school. For example, as principals lead the development of social and citizenship skills for their students, they must know how schools have typically shaped teen-agers' experiences with one another and with the wider world. They further must understand how these school effects might relate to productive future citizenship. What evidence is there that the high school's climate and disciplinary structures shape social attitudes and behaviors for the future? What does this evidence suggest for the school's goals and policies? Similar lines of inquiry must be a part of the principal's intellectual and philosophical repertoire if he or she is to lead in the formulation of academic, moral, vocational, and social purposes. An appreciation of the history of secondary school functions and practices, I believe, is essential to developing the vocabulary of purposes that permits such leadership.

Second, the principal must *develop the intellectual tools necessary to understand the local condition*. Knowing the broad philosophical purposes and history of high schools is important, but any one school's purposes must to a degree match local societal values, occupational expectations, and academic focus. This requires that the principal lead in building a rationale for each major curricular and cocurricular program that is anchored in the social, economic, and cultural needs of the school's students. Successful mission-building involves knowing how local authorities, local adults, and students themselves think about the school's purposes and learning about the real social, occupational, and intellectual patterns of the area. Such work calls on the principal to monitor local trends and to watch and listen to the local scene with insight. He or she must also feel comfortable with basic social science concepts in order to understand how social, economic, and cultural forces bear on the school's curriculum, cocurriculum, and goals.

Third, the principal must *be able to express these purposes*. This ability necessarily comes into play *after* purposes are formulated and framed in the staff's and principal's mind. But it is as important *during* the formulation and the framing when the principal's articulation of possible purposes helps center the collective mission-building effort. Here again, the principal needs a level of conceptual sophistication to find the words and ideas necessary to explain to both students and staff why they are there. That ability hinges on the principal's vocabulary of ideas, words, and other symbols and on his or her sensitivities to the vocabularies of students, faculty, parents, and others. Clearly, principals need a broader repertoire of ideas and words than does any one constituency in order to express clearly the same few fundamental purposes to each constituency in terms they will understand. The principal, through actions, words, and other forms of communication, must be adept at "adapting and modifying shared symbols that signal and reinforce the [school's] mission" (Bennis and Nanus, 1985, p. 143).

Fourth, the principal must *be able to summon forth these central purposes when they are necessary for the institution*. Most of my activities as principal were reactive, short-term, and immediate. The same is true for most teachers. In most high schools, routine activities determine actual purposes. The principal must recognize when students, staff, community, and board need reminders of the school's direction. Most importantly, he or she must find the appropriate means to remind and redirect people. Here again, the principal must appreciate the value of a structure of purposes that provides task-orientation to the institution in such a way that each person sees better his or her own tasks. Such a structure of purposes grows from a conception of the organization as a whole as well as from understanding practical organizational models that relate each teacher's and each student's work to meeting the organization's purposes. Activities that cannot be related to this structure should be either adapted to it or eliminated. Like the team formed by navigator, chief mate, and captain, the principal must eye the chart, the winds, and the sails, and while keeping the destination and ship's position in mind, use these sources of information to decide how to deploy crew and plot courses. For this, the principal must conceive of the school as an organization with a life bigger than the individual lives of any of its occupants. In large measure, such a perspective can be learned. More to the point, the principal must appreciate the need to use it continually in adapting the work of teachers, students, and herself or himself to fit the school's purposes.

A CAPACITY TO TRANSLATE PURPOSES INTO THE SCHOOL'S DAILY ROUTINES

High purposes do not a successful principal make. As my case demonstrates, a principal can be viewed as friendly, professional, and academically oriented yet his or her contributions to school outcomes may remain indistinct and even debatable. Those fine purposes, those "right" altruistic motives, will come to no avail if the principal cannot see them through. This capacity is the key to the principal's having more than a salutary effect on the school. Without it, principals can be little more than figureheads and public relations agents.

The translation capacity is essential to the principal's ability to stay the course once he or she has successfully helped identify and voice the purposes of the school. With it, the principal's leadership becomes real: he or she reifies the goals of the school in the actual events and routines of students, teachers, and staff. The principal's capacity to do this hinges on his or her distinguishing between the espoused purposes and the actual purposes and activities of the school (Argyris and Schon, 1974). The principal is simultaneously realistic about what *does* go on in the school and cognizant of where the school *ought* to be headed. Further, he or she can help others recognize how their activities specifically assist—or do not assist—in the attainment of purposes and how improvements can be made. This translation capacity operates constantly, making staff and students proud of their accomplishments, setting new goals for improvement, and spurring curricular, cocurricular, and pedagogical assessment and innovation.

The capacity to translate goals into action requires, first, the *ability to analyze the possible effects of school on its occupants*. This ability is founded not only on experience in schools but also on organizational sophistication. The principal must have command of social and psychological concepts and organizational theories to help evaluate how a certain event or routine might influence students and faculty. Formal knowledge and skills in program evaluation, student assessment, and staff and peer observation are important. Similarly, the principal must learn informally to read the environment, judging the fatigue levels of staff, the commitment levels of parents, and the climate among students at any given moment. If we were to abolish tracking, a principal might ask, how might students, teachers, and parents respond? Where might we encounter support or resistance? These analytic skills—along with the will to see things as they honestly are—permit the principal to develop with others practicable strategies toward specific improvements.

Analyses of school practices lead to the exploration of alternative strategies and programs. The second skill the principal needs is the *ability to negotiate progress* as faculty, parents, students, central office, and school board consider these alternatives. Leadership of high school change involves stewardship of improvement ideas, sensitivity to the dynamics of faculty interests and decision-making, and usually mediation among separate groups and purposes. As I discovered in Ellsworth, a high school faculty is a reluctant if not recalcitrant partner to change. To effect a change in, for example, academic advising, I found I needed to be both assertive and consultative simultaneously. I needed to mold consensus about the problem we faced, collect solutions from all sides, then lead open discussion to ensure that all interests were heard. Through it all, I had to keep the issue of academic placement in the limelight, for in a busy high school, most needs will perish in the daily maelstrom if they are not championed. The principal, I found, needs to encourage or even instigate change, but can neither assert solutions nor desert staff to create solutions alone. Change, as a range of scholars have documented (Fullan, 1982; Sarason, 1982; Sergiovanni and Moore, 1989), happens slowly and conjointly.

Negotiating progress frustrates many principals and faculty because it takes so long. So too is our desire to see our decisions and our practices bear fruit frustrated by time and the complexities of students and the school. In translating purposes into action, the principal must *be capable of recognizing progress and achievement,* a skill contingent upon understanding how the goals of the school might actually show up as outcomes. Certainly, some work bears immediate fruits: students score well on a unit test; a disciplinary policy succeeds in driving students who smoke from the bathrooms; students respond well to a career-day program. But the grand goals of the high school seek more permanent and less observable student effects than these. To know whether the school has successfully translated a purpose into a productive pattern of activities, the principal must expect to look down the line and must discern patterns of productive outcomes, not just single events. This requires knowing what to look for in evaluating effects, patience, and a willingness to celebrate and reward both students and staff who create and sustain those patterns. The principal must identify indicators of long-range progress and must seek these out in his or her daily rounds.

In counterpoint to the principal's abilities to stimulate and recognize change, the principal must also sustain a measure of order and predictability. Students need such security to learn; staff demand it in order to be free to teach; school boards and parents require it as a matter of course.

The challenge for the principal is to *be able to convey a dependable organizational structure to everyone involved in the high school*. This ability is a necessary precondition to all other work. The principal must create a system of rules, roles, and relationships that can be counted upon to curb behaviors and attitudes that do not serve the goals of the school while, simultaneously, they invite behaviors and attitudes that promote learning, social responsibility, and community. The correct balance of tight and loose structure is elusive; the search for it is eternal. The principal must appreciate and embrace the paradoxical nature of this balancing act: he or she will forever tend the balance, seeking that equilibrium between satisfaction and control, on one hand, and self-improvement and growth on the other.

Running throughout each of the above abilities is the presumption that the principal will see and understand the activities and attitudes of people accurately. This *ability to be objective* about what goes on and about people allows the principal to collect data in the school environment that can inform fair decisions. It at once provides valid information for key program, policy, and personnel decisions and builds a sense among students and teachers that they will be treated according to fact rather than personal preference. Hence, most staff will understand and respect the principal's activities and attitudes, as I learned in Ellsworth, even if some do not like the principal or a decision he or she has made. This ability to be objective is tricky. The principal can learn to observe carefully and to respect fact over hearsay, but his or her personality and experience with people will likely impede total objectivity. Similarly, the principal must feel reasonably free from threat in order to see things and people as they are.

A CAPACITY TO COMMUNICATE WITH AND TO DIRECT AND MOTIVATE ADULTS

If principals understand the school's purposes and can translate them into daily practices, they yet must master a third major capacity to meld the adults in the school around those common purposes. The first two capacities rely heavily on conceptual and perceptual abilities: they require observing, analyzing, consulting, deliberating choices, and taking action. To execute successfully the principal's role, a set of interpersonal capacities must be present as well. The principal must have the ability to communicate clearly and efficiently with the staff, a process involving speaking *and* listening. And the principal must be able both to motivate *and* direct that staff, managing in the process to resolve the sometimes dichotomous nature of these two activities. This difficult work casts the principal as a catalyst for disparate interests and personalities.

This "catalyst" capacity is particularly challenging in the high school where larger populations and plants, greater student activity and autonomy, and more fragmenting of staff occur than in most lower schools. The principal who succeeds at it is able to be understood and to understand others most of the time. Staff feel an organization exists in their work with students and that they have contributed to its formation. The principal has engaged the faculty in frank discussion of issues important to teaching, student activities, and school planning. Staff feel that their perspectives and opinions have been valued by the principal and by colleagues. In short, the principal has created an ethos among the faculty and staff that stimulates open exchange about professional matters and honors risk-taking in the service of professional improvement.

Communication itself will not generate collective action. The principal must be capable of directing and motivating faculty to play their appropriate parts in the complex work of high schools. I say this not because I believe adults need direction and motivation; most do not. Rather, it has been my experience that high schools are so loosely coupled and serve so many masters and mistresses that, left to their own devices, they are apt to serve none well. The adults in the high school, to maintain a focus on long-term progress, must have confidence in their sole and collective abilities to make school productive for all students. The principal occupies a position of significant influence over the organization of work and the climate in which it is done. This climate is most robust—and faculty feel most confident in themselves as a unit—when faculty see the principal directing and motivating them all toward the common good of students (Weindling and Earley, 1987).

The principal's function is not necessarily to *be* the motivator and supporter for *each* staffer. I tried that and found that time, energy, and personality limitations made such a goal impossible to reach in a high school. The principal's function, instead, is to structure an interpersonal environment for staff that motivates and supports optimism, effort, and an innovative spirit. Because staff are frequently the most powerful influences in one another's work climate, the principal must function more as a catalyst for the group than as an inspirer or director of individuals.

What specific abilities cluster in this broad capacity? Basic to communication, direction, and motivation is the *ability to employ working models for understanding adult behavior*. We are too often myopic in our assessments of adult motives. High school principals, as I found for myself, fall into a defensive mindset in which all teachers' actions and words are viewed suspiciously as schemes to resist or retrench. Efforts to motivate degenerate into efforts to seek compliance; efforts to include staff in decisions become efforts to placate or to engineer approval. The high school principal must learn and appreciate the *diverse* motives staff bring to their work and the *various* means through which adults may be motivated. Adults, and particularly adults who we urge to be creative, learn and teach in different natural styles (Cross, 1981; Levine, 1989). The principal, as I painfully discovered, who insists on uniform relationships and strict compliance risks not only alienating many staff but undercutting the spirit of diversity teachers themselves should cultivate in classrooms. Principals cannot persist in viewing their faculties as their students; they must entrust teachers with important schoolwide responsibilities, support their decisions and initiatives, and help them evaluate honestly the outcomes.

Given this ability to understand the diverse "places" staff "are coming from" and their implications for the principal's approach to each staffer, the principal must then *be able to read accurately interpersonal signals, both individual and group.* As a new principal in a new community, my greatest regret was that I did not have the skills or time to know staff and faculty before we had to make tough decisions together. Perhaps as a result, I believe the most critical interpersonal skill the principal needs is empathy, the ability to listen to and watch another person carefully enough to obtain a good idea of what he or she is thinking and feeling. The principal who can do this reasonably efficiently has greatly enhanced abilities to motivate and direct staff effectively. Words, tone, and actions are interlaced with the current thinking and moods of the individual or group. Similarly, adeptness at understanding nonverbal cues, at directly assessing opinion and mood, and at group decision-making are important skills. The principal who can read interpersonal signals well does not rely on blind policies or formulaic approaches based on theory, a textbook, or advice from the good old boys. He or she instead shapes strategies, decisions, and personal postures to the people involved.

Successful motivation and direction of adults requires, as well, a measure of self-knowledge that will permit successful self-management (Bennis and Nanus, 1985). As a thirty-year-old principal who never before had been at the helm of an 850-person organization, my sense of how my actions and words would be understood was largely hypothetical. I learned by groping and by following my instincts for dealing with people in general. As time went along, my understanding of how I was affecting staff and students grew and, for most staff, led to more effective relationships. The principal's *ability to understand and shape his or her own words, feelings, and behavior* stands at the intersection of successful and unsuccessful leadership. The principal can grasp conceptually school purposes and accurately interpret staff thinking and affect, but unless he or she understands how subsequent behaviors are likely to influence staff, his or her next moves will be little better than haphazard.

In a bubbling high school environment, this ability takes on monstrous proportions; the principal cannot respond to all interpersonal stimuli in effective or like fashion. But he or she can develop skills and procedures for monitoring how his or her responses are influencing others. Key to these is the will to be self-reflective. But, most importantly, the principal needs feedback from others. Teachers, counselors, secretaries, superintendents, and students know best the impacts of the principal's personality, words, and actions. As the principal attempts to build a mission and a team to fulfill it, he or she needs to check in regularly on how he or she is managing his or her own skills and qualities. That takes self-assurance, awareness of one's public and private selves, and a willingness to adapt behaviors and beliefs.

Finally, to succeed in communicating, directing, and motivating adults the principal must combine two qualities: trust and professional energy. The principal needs to *be able to project personal trust and professional dissatisfaction simultaneously*. The principal must believe that most staff are effective with children and want to do the best for them. At the same time, he or she must project a desire to improve. This ability derives in part from the principal's understanding that a faculty member is at once a person in his or her own right and an employee of the school with a mission to accomplish. The principal has a basic faith in each staff member's good intentions and competencies as a person and believes, as well, that the school's—and thus each staff member's—performance can be made better. He or she generates personal security while fomenting professional unrest. Such work requires tremendous energy, an empirical mind, acceptance of the constant risk of failure, and interpersonal constancy. The melding of collegial trust and professional dissatisfaction fosters the self-confident but critical spirit so essential to the good high school (Lightfoot, 1983, pp. 309 ff.).

The ability to at once spawn support and trust in staff *and* make institutional and individual self-criticism legitimate requires that the principal understand the dual nature of school leadership. The school world operates as a system of people with personal needs and agendas and it operates as an institution with goals and business to do. To lead, the principal must work simultaneously on both levels, as caretaker and nurturer of the system of people and as guide and captain of the school's business. The principal needs to understand how his or her activities in one sphere shape his or her effects in the other. The principal must decipher the signals of the staff and students using two codes, one of the heart and one of the head. Three questions guide the principal's daily work: How are folks feeling about being here? How are their actions serving the purpose of educating our students? and How do the answers to these two questions affect one another as I plan my work for today? The principal who can use these questions to integrate the socioemotional world of the school with the instrumental world of the school has found a key to purposive leadership.

THREE ROOTSTOCK QUALITIES

The high school principalship in Ellsworth placed demands upon me that taxed not just my education and my experience base in schools but the qualities of my personality. The role was so public and so fast-paced that I often could not act in a planned or even logically consistent manner. I did what felt right. I did what seemed best at the time. I more often acted according to a few basic principles, shared earlier in this book, than to a coherent strategy. The consequence of this fact was that my temperament, interpersonal manner, and sense of humor made their mark on my leadership as much as did my philosophy and trade knowledge. Deeply rooted personal qualities play significant roles in the success of principals. I present three here that I believe are prerequisites for success in U.S. high school leadership.

The first of these is *self-confidence*. I have abundantly documented the complex of forces impinging upon my principalship. Daily decisions and judgments required that I deal with a wide range of philosophies and emotions to keep the school moving toward its goals. The public visibility of the high school principalship requires that the leader be clear-minded, interpersonally open, comfortable with the many tasks of school work. Central to these tasks is organizing adolescents, teachers, and many daily events, creating authoritative order without repression. The principal must personify this organized authority, sending messages by his or her personal style and visibility that the helm is in steady, capable hands. The principal must not only *look* confident as he or she handles school functions; he or she must *be* confident. The foundation stone of this professional confidence is personal self-confidence. This is a special quality, however, and is not to be confused with egotism, self-promotion, or arrogance.

We for decades have mistaken this self-confidence for quick, unilateral decision-making. It is vital that we not persist in this error. Principals need to be confident of their ideas and ideals and they must be interpersonally secure; they do not need to have every answer for every classroom. True leadership is self-reinforcing. Confident principals draw on the expertise of those around them while fashioning a coherent, purposeful program for the school that, in turn, feeds everyone's sense of solidarity and achievement—and everyone's professional confidence. To succeed at consultation, the principal must be interpersonally self-assured and his or her grasp of secondary school philosophy and pedagogy must make the principal conversant in most aspects of the school's work. Hence, the self-confident principal welcomes disparate ideas and personal interests into the decision-making fray. The principal's experience with people and comfort level with various and divergent viewpoints make collaboration both possible and extraordinarily productive.

Although we want principals to establish collaborative decision-making, principals make many decisions—or endorse many final decisions at the end of the collaborative process—alone. Principals still must "fish or cut bait"; they must rely on their judgment-making capabilities, those mysterious machinations of our intellects, our value systems and our interpersonal antennae. The moment of decision is, to me, like the moment of performance when the soprano sings the opening note or the pitcher releases the ball: we cannot intellectually fathom and control what we are doing; we must have confidence that we will do it and it will work. This confidence stems in large measure from knowing that we can handle what follows; it is comprised of what John Gardner (1987, p. 15) calls "courage, resolution, and steadiness." Principals live in environments where it seems someone always gripes, someone always has a better way than the one the principal chose. The more far-reaching the decision, it seems, the more diverse will be the reaction. The principal's psychological preparation for leading, his or her level of self-confidence, must permit him or her not only to weather being told he or she is wrong, but to accept the fact that he or she *will* be wrong. Trust in oneself and in others is proven most when the principal can seek help from others to resolve a problem he or she has created.

The proof of one's professional self-confidence lies in one's willingness to take risks. The opportunity presents itself daily to the high school principal. Where choices are seldom clear-cut and the role is undergirded by a web of paradoxes and interpersonal crosscurrents, actions are guided by what one can *reasonably predict* as likely outcomes, not by certainties. Principals constantly balance a range of possible positive impacts with a range of possible negative impacts, then chart people, schedules, and ideas onto a course that is admittedly imprecise. Here, acknowledging an issue and the need to make a decision means taking risks. So does the important work of making collective decisions and of seeing them into action. Progress is often obtained not through historic single decisions but through a series of successive small variations on a single major decision (Lindblom, 1959).

Ultimately, the principal's self-confidence is a function of his or her professional self-knowledge. Do I *know* that I *can* deal with students and adults? The answer to this question resides in the principal's past experience, no doubt, but it also is affected by a broader sense that he or she is comfortable with people and that he or she likes people. Such an awareness of one's capabilities must, as well, be realistic and accurate. Many aspiring educators want to teach because they like children and want to serve them, but some of them clearly do not succeed despite these altruistic motives. So too are principals limited by personal qualities and incapacities; knowledge of these, counterintuitively, *builds* self-confidence and professional competence. In a job where one feels commissioned to do it all, making accurate decisions to deploy staff or students who can do it better than the principal is crucial. Fundamental to these decisions is the principal's ability to see him- or herself as he or she is, to admit that he or she cannot exercise all the functions of the principalship alone. Perhaps the greatest self-confidence is called forth in the request for a partnership of faculty, students, and community members in running the school. Certainly, as my successes and failures with staff partnerships attest, the potential professional fulfillment that can emerge is well worth the risk.

While self-confidence takes on many faces and conjures up psychological undertones, the second personal quality is more straightforward. It is an *appreciation of diversity.* Not to be confused with the intellectual comprehension of diverse elements, this is a quality of one's value system, one's ethical orientation. It permits the principal to respect and even nurture the diverse and sometimes incompatible elements in the secondary school environment. This appreciation starts with the recognition that, in every U.S. high school, purposes are crossed, clienteles speak with many voices, students bring diverse needs, staff's strengths and weaknesses vary widely, and resources seldom are plentiful enough to meet all documented needs. The principal, too, must understand how this variety makes his or her work paradoxical. The principal's way is not defined in a lucid, cohesive plan; thought and action cannot therefore be dogmatic or formulaic, as if the school needed a single "right" system. This conceptual base is built partly through experience, partly through access to other principals, partly through reflection, and partly through intellectual effort.

Essential to preserving this appreciation of diversity is the ability to tolerate the ambiguities that inevitably accompany the recognition of incongruities. The principal needs the psychological equipment to permit him or her *not* to react by cramming odd-fitting pieces into the available holes in the organizational chart or eradicating altogether events and people that do not fit policies and regulations. In fact, the principal must see in the diversity of the school a strength. As Richard Sennett (1970) argues in a different context, the principal must see uses for the disorder of the school and seek means of forming complementary webs of different activities and people. Where high schools have dwelt largely on creating order as an end in itself, the principal must appreciate the miseducating effects of order for its own sake. Instead he or she must seek the all-important balance discussed earlier between centralized organization and individual educational needs and professional styles. To do this, the principal must be comfortable with many agendas and divergent activities and with the impossibility of controlling it all.

Most importantly, however, he or she must not view this as an argument for inaction or for the futility of intention. To the contrary, the principal's appreciation of diversity must fuel his or her sense of purpose. Public high schools in the United States, after all, are diverse by nature: they accept everyone who comes to them and they seek to fulfill each pupil's aspirations. Barth (1990), Lightfoot (1983), and Sizer (1983) eloquently argue in the tradition of Dewey that the heartbeat of educational purposes in the U.S. public school is sustained by the energy of our many students and their diverse needs. The principal, more than any other single person in the high school, must admire the mix of personalities, feelings, and purposes students bring to school. He or she then must steer a course for staff, parents, and students that matches these, to the extent possible, to a varied staff and to an adaptable plant and program.

The qualities in a person that permit him or her not only to tolerate ambiguity but to see strengths in diversity are not perfectly clear. Certainly, the principal must be comfortable with the fact that people come in different personality types and with different philosophies. He or she must further believe that the multiplicity of personal factors in a school *can* coexist under one orderly structure of policies and procedures. The high-achieving child of the lawyer has a place alongside the child of a millworker who has a place alongside a severely retarded child who has a place alongside the star athlete. . . . Similarly, the principal must see the complementary strengths of a diverse staff, understanding how the encouragement of diverse skills and styles among staff helps meet the diverse needs of students. Undergirding these abilities, the principal must be a relativistic thinker, to see the landscape of ideas, programs, and procedures in the school relative to the diverse needs of children, not in the image of a single absolute plan for the best high school. The principal who can be such a thinker *and* persist in staying the course of the school toward its purposes is an energetic learner him- or herself. Conflict and incongruity cannot be the principal's measures of failure; rather they must be welcomed as opportunities for learning and for asserting the purposes of the school.

A value system that embraces diversity may be as discomforting as it is novel to many secondary administrators and faculty. To some of my staff, my desire to consider all sides of issues and to support conflicting practices, people, and philosophies was alien; it offended their need for a uniform, rational system in school life. In many respects, my life would have been simpler had I ruled with an iron hand and asserted orderly management and instruction. I might have barracaded myself behind the trappings of my office and drawn sustenance from my power and the "rightness" of my superior judgments. But here is the rub: teaching, learning, and social development require personal flexibility and extensive discretion; in the highly centralized high school, conscientious educators will eventually resist and lose respect for principals who discredit this basic fact. More significantly for me, however, such a leadership strategy would have created a personally impoverishing work life. As I discovered this, I uncovered a third fundamental quality: the principal must *enjoy the daily personal contacts* of his or her work and, in doing so, draw sustenance from them and give sustenance to others.

This quality seems simple-minded, obvious, and unscientific. But I have come to believe that it has profound effects on both the principal's satisfaction and the school community's faith in itself. The principal who enjoys the contacts of daily work welcomes children and adults to his or her school and his or her activities and, in doing so, communicates interest and acceptance to them. Those contacts have authenticity, whether they are pleasant or not, and leave others with the sense that their life in the school means something to the person on top. It gives their work and their presence purpose and a value beyond the immediate objectives of their particular assignment. The principal's enjoyment of people opens two-way communication and reflects respect for the integrity of the student, staff member, or member of the public.

This quality contributes to the principal's leadership an ease with people and a comfort with the role that can offset the stress of working in the ambiguous high school environment. Student contacts are centrally important in this regard. The enjoyment the principal derives from simply watching a class of sophomores explore a short story, or discussing a problem with a student, or planning a fund raiser with the student council, or watching a tough kid make a pine table is satisfaction enough for the work one does in a day, some days. These *are* prime satisfactions the principal can draw from work that is long-term, ill-defined, and often unappreciated explicitly by others. The challenge, of course, is to find the person who can feel rewarded and invigorated by such interpersonal contacts but who can withstand the natural inclination to make them the only goals one seeks.

Personal contact with students, staff, parents, and other educators requires adaptability, warmth, and authenticity. Vital norms of affiliation within the school culture are established. The principal must feel comfortable talking with a range of people and this comfort must communicate to them respect and interpersonal esteem. While the principal need not be gregarious, he or she must be authentically enthusiastic about the ideas and feelings of others. Such enthusiasm creates self-confidence and reciprocal respect even in tough high schools (Foster, 1971). The fact that the principal *enjoys* those contacts models for everyone the importance of expressing personal acceptance and encouragement to one another. These are the norms of a healthy school climate; they create a community ethos that is personally and collectively validating. The benefits are two-sided: the principal draws encouragement and energy from personal contacts and the school community discovers a visible, affirming, and engaged leader.

This final personal quality operates in all realms of the principal's world. It is vital to his or her success simply because that world is so full of people. The origins of the principal's ability to relax, to show warmth, humor, and interest, and to share a part of another's perspectives and emotions are mysterious. They seem rooted deeply in his or her personality and history. No test provides a measure of it, save the test of the community within which one works and lives. Insofar as teaching calls on the same abilities, a principal's professional history in teaching affords a chance to identify the degree to which a person enjoys these daily contacts of his or her work. Some teachers apparently aspire to the principalship to escape the intensity of daily contacts, to use the office as a refuge from the demands and responsibilities of educating and managing children. Recruiters of principals, however, have ample opportunity to investigate this aspect of a candidate's past, to seek evidence of this enjoyment factor, and to make employment decisions using such evidence. In my experience, its presence in a person spells the difference between a technically expert educator and an educator who succeeds in influencing those he or she teaches or leads.

The three rootstock qualities I have described form an important trio in the principal's success. Self-confidence, appreciation for diversity, and enjoyment of personal contacts complement one another, providing steadiness of purpose, adaptability, and interpersonal affirmation. They undergird the principal's ability to build the capacities described earlier in this chapter and, in turn, to perform well the three major functions explored in this book. Without them, setting purposes, translating those purposes into the various realities of the school population, and effective communication and motivation are impossible.

My years as a principal repeatedly tested these qualities in me. Every personnel dispute, curriculum debate, student conflict challenged my self-confidence, threatened to narrow my appreciation of diversity, and flirted with interpersonal alienation. To the extent that I was able to withstand these dissembling forces, my leadership was strengthened. Indeed, it is difficult to envision a vibrant, optimistic, and purposeful school without a principal who is personally secure, attentive to all shades of student need, and interpersonally affirming.

ON THE EDUCATION OF PRINCIPALS

In 1923 Ellwood P. Cubberley published the first influential textbook on the principalship, *The Principal and His School,* in which he cataloged the many functions and activities of the school principal. The book contains an irony of which Cubberley himself seemed only faintly aware. He began by asserting that "there is [now] a definite body of concrete experience and scientific information which should be taught to those [aspiring to the principalship]" (p. vi). He then devoted 566 pages to his catalog of such experience and information only to conclude with a lengthy quote from Leonard Ayres that stated "education for leadership largely means . . . self-education" (p. 565). If the principal's education as a leader ultimately boiled down to self-education, what was the purpose of Cubberley's detailed curriculum for a course in the principalship? The irony lives on. We continue to train for the principalship in courses with texts like Cubberley's, but we understand that our education as leaders will occur in the course of our practice, in vitro, and largely at the hands of ourselves.

This book has followed my learning about myself as a leader. True to

Ayres' observation, my self-education consisted largely of examining the cues given by those I was hired to lead. It was an education about my choice of activity patterns, my judgment of people, and my relationships with people. Students, teachers, staff, and other colleagues provided the instructional incidents in that education. As for many principals, the value of this education seemed far to outweigh that of my formal learning about the science of the principalship or leadership. What then is the optimal preparation for the school principalship? Are university programs and texts useless? Must we leave principals only to self-educate?

We need first to agree on the nature of the task. We frequently speak and write about training principals, as if a universally applicable regimen of knowledge and technique existed that principals needed to acquire and to adapt both their behavior and thinking to. The model is that of the athlete or technician making performance tasks second nature through drill. Clearly, succeeding as a leader of school requires more than that. Schools are unruly because children and learning are varied and difficult to prescribe, demanding that teachers constantly scan for cues and constantly weigh choices about instructional strategies and environments. Principals must be capable of scanning and weighing choices just as constantly in order to make decisions about schedules, student placement, resources, curriculum, and instruction.

School leadership is a discretionary activity. Rather than training to learn every tactic for every eventuality, principals need to educate themselves to use discretion appropriately. The purpose of a principal's education is to learn how to learn what the school community's needs are and how the principal and staff, primarily, can manage and deploy their talents and resources to match them. Plainly, education for the principalship never ends. As long as we are leading effectively, we are learning new things about the dynamic mix of children, teachers, parents, their aspirations and capabilities and about how adults can respond to the challenges of student development.

The training paradigm has misled us in our thinking about the preparation of principals. It is responsible for the frequent polarization of university and workplace, of theory and practice, of textbook and experience. We assume that the university with its theories, textbooks, and erudite professors should train us to succeed; they should make us ready for all those eventualities we will face as principals. When we find that they do not (as we inevitably do), we conclude that the university had the wrong stuff. But the paradigm is wrong. No amount or quality of pre-service training will prepare a principal to hit the ground running.

School leadership requires an education, not training. It requires us to learn how to learn about leadership needs and about pedagogical needs. It must happen in the workplace where the people and problems are the instructional experiences. Viewed in this manner, the polar opposites of theory and practice or textbook and experience can be seen as *complements* to one another. The development of a leader involves melding what textbooks and experience say, integrating the thinking and writing one can do at a university with the people and problems of the workplace, and drawing insights about theory and practice from one another. It is in the integration of these different ways of looking at one's work that the principal can ultimately make sense of his or her complicated work environment, his or her purposes as a leader within that environment, and how his or her talents enhance or inhibit fulfillment of those purposes. Each principalship and each day in the principalship is an opportunity for learning. If those opportunities are not seized, the teachers, students, and parents who seek stimulation for their own learning in the school will be disillusioned and feel oppressed. The school will have no true leader.

How, then, are principals to gain an education? I propose that we view the preparation of principals as *the beginning of a continuous process*. If I think about how I would have liked to be brought into the profession, I can see four phases to this beginning.

1. *Orientation to the Role* in which I have access to theory, generalized knowledge, and others' reflected experience as principals. Universities are good places to ingest much of this formally contained information about the role. As long as I remembered that I was largely orienting myself to the information and the role, I would not expect to use what I learned immediately.

2. *Immersion in the Role* in order to (a) learn about the school as an organization and (b) learn how to use the constant stream of this information to determine how to fulfill the three functions depicted in this book. The purpose of immersion is not to act as a principal but to learn how to learn from the school environment about leadership needs and oneself. Immersion can be accomplished through simulations, internships, practica, and activity-based assessment procedures such as the National Association of Secondary School Principals Assessment Centers.

3. *A Career Decision Point* when the future principal, with the assistance of mentors or others, collects data and advice about his or her suitability to the principalship. Using feedback from others, self-observation, and descriptions of the personal qualities one might need for certain types of principalship, the future principal must judge the match between himself or herself and the demands of leading schools. Vital to this judgment is a readiness to admit that he or she will make a capable leader for some, but probably not all, schools. The career decision to become a principal must identify what the best match of person and school is apt to be.

4. *Mature Professional Development* in which the person who accepts a principalship gathers information about the school and feedback about him- or herself and, through the medium of professional circles, learns how to use this information to fashion judgments and strategies for his or her activities as a leader. Professional development permits the principal to integrate as wide a

range of ideas and resources as he or she can consider with the real challenges of his or her school. It never ends.

Implied in this sequence of Orientation-Immersion-Decision-Development is a very different role for universities and professional administrator groups. University degree programs must see themselves as principals have seen them for years: places to become cognitively oriented to the role and the knowledge it may require. This is a downsized role when compared to the one in our traditional training paradigm. The part that university programs play is further diminished in my model by the appreciably grander role of the profession itself. Professional associations—whether formal affiliates of larger principal organizations, principals' centers or academies, or ad hoc gatherings of neighboring principals—are the keepers and purveyors of craft knowledge and professional wisdom. Their importance in the true education of school leaders is vast.

These professional circles can foster reflective learning for more principals on a more regular basis than any form of centralized or standardized in-service education can. The principals' center and academy movement (Wimpelberg, 1988) and a growing literature on leader learning-in-action (Jentz and Wofford, 1979; Schon, 1983) provide insight into the way these circles might best function. Two things are clear: They can legitimize the sharing of practical problems and stories as the beginning places of principals' learning; and they can establish trusting yet professionally challenging environments that will stimulate principals to share with one another and to cull useful lessons from outside sources. Professional circles need not be limited in membership to principals, as others who seek to expand their own repertoires as educators, leaders, and students of leadership can benefit from membership as well.

As long as we persist in the belief that we can educate or, worse, train principals through the delivery of knowledge, we will violate a basic reality of both school and leadership. Schools and leaders succeed best when they respond to the hopes, fears, and characteristics of the people toward whom they are directed. Put simply, one cannot be taught to educate or to lead; one certainly cannot be taught to lead educators. Instead, leaders and educators must develop themselves, but not by themselves. Just as they must establish conditions in which teachers and students learn and grow, principals and others can establish conditions in which principals can engage in the important syntheses of work and thought, of action and reflection, that constitute the center of professional learning.

Principals' dominant task is to learn what questions to ask of their schools, what resources to seek in order to answer those questions, and what personal talents are called forth from them and others if the school is to act productively. To persist in our belief that principals can be taught by those with the wisdom and knowledge is to promote the fiction that principals need not learn about or from their schools and communities. It is but one short step from there to the conclusion that principals, in order to be effective leaders, need not take directions or seek feedback from those whom they lead.

We who are engaged in the preparation and development of principals shape their understanding of school leadership. Whether we view principals as actors on the school environment or actors within that environment spells the difference between our encouraging principals to view themselves, in Roland Barth's (1989, p. 146) words, as heroes or heromakers. Our own approaches to principals as they seek development and education will illuminate our conceptions of their work. If we persist in activities that transmit knowledge only, we model an oligarchic conception of learning *and* of leadership. If, on the other hand, we approach principals with the goal of aiding them as they develop ideas, attitudes, and behaviors that answer the questions they have about their schools and themselves, we demonstrate for them the value of viewing themselves as developers of talent and growth in their schools. Even in the most hidebound of U.S. high schools, talents and a desire for growth abound, both among students and among faculty and staff. What better purpose exists for educational leadership than to see these flower in everyone?

Appendix: Principal Leadership Study Survey

In mid-summer 1984 I mailed a survey to staff members who had worked with me for more than two of my seven years in the Ellsworth, Maine, schools. The survey addressed my performances as a principal, a position I held in a variety of circumstances over the seven-year period (including grades 7–12 and secondary vocational schools). Staff were invited to respond anonymously and were assured that I would not even read written comments in order to preserve anonymity. An intermediary entered all data into a computer and typed all comments for me to use in analysis.

The following pages present the characteristics of respondents and the survey instrument itself.

The Respondent Group

    A. Response Rate   67 questionnaires mailed
                           54 returned
                           81% rate

    B. Distribution*

        1. By school   High School–47
                           Junior High–13
                           Voc. School–9

        *A number of staff worked with me in more than one school.

        2. By position

*Classroom Teacher	27
*Special Area Teacher	16
*Guidance	4
*Administration	2
Aide	2

           *Include duplicates.

Staff Perception Questionnaire

Gordon Donaldson served as supervising principal from 1976 through 1983. Though his title remained nearly the same through that period, his responsibilities changed. For reference, here are the roles he filled:

1976-78   Supervisory resp. gr. 7-12; administrative role 9-12

1978-80   Supervisory resp. gr. 7-12; staff leadership 7 & 8 and 9-12 (S. Taylor Assistant Princ., 7-12)

1980-83   Supervisory resp. gr. 7-12; all aspects of 9-12 but daily management; all aspects of Vocational School; limited curricular resp., K-12.

The questionnaire has two parts. The first asks you to describe Gordon's activities as principal. The second asks you to evaluate those activities.

Part I.   What Donaldson Did as Principal

1. The items below list situations in which you may have seen, heard, or spoken with Gordon in the course of a week. Indicate how frequently you <u>usually</u> came into contact with him in each situation. <u>Check one column for each letter</u>.

Situation	Often (once a day or more)	Sometimes (2-4 times a week)	Seldom (once a wk. to once a mo.)	Almost Never (Once a semester or less)
a. in corridors	___	___	___	___
b. in my classroom	___	___	___	___
c. in main office	___	___	___	___
d. teacher's room	___	___	___	___
e. at school events	___	___	___	___
f. through P.A. system	___	___	___	___
g. through memos	___	___	___	___

Appendix

	Situation	Often (once a day or more)	Sometimes (2-4 times a week)	Seldom (once a wk. to once a mo.)	Almost Never (Once a semester or less)
h.	through personal notes	___	___	___	___
i.	in faculty meetings	___	___	___	___
j.	in small, specific-purpose meetings	___	___	___	___
k.	other (specify) _____	___	___	___	___

2. The following is a list of types and topics of communications you may have had with Gordon. Indicate how frequently you <u>usually</u> had an interchange with him of each type or on each topic. <u>Check one column for each letter</u>.

		Often (once a day or more)	Sometimes (2-4 times a week)	Seldom (once a wk. to once a mo.)	Almost Never (Once a semester or less)
a.	I received <u>information</u> from him (e.g. about a student or program)	___	___	___	___
b.	I received <u>general instructions from him</u> (e.g. about scheduling or an assembly)	___	___	___	___
c.	I received <u>personal instructions</u> from him e.g. what my responsibility was)	___	___	___	___

		Often (once a day or more)	Sometimes (2-4 times a week)	Seldom (once a wk. to once a mo.)	Almost Never (Once a semester or less)
d.	I received <u>suggestions</u> from him (e.g. what to do with a student or problem)	_____	_____	_____	_____
e.	I received <u>requests</u> from him (e.g. Would you cover a class help a group of students)	_____	_____	_____	_____
f.	I received <u>orders</u> from him (e.g. what I <u>must</u> do/not do)	_____	_____	_____	_____
g.	We engaged in <u>discussion</u> of mostly professional issue	_____	_____	_____	_____
h.	We engaged in <u>casual talk</u> (e.g. gardening, ballgames, family)	_____	_____	_____	_____
i.	I sought him out for <u>specific information</u> (e.g. What's tomorrow's schedule)	_____	_____	_____	_____
j.	I sought him out <u>for advice</u> (e.g. how to handle a situation)	_____	_____	_____	_____

	Often (once a day or more)	Sometimes (2-4 times a week)	Seldom (once a wk. to once a mo.)	Almost Never (Once a semester or less
k. I sought him out to <u>inform him</u> of something I thought he should know (e.g. to handle problem; change a procedure)	____	____	____	____
l. I sought him out <u>to tell him</u> what to do (e.g. to handle a problem; change a procedure)	____	____	____	____
m. Other: Specify ____	____	____	____	____

3. Listed below are possible goals a principal might hold. Using the following rating scale, indicate how important <u>you believe</u> each was to Gordon.

   1 = of <u>utmost importance</u> to him
   2 = <u>quite important</u> to him
   3 = <u>slightly important</u> to him
   4 = <u>no importance</u> to him

                    Importance
                    Rating
                    (1, 2, 3, or 4)

  a. to raise student performance   ____

		Importance Rating (1, 2, 3, or 4)
b.	to befriend staff	___
c.	to implement management's desires	___
d.	to create cooperative faculty team	___
e.	to inspire students to achieve and behave	___
f.	to use staff for his purposes	___
g.	to force students to behave	___
h.	to involve students actively in school	___
i.	to exercise his authority	___
j.	to encourage staff creativity	___
k.	to befriend students	___
l.	to lead Ellsworth out of the Dark Ages	___
m.	to make teachers accountable for teaching	___
n.	to earn a good income	___
o.	to keep everyone on the defensive	___
p.	to put his own ideas to work	___
q.	to make the school its best	___
r.	to make school comfortable for staff and students	___
s.	to work his way up the job ladder	___
t.	to make school run smoothly and quietly	___
u.	to force some teachers out	___
v.	to make fair decisions, treat everyone fairly	___
w.	to create public support for schools	___
x.	other (specify) _____	___

Appendix

4. Describe Gordon <u>as you remember him at school</u> by circling the appropriate number between each pair of terms.

Pleasant	1	2	3	4	5	6	7	8	Unpleasant
Friendly	1	2	3	4	5	6	7	8	Unfriendly
Rejecting	1	2	3	4	5	6	7	8	Accepting
Helpful	1	2	3	4	5	6	7	8	Frustrating
Unenthusiastic	1	2	3	4	5	6	7	8	Enthusiastic
Tense	1	2	3	4	5	6	7	8	Relaxed
Distant	1	2	3	4	5	6	7	8	Close
Cold	1	2	3	4	5	6	7	8	Warm
Cooperative	1	2	3	4	5	6	7	8	Uncooperative
Supportive	1	2	3	4	5	6	7	8	Hostile
Boring	1	2	3	4	5	6	7	8	Interesting
Quarrelsome	1	2	3	4	5	6	7	8	Harmonious
Self-assured	1	2	3	4	5	6	7	8	Hesitant
Efficient	1	2	3	4	5	6	7	8	Inefficient
Gloomy	1	2	3	4	5	6	7	8	Cheerful
Open	1	2	3	4	5	6	7	8	Guarded

5. Is there an aspect of Gordon's work as a principal--either positive or negative--that was not addressed above? If so, briefly describe him in that regard.

_____

_____

_____

Appendix

Part II How Gordon Did As Principal

1. The following statements might be used to describe a principal's purposes, both personal and professional. Using the following rating scale, indicate <u>your evaluation of Gordon's success</u> at accomplishing each of these activities.

       1 = <u>high</u> success rate
       2 = <u>good</u> success rate
       3 = <u>slight</u> success
       4 = <u>no</u> success

		Success Rating (1, 2, 3, or 4)
a.	to raise student performance	_____
b.	to befriend staff	_____
c.	to implement management's desires	_____
d.	to create cooperative faculty team	_____
e.	to inspire students to achieve and behave	_____
f.	to use staff for his purposes	_____
g.	to force students to behave	_____
h.	to involve students actively in school	_____
i.	to exercise his authority	_____
j.	to encourage staff creativity	_____
k.	to befriend students	_____
l.	to lead Ellsworth out of the Dark Ages	_____
m.	to make teachers accountable for teaching	_____
n.	to earn a good income	_____
o.	to keep everyone on the defensive	_____
p.	to put his own ideas to work	_____

Appendix

		Success Rating (1, 2, 3, or 4)
q.	to make the school its best	____
r.	to make school comfortable for staff and students	____
s.	to work his way up the job ladder	____
t.	to make school run smoothly and quietly	____
u.	to force some teachers out	____
v.	to make fair decisions, treat everyone fairly	____
w.	to create public support for schools	____
x.	other (specify) _____	____

2. In his contacts <u>with me</u>, Gordon was:

		Strongly Agree	Moderately Agree	Moderately Disagree	Strongly Disagree
a.	aloof and distant	1	2	3	4
b.	critical of my performance	1	2	3	4
c.	helpful to my teaching skills	1	2	3	4
d.	impatient	1	2	3	4
e.	fair	1	2	3	4
f.	encouraging	1	2	3	4
g.	not conerned with me personally	1	2	3	4
h.	supportive in tight spots	1	2	3	4
i.	relaxed and friendly	1	2	3	4
j.	guarded in expressing himself	1	2	3	4

		Circle the Appropriate Number			
		Strongly Agree	Moderately Agree	Moderately Disagree	Strongly Disagree
k.	mainly concerned about my work	1	2	3	4
l.	an effective motivator	1	2	3	4
m.	difficult to understand	1	2	3	4
n.	not a significant force	1	2	3	4
o.	trusting and accepting	1	2	3	4
p.	close-minded to my views	1	2	3	4
q.	hard to satisfy	1	2	3	4
r.	a professional	1	2	3	4
s.	other (specify) _____	1	2	3	4

3. In summary, state briefly your overall assessment of Gordon's work in Ellsworth as principal. Feel free to use the reverse side as well.

_____

_____

_____

4. If you are aware of any circumstances affecting Gordon's performance that were beyond his control while working in Ellsworth, briefly note them below.

<u>Circumstance</u>   <u>Effects on Gordon</u>

Thank You For Your Time

References and Bibliography

Argyris, C. and Schon, D. (1974). *Theory in practice: Increasing professional effectiveness.* San Francisco: Jossey-Bass.
Bacharach, S. and Conley, S. (1989). Uncertainty and decision-making in teaching: Implications for managing line professionals. In T. Sergiovanni and D. Moore (Eds.), *Schooling for tomorrow* (pp. 311–329). Boston: Allyn and Bacon.
Barnard, C. (1938). *Functions of the executive.* Cambridge, MA: Harvard University Press.
Barth, R. (1979). *Run school run.* Cambridge, MA: Harvard University Press.
——— (1985). The leader as learner. *Educational Leadership, 42*(6), 92–93.
——— (1988). School: A community of leaders. In A. Lieberman (Ed.), *Building a professional culture in schools* (pp. 129–147). New York: Teachers College Press.
——— (1990). *Improving schools from within.* San Francisco: Jossey-Bass.
Begley, P. (1988). The influence of values on principals' problem-solving processes: An empirical study. Presented at the Annual Meeting of the American Educational Research Association, New Orleans.
Bennett, W. (1989). James Madison High School. In H. Walberg and J. Lane (Eds.), *Organizing for learning: Toward the 21st century.* Reston, VA: National Association of Secondary School Principals.
Bennis, W. and Nanus, B. (1985). *Leaders: The strategies for taking charge.* New York: Harper & Row.
Blase, J. (1988). An ethnographic study of the politics of teaching. Presented at the Annual Meeting of the American Educational Research Association, Washington DC.

Blumberg, A. (1989). *School administration as a craft: Foundations of practice*. Boston: Allyn and Bacon.

Blumberg, A. and Greenfield, W. (1980). *The effective principal: Perspectives on school leadership*. Boston: Allyn and Bacon.

Boyer, E. (1983). *High school: A report on secondary education in America*. New York: Harper & Row.

Bradford, D. and Cohen, A. (1984). The postheroic leader. *Training and Development Journal, 17*(1), 40–49.

Brandt, R. (Ed.). (1989). *Effective schools and school improvement*. Alexandria, VA: Association for Supervision and Curriculum Development.

Bridges, E. (1986). *The incompetent teacher*. Philadelphia: Falmer Press.

Brookover, W. and Lezotte, L. (1979). Changes in school characteristics coincident with changes in school achievement. East Lansing: Michigan State University Institute for Research on Teaching.

Burns, J. M. (1978). *Leadership*. New York: Harper & Row.

Carmichael, L. (1981). *McDonogh 15: Becoming a school*. New York: Avon Books.

Castetter, W. B. (1986). *The personnel function in educational administration* (4th ed.). New York: Macmillan.

Cooper, L. (1988). The professional development of principals: The principal's perspective. Unpublished doctoral thesis, Harvard Graduate School of Education, Cambridge, MA.

Corbett, H., Firestone, W., and Rossman, G. (1987). Resistance to planned change and the sacred in school cultures. *Educational Administration Quarterly, 23*(4), 473–498.

Cousins, J. (1988). Performance improvement as problem solving: Principals' use of information concerning their own performance. Presented at the Annual Meeting of the American Educational Research Organization, New Orleans.

Cross, K. P. (1981). *Adults as learners*. San Francisco: Jossey-Bass.

Cubberley, E. (1923). *The principal and his school*. New York: Houghton Mifflin.

Deal, T. (1990). Images of leadership. Presented at the Annual Meeting of the American Educational Research Association, Boston.

DeBevoise, W. (1984). Synthesis of research on the principal as instructional leader. *Educational Leadership, 41*(7), 14–20.

Devaney, K. (1987). *The lead teacher: Ways to begin*. New York: Carnegie Forum on Education and the Economy.

Donaldson, G. (1972). Rx for school leadership: The Maine Principals' Academy. *Phi Delta Kappan, 63*(6), 400–402.

――― (1985). Sisyphus and school improvement: Fulfilling the promise of excellence. *Educational Leadership, 42*(5), 4–7.

Donaldson, G. and McCaul, E. (1986). *The Maine Principals' Academy: A five year evaluation study*. Orono: University of Maine.

Donaldson, G. and Quaglia, R. (1989). *Integrating knowledge in educational administration: Moving beyond content*. Charlottesville, VA: National Policy Board for Educational Administration.

Duke, D. (1987). *School leadership and instructional improvement*. New York: Random House.

Dwyer, D., Barnett, B., and Lee, V. (1987). The school principal: Scapegoat or last great hope?. In *Leadership: Examining the elusive*. Alexandria, VA: Association for Supervision and Curriculum Development.

Edmonds, R. and Frederiksen, J. (1978). *Search for effective schools*. Cambridge, MA: Harvard University Center for Urban Studies.

Erickson, F. (1987). Conceptions of school culture. *Educational Administration Quarterly, 23*(4), 11–24.

Fiedler, F. E. (1967). *A theory of leadership effectiveness*. New York: McGraw-Hill.

Firestone, W. and Wilson, B. (1985). Using bureaucratic and cultural linkages to improve instruction: The principal's contribution. *Educational Administration Quarterly, 21*(2), 7–30.

Foster, M. (1971). *Making schools work: Strategies for changing education*. Philadelphia: Westminster Press.

Fullan, M. (1982). *The meaning of change*. New York: Teachers College Press.

Gardner, J. W. (1987). *Attributes and context of leadership*. Leadership Papers, No. 6. Washington DC: Independent Sector.

Goldman, C. and O'Shea, C. (1990). A culture for change. *Educational Leadership, 47*(8), 41–43.

Goodlad, J. (1983). *A place called school*. New York: McGraw-Hill.

Grant, G. (1988). *The world we created at Hamilton High*. Cambridge, MA: Harvard University Press.

Greene, M. (1984). How do we think about our craft? *Teachers College Record, 86*, 55–67.

Griffiths, D., Stout, R., and Forsythe, P. (1988). *Leaders for America's schools: The report and papers of the national commission on excellence in educational administration*. Berkeley, CA: McCutchan.

Hallinger, P. and Murphy, J. (1987). Assessing and developing principals' instructional leadership. *Educational Leadership, 45*(8), 54–61.

Hampel, R. (1986). *The last little citadel: American high schools since 1940*. Boston: Houghton Mifflin.

Herndon, J. (1968). *The way it spozed to be*. New York: Simon and Schuster.

Jentz, B. (1982). *Entry: The hiring, start-up and supervision of school administrators*. New York: McGraw-Hill.

Jentz, B. and Wofford, J. (1979). *Leadership and learning*. New York: McGraw-Hill.

Kammeraad-Campbell, S. (1989). *Doc: The story of Dennis Littky and his fight for a better school*. Chicago: Contemporary Books.

Kennedy, A. and Deal, T. (1982). *Corporate cultures: The rites and rituals of corporate life*. Reading, MA: Addison-Wesley.

Kidder, T. (1989). *Among schoolchildren*. Boston: Houghton Mifflin.

Kleine, P. (1990). Women in educational administration: A matter of choice?. Unpublished doctoral dissertation. Orono: University of Maine.

Kohl, H. (1967). *36 children*. New York: New American Library.

Lane, J. and Walberg, H. (Eds.). (1987). *Effective school leadership: Policy and process*. Berkeley, CA: McCutchan.

Leithwood, K. (1988). The nature, causes, and consequences of principals' practices: A framework for research and review of recent literature. Presented at the Annual Meeting of the American Educational Research Association, New Orleans.

—— (1990). The principal's role in teacher development. In B. Joyce (Ed.), *Changing school culture through staff development*. Alexandria, VA: Association for Supervision and Curriculum Development.

Leithwood, K. and Jantzi, D. (1990). Transformational leadership: How principals can help reform school cultures. Paper presented at the Annual Meeting of the American Educational Research Association, Boston.

Levine, S. (1989). *Promoting adult growth in schools: The promise of professional development*. Boston: Allyn and Bacon.

Lieberman, A. (Ed.). (1988a). *Building a professional culture in schools*. New York: Teachers College Press.

—— (1988b). Teachers and principals: Turf, tension, and new tasks. *Phi Delta Kappan, 69*(9), 648–653.

Lightfoot, S. L. (1983). *The good high school: Portraits of character and culture*. New York: Basic Books.

Lindblom, C. (1969). The science of "muddling through." In A. Etzioni (Ed.), *Readings on modern organizations* (pp. 153–166). Englewood Cliffs, NJ: Prentice-Hall.

Lipham, J., Rankin, R., and Hoeh, J. (1985). *The principalship: Concepts, competencies, and cases*. New York: Longman.

Lipsitz, J. (1984). *Successful schools for young adolescents*. New Brunswick, NJ: Transaction Books.

Lipsky, M. (1980). *Street level bureaucracy: Dilemmas of the individual in public services*. New York: Russell Sage Foundation.

Little, J. W. (1982). Norms of collegiality and experimentation: Workplace conditions of school success. *American Educational Research Journal, 19*(30), 325–340.

Lortie, D. (1975). *Schoolteacher: A sociological study*. Chicago: University of Chicago Press.

Martin, W. and Willower, D. (1981). The managerial behavior of high school principals. *Educational Administration Quarterly, 17*(1), 69–90.

McEvoy, B. (1987). Everyday acts: How principals influence the development of their staffs. *Educational Leadership, 44*(2), 73–77.

McPherson, R., Crowson, R. and Pitner, N. (1986). *Managing uncertainty: Administrative theory in education*. Columbus, OH: Merrill.

Meyer, J. and Rowan, B. (1978). The structure of educational organizations. In M. Marshall and Associates (Eds.), *Environments and organizations* (pp. 78–109). San Francisco: Jossey-Bass.

Morris, V. C., Crowson, R., Porter-Gehrie, C., and Hurwitz, E. (1984). *Principals in action: The reality of managing schools*. Columbus, OH: Merrill.

Murphy, J. (1988). The unheroic side of leadership: Notes from the swamp. *Phi Delta Kappan, 69*(9), 654–659.

National Association of Secondary School Principals. (1985). *The principal assessment center*. Reston, VA: NASSP.

National Center for Educational Statistics. (1988). *Public education agency universe, 1986–87: Final tabulations*. Washington DC: Department of Education (OERI).

National Network of Principals' Centers. (1986, 1987, 1988, 1989). *Reflections.* Cambridge, MA: Harvard Graduate School of Education.

National Policy Board for Educational Administration. (1989). *Improving the preparation of school administrators: An agenda.* Charlottesville: University of Virginia.

Persell, C. and Cookson, P. (1982). The effective principal in action. In *The effective principal.* Reston, VA: National Association of Secondary School Principals.

Peshkin, A. (1978). *Growing up American.* Chicago: University of Chicago Press.

Peters, T. (1989). A Conversation with Tom Peters. *Educational Leadership,* 46(3), 27–31.

Peters, T. and Waterman, R. (1982). *In search of excellence: Lessons from America's best-run companies.* New York: Harper & Row.

Peterson, K. (1990). Leadership and culture: Qualitative studies and insights. Presented at the Annual Meeting of the American Educational Research Association, Boston.

Pfeffer, J. (1981). Management as symbolic action: The creation and maintenance of organizational paradigms. In L. Cummings and B. Staw (Eds.), *Research in organizational behavior,* Vol. 3. Greenwich, CT: JAI Press.

Powell, A., Farrar, E., and Cohen, D. (1985). *The shopping mall high school: Winners and losers in the educational market place.* Boston: Houghton Mifflin.

Roe, W. and Drake, T. (1986). *The principalship.* New York: Macmillan.

Rosenholtz, S. (1986). *Teachers' workplace: The social organization of schools.* New York: Longman.

Rutter, M., Maughan, B., Mortimore, P., and Ouston, J. (1979). *Fifteen thousand hours: Secondary schools and their effects on children.* Cambridge, MA: Harvard University Press.

Sarason, S. (1982). *The culture of the school and the problem of change.* Boston: Allyn and Bacon.

Schein, E. (1985). *Organizational culture and leadership: A dynamic view.* San Francisco: Jossey-Bass.

Schon, D. (1983). *The reflective practitioner.* New York: Basic Books.

Sennett, R. (1970). *The uses of disorder.* New York: Vintage.

Sergiovanni, T. (1987). *The principalship: A reflective practice perspective.* Boston: Allyn and Bacon.

——— (1989). The ameoba theory of leadership. Working paper. San Antonio, TX: Trinity University.

Sergiovanni, T. and Moore, D. (1989). *Schooling for tomorrow.* Boston: Allyn and Bacon.

Shakeshaft, C. (1987). *Women in educational administration.* Newbury Park, CA: Sage Publications.

Shepard, H. (1985). Rules of thumb for change agents. *Organization Development Practitioner,* 17(4), 1–5.

Shulman, L. (1989). Teaching alone, learning together: Needed agendas for the new reforms. In T. Sergiovanni and D. Moore (Eds.), *Schooling for tomorrow* (pp. 241–264). Boston: Allyn and Bacon.

Sizer, T. (1983). *Horace's compromise.* Boston: Houghton Mifflin.

Smith, W. and Andrews, R. (1989). *Instructional leadership: How principals make a difference*. Alexandria, VA: Association for Supervision and Curriculum Development.

Stager, M. and Leithwood, K. (1988). Cognitive flexibility and inflexibility in principals' problem solving. Presented at Annual Meeting of the American Educational Research Association, New Orleans.

Stanley, S., and Popham, W. J. (1988). *Teacher evaluation: Six prescriptions for success*. Alexandria, VA: Association for Supervision and Curriculum Development.

Tyack, D. and Hansot, E. (1982). *Managers of virtue: Public school leadership in America, 1820–1980*. New York: Basic Books.

Warren-Little, J. (1985). *What schools contribute to teachers' professional knowledge*. San Francisco: Far West Laboratory.

Weber, M. (1947). Power and bureaucracy. In T. Parsons (Ed.), *The theory of social and economic organization*. Glencoe: Free Press.

Weick, K. (1982). Administering education in loosely coupled schools. *Phi Delta Kappan, 63*, 673–676.

Weindling, D. and Early, P. (1987). *Secondary leadership: The first years*. Philadelphia: NFER-Nelson.

Wimpelberg, R. (1988). The inservice development of principals: A new movement, its characteristics, and future. In J. Thurston and T. Lotto (Eds.), *Advances in educational administration* (pp. 279–312). Greenwich, CT: JAI Press.

Wolcott, H. (1973). *The man in the principal's office*. New York: Holt.

Wood, C., Nicholson, E., and Findley, D. (1985). *The secondary school principal: Manager and supervisor*. Boston: Allyn and Bacon.

Index

Academic program. See Instructional program
Accountability, 58–60, 72–73, 164–65, 173–75
Accountability Paradox, 175–76
Activity patterns, 7–8, 15–46, 156–59
Administrative culture, 80, 105
Adults, understanding, 191–94
Affiliation, norms of, 199
Agenda Paradox, 176–78
Ambiguity, 45, 182–84, 197–99
Analytic skills, 189, 191
Assertiveness, 62–64, 98–100. *See also* Leadership
Assistant principal, 23
Authority, 54, 58, 130–34, 144–48, 176–78, 195
Authority Paradox, 178–80
Availability: to clientele, 17–20, 180–82; to teachers, 25–28, 68–70, 104–5
Ayres, Leonard, 200

Barth, Roland, 3, 45, 168, 186, 197, 204
Bennis, Arthur, 87, 169
Blanchard, Kenneth, 161
Blumberg, Arthur, 3, 119
Bridges, Edwin, 160
Building supervision, 34–35
Bureaucratic relationships, 43–45, 54–55, 60, 80, 104, 166–67, 178–80

Carmichael, Lucianne, 3
Certification, 2
Change strategies, 39–40, 97–98, 184, 189–91. *See also* Innovation
Climate: faculty, 74–75, 83–84, 175–76, 191–92, 199; setting, 20–21, 39–40, 42–43
Cocurricular activities, 27, 93
Collaborative leadership, 65–66, 71–72, 112–14, 133, 151–52, 159–60, 175–80, 185, 191ff., 203–4

Communication: patterns, 48–51, 168–69; skills, 188, 191–94
Community: learning about, 94–98, 187–88; values of, 97–99, 145–46
Community of learners, 162–63, 184
Confidence in staff, 78–82, 85, 148–52, 160–64, 194
Conflict: among people, 22, 106–8, 150–51, 197–99; with teachers, 114–17, 128–29, 141–43, 146
Consulting skills, 195
Contact: between principal and staff, 48–51, 198–99; enjoyment of, 197–200
Control, need for, 81, 177, 197
Cooper, Laura, 184
Cubberley, Ellwood P., 200
Curriculum planning, 24, 38–39, 91–94, 109–10

Decision-making, 93–94, 99–100, 194–96, 201; shared, 71–72, 92–94, 112–14, 151–52
Delegation, 43, 196. See also Collaborative leadership
Department functioning, 104, 110
Dewey, John, 197
Dissatisfaction, professional, 194
Diversity: appreciation of, 197–99; of staff, 114–17, 162, 165–66

Education of principals, 2–3, 6–7, 182–84, 200–204
Effectiveness of principals, 3–5, 29, 45–46, 101–2, 124–28, 133–36, 144–52, 167–69, 186ff.; difficulty evaluating, 138
Effective schools, 4, 171–72
Efficacy, principals' sense of, 82–85, 98–100, 116–17, 128–33, 142–48, 151–52, 167–69, 173–74, 185
Efficiency, 19–20, 176–78
Ellsworth Junior-Senior High School, 10–11
Ethical treatment, 132, 140–42, 147–48, 197–99
Ethos, 4, 20–21, 39–40, 88. See also Climate

Evaluation: of outcomes, 106, 190; of principal, 119–134, 135–152; of teachers, 24, 72–78, 82–85, 164–65. See also Effectiveness of principals
Expectations: clarity of, 122–24, 180–82; compromising, 114–17, 171–75; setting high, 56–58, 61–62, 89–91, 127, 140–43

Faculty meetings, 26, 71–72, 103–8, 112
Fair, on being, 103–8, 126–27, 132, 141, 147–50, 191
Faith: in principal, 142–48, 150, 175, 181; in staff, 84, 148–49, 160–61, 163–64, 194
Feedback: need for, 116–17, 119–20, 128, 183–84; uses of, 186, 193–94
Financial management, 26, 42–43
Foster, Marcus, 3
Fragmentation of role, 19, 21, 156, 176–79
Functional Approach, 6–9, 153, 156

Gardner, John, 196
Goals: altruistic versus authoritarian, 58–59, 131–33; attainment of, 128–33, 189–91; based on students, 88–91, 156–57, 186–87; establishing coherent, 55–61, 122–24, 176–78
Goodlad, John, 177
Grant, Gerald, 5, 13–14
Greenfield, William, 3, 67, 119
Group dynamics, 150–52

High Expectations Paradox, 173–75
High schools, history of, 187
Hiring staff, 161
Hope, sense of, 139, 143, 148, 157–58, 163, 192, 198–200
Hopelessness, sense of, 115–17, 127–28, 139–40, 150

Ideals, melding with action, 13–14, 78–79, 134, 156–57, 176–78, 189–91

Information, providing, 18–19
Informed, on being, 19–21, 31–35, 53–54, 93–94; about staff, 68–70, 161
Innovation, 39–40, 112–14, 146, 163, 172–73
Instructional leadership, 43, 107–12, 115–16, 154, 171–184
Instructional program, 34, 38–41, 87–88, 93–94; coordination of, 84–85, 106–10
Instructional supervision, 23–25, 44–45, 74–78, 110–11
Integrity, 112–14, 135–52, 149–52
Interpersonal: aspects of leadership, 3–4, 120–24, 140–42, 148–52, 160, 191–95, 198–99; perceptiveness, 193

Job description: clarification of, 183; Ellsworth, 10–12; typical principal's, 138–39, 143, 146–47, 177–78

Leadership: activities, 50–51; capacities and qualities for, 135–44, 147–52, 186ff.; heroic, 155–56; learning about, 79–82, 116–17, 179, 183–84, 198; new conceptions of, 13–14, 28–29, 153–54, 167–69, 186ff., 200–204; responsive versus assertive, 28–29, 96–100, 133–34, 173; style, 108, 113–26, 136, 176–68; successful, 3–5, 29, 45–46, 67, 96, 101, 117, 133–36, 142–48, 177–78; symbolic, 14, 30, 105–8, 156, 167–69; team, 23, 65–66, 151–52, 159–60, 175–76
Learning: principals', 73–74, 155–56, 198, 200–204; styles, 192
Least Preferred Coworker Scale (Fiedler), 120–22
Leithwood, Kenneth, 4, 183
Lieberman, Ann, 5, 162, 185
Lightfoot, Sarah Lawrence, 5, 182, 197
Loosely coupled, 81, 177, 192

Maine Principals' Academy, 38, 172–84

Management by walking around, 17–20, 31–35, 61–63, 88
Management functions, 26, 77, 80, 139, 156–57, 176–80; effects on teachers, 104, 107–8
Mission: articulating, 108, 156–57, 167–69, 186–89; building, 61–63, 70, 79, 82, 91–94, 108, 114–17; maintaining, 2, 29, 55–61, 88, 98–100, 113–14, 173–78
Modeling learning, 158–59, 162, 196–98
Motivating adults, 122–24, 127–28, 191–94
Murphy, Jerry, 155

Nanus, Bert, 87, 169
National Network of Principals' Centers, 184
Negotiation, 183, 190
Nonrational factors, 163–69, 171–72, 178–80, 182–83, 194–95, 197
Norm setting, 148–52, 158–59, 199–200

Observation skills, 31–35
Office procedures, 41–43
Open, on being, 68–70, 103–8, 120–22, 127–28, 197–99
Order: creating, 176–78, 195, 197; maintaining, 182, 191
Organizational sophistication, 188–90
Overburdened principal, 45–46, 155–56, 159–60

Paradoxes of leadership, 172–84
Parents: complaints, 76, 97–98; goals, 94–98; responsiveness to, 97–100
Personal demands of role, 37–38, 45–46, 116–17, 171–84, 194–97
Personality, effects of on leadership, 114–17, 122–24, 133–34, 140–42, 147, 150–51, 194–95
Personnel: assessment, 78–85, 164–65, 175–76; selection and deployment, 8, 64–85, 161. *See also* Evaluation
Philosophical foundation, 186–89
Planning, 27, 38–41, 87

Political considerations, 99–100, 144–48
Power, 140, 144–48, 167–69, 175–76, 178–80
Principals' centers/academies, 184, 202–4
Principalship: conceptions of, 2–4, 29, 154, 171–73, 186ff.; expectations for, 13, 19, 28, 137–40, 155, 171–72, 179–82; preparation for, 4–6, 182–84, 200–204; study of, 4–6
Problem-solving, 70, 112–13, 174–75
Professional: associations, 37–38, 203–4; circles, 202–4; integrity, 149–50
Program. *See* Instructional program
Public figure, 99–100, 157–58
Public relations, 32–33, 35–38, 94–100
Pupil Evaluation Team, 71, 89, 97, 111–12
Purpose, sense of Donaldson's, 28–29, 33, 55–61, 91–94, 98–100, 123, 140–41, 150, 186–89; distraction from, 20, 45, 176–78; translating into action, 61–63, 99–100, 109–10, 133–34, 143–44, 155–69, 189–91, 194

Questionnaire of staff views, 47–48, 119ff., 205–14

Recalcitrant staff, 114–17, 146, 150–51
Reflection: Donaldson's strategy for, 9–10, 21; principal's need for, 152, 183–84, 196–97, 200–4; staff, 40–41, 162–63
Reform movement, 4–6, 171–72, 185–86. *See also* Innovation
Relationships: 8–9, 36–37, 52, 82–85, 101–2, 110, 116–18; Donaldson's with staff, 103–52, 179–80; establishing with staff, 60, 64–85, 103–8, 135–36, 160, 163–67; failed, 150–52; importance of, 127–29, 133, 136, 142, 148–52, 198; need to monitor, 117–18, 166–67, 193–94

Responsiveness: to parents, 17–19, 25, 96–97, 180–82; to students, 16–17, 174; to teachers, 78–70. *See also* Collaborative leadership
Rewards of principalship, 198–99
Risk-taking, 192, 196–97
Role expectations for principal, 13, 19, 28, 32, 137–40, 155, 171–72, 179–82

Scheduling, 38–41
School board, 44, 95–96, 144–48
School district effects on principal, 123–24, 138–40, 144–48
Self-confidence, 33, 99–100, 116, 131–32, 151–52, 194–97
Self-criticism, 161–62, 164–65, 175–76, 182, 193–94, 200
Self-management, 151–52, 193–94
Sennett, Richard, 171, 197
Sizer, Theodore, 5, 197
Special education, 22–23, 111–12
Staff development, 74–78, 112. *See also* Collaborative leadership
Structuring: programs, 23–25, 38–41; school, 21–23, 31–35, 191–92
Students: academic placement, 22, 38–41, 87, 105–6; being informed about, 88–91; complaints about, 75–77, 96; "problem," 89, 93–94; supervision of, 20–21, 31–35, 61–63
Subjectivity, 67–68, 74–78, 132, 191
Success Paradox, 180–82
Superintendent, 43–45, 144–48
Supervision. *See* Instructional supervision
Symbolic impacts, 7–8, 13, 31, 105–8, 156–59, 167–69

Task orientation, 120–24
Teachers' Association, 73, 76. *See also* Union-management relations
Teachers: consultation with, 3–4, 25–27, 195; culture, 5, 83–84; Donaldson's communication with, 51–55, 122, 126–27; Donaldson's contact with, 48–51; establishing relation-

ships with, 8–9, 24, 51, 103–8, 159–60, 198–99; learning about, 67–69, 70–78; perceptions of principal, 47–63, 119–34, 135–52
Team building, 26, 106–8, 113–14, 128–29, 133–34, 160–64. *See also* Collaborative leadership
Time, lack of, 68, 91
Time versus activity chart, 15–16
Training of principals, 4–6, 182–83, 200–4
Trust: establishing, 78–82, 85, 120–22, 127, 144–48; in one's faculty, 164–65, 194

Uncertainty, 1–3, 28, 196–97
Union-management relations, 80–81, 116, 160
Unity: among staff, 78–82, 106–8, 110–11, 114–17, 134, 143–44, 150–51, 165; of staff views, 61–63, 119–34, 135–52

Values, establishing, 97, 106, 148–52, 158–59, 168–69, 197–98

Warren-Little, Judith, 162
Wolcott, Harry, 3
Workplace, school as, 183–84

ABOUT THE AUTHOR

GORDON DONALDSON received B.A. and Ph.D. degrees from Harvard. He taught in Philadelphia, Boston, and North Haven, Maine, in addition to being principal in Ellsworth, Maine. Since 1983, he has served on the graduate faculty at the University of Maine, Orono. Donaldson helped found the Maine Principals' Academy in 1979 and has been a member of the Advisory Board of the National Network of Principals' Centers since its inception. He has served on committees of the National Association of Secondary School Principals and as editor of the *Journal of Maine Education*. He has published frequently on school leadership and improvement, education for school leadership, rural schools, and school climate.